FRIEDRICH NIETZSCHE

FRIEDRICH NIETZSCHE
PHILOSOPHER OF CULTURE

BY

FREDERICK COPLESTON, S.J.

*Professor of the History of Philosophy
in the University of London*

SEARCH PRESS LONDON

BARNES & NOBLE BOOKS NEW YORK
(a division of Harper & Row Publishers, Inc.)

SEARCH PRESS LIMITED
2-10 Jerdan Place, London SW6 5PT
First published, 1942
This edition with new material, 1975
© Frederick Copleston, 1942, 1975
ISBN 0 85532 342 6

Published in the USA 1975 by
Harper & Row Publishers, Inc.
BARNES & NOBLE IMPORT DIVISION
ISBN-0-06 491283-3

DE LICENTIA SUPERIORUM ORDINIS: FRANCISCUS MANGAN, S.J., PRAEP.
PROV. ANGLIAE. NIHIL OBSTAT: ENGELBERT GUTWENGER. S.J., CENSOR
DEPUTATUS. IMPRIMATUR: ✠THOMAS, ARCHIEPISCOPUS BIRMINGAMIENSIS.
DIE 29A JANUARII 1942.

REPRODUCED AND PRINTED BY PHOTOLITHOGRAPHY AND BOUND IN
GREAT BRITAIN AT THE PITMAN PRESS, BATH

CONTENTS

PREFACE TO THE SECOND EDITION

MY first book, *Friedrich Nietzsche: Philosopher of Culture*, was published in 1942. It was a favourable time for publishing such a work. For though it is probably true to say that in the second World War there was less inclination than in the first to find in the German philosophers the spiritual source of contemporary conflict, the name of Nietzsche was not infrequently mentioned in connexion with the Nazi movement and the ideas of Adolf Hitler and his colleagues. In 1941 I had published two articles on this topic: 'Nietzsche and National Socialism' in *The Dublin Review* and 'Nietzsche versus Hitler' in *The Month*. If I remember correctly, Dr. Oscar Levy, the general editor of the English translation of Nietzsche's *Works*, told me that the title of the second article was as music to his ears. Thus encouraged, I produced a book, the title of which gave further pleasure to Dr. Levy. To be sure, he must have disagreed with a great part of the contents of the book. But in regard to Nietzsche he much preferred attack to silence, going on the principle that bad publicity is better than no publicity. Further, being both a devoted Nietzschean and a Jew, he was pleased with any author who dissociated Nietzsche from the anti-Semitism of the Nazis.

The book was generally well received, a fact which naturally gave considerable satisfaction to its author. In wartime conditions, however, stocks were soon exhausted, and after a while the work went out of print. Some years after the war suggestions were made that it should be reissued. But they did not meet with my acceptance, partly because the book had come to seem to me both philosophically naïve and emotively over-charged, partly because I had become thoroughly dissatisfied with my treatment of Nietzsche's thought. There was also another reason. The ecclesiastical censorship had insisted that before I could submit the book for publication I must insert into the original text some unambiguous condemnation of Nietzsche. As protest proved unavailing, I complied with this demand and introduced into the Preface and into various places in the text personal condemnations of Nietzsche of a strength sufficient to satisfy the censors. Obviously, though my compliance was doubtless regarded as commendable by the official ecclesiastical mind, other people might look on it in quite another light. The point is however that I became more and more reluctant to allow a work to be republished which had been disfigured in this way. And I was more than content to let the relevant two chapters in the seventh volume of my *History of Philosophy* (1963) serve as an expression of my views on Nietzsche. They may perhaps be both inadequate and dull; but at any rate they do not include any features inserted at the behest of ecclesiastical censors.

The book is however available in some libraries, and it is mentioned in a number of bibliographies, including my own bibliography for the chapters on Nietzsche in my *History*. As therefore I have been given to understand that there is a certain demand for its republication, I have consented, even if without marked enthusiasm. The original text has been left unchanged, including the quotations. These were made, with due permission from Dr. Levy and Messrs. Allen and Unwin, from the English translation of Nietzsche's *Works*, whereas in the chapters on Nietzsche in my *History* I translated from K. Schlechta's three-volume (and incomplete) German edition of the *Werke*, though I also supplied references to Levy's translation for the convenience of readers. The critical German edition of Nietzsche's writings is still unfinished. And in any case it is obviously more convenient to printers if the whole text of the 1942 book, including quotations, is left as it was. Readers can always consult more recent translations, such as Walter Kaufmann's *The Portable Nietzsche* (New York, 1959) and *Basic Writings of Nietzsche* (New York, 1968), if they so wish.

Though however the text of the 1942 book has been left unchanged, I have added, by way of indirect comment, three hitherto unpublished papers on Nietzsche. The first two, 'Remarks about Nietzsche' and 'Nietzsche as a Philosopher', were written for undergraduate societies. They are simple talks, intended to serve as material for discussion;

and they are unencumbered by any apparatus of scholarship. The third paper, 'After Twenty-Two Years', introduces some more direct comment on the 1942 book, though it is of a general nature. To supply detailed comment would be to attribute too much importance to the book.

(London, 1973)   *Frederick C. Copleston*

PREFACE TO THE FIRST EDITION

AT the present time there can scarcely be any excuse required for writing about Friedrich Nietzsche. The philosopher of the Will to Power and the Superman has been cited as one of the chief progenitors of Nazi dynamism, as in part responsible for modern German restlessness and activism, as patron of the notion of a *Herrenklasse*. The opponent of Statolatry, the scorner of Socialism, the derider of the German Empire, has been defended as essentially an anti-Nazi. This conflict of attitudes towards Nietzsche would seem to supply an excuse ready-made for a further book on his philosophy.

There is another reason why Friedrich Nietzsche is of importance at the present time. We are fighting, not only in order to fulfil our plighted word, not only even for an independent and free existence as a nation, not only for the independence of other nations that have been subjected to the rule of the tyrant, but also for the preservation of the cultural values of Europe. This war is many-sided, but one of its essential aspects is that of a war for the preservation of the cultural heritage of Europe against the attack of the New Barbarian. If this be so, it is obviously of importance to consider the nature and foundations of true culture. In this question Friedrich Nietzsche was passionately interested. His work may be said to centre round the problem of human culture: he summoned man to a new cultural ideal, the surpassing of man in Superman, *der Übermensch*. Scorning what he regarded as herd-moralities, and the ideologies of the mediocre, he preached the noble and aristocratic values, and the ascent of the human species to its self-surpassing.

All honour to Nietzsche that he was so earnestly, so passionately, and so whole-heartedly devoted to the cause of culture. He judges of all particular phenomena—the State, morality, religion—in their relation to what he considers to be the true ideal of culture. In so far as they favour that ideal, they are commended: in so far as they tend to hinder

its realization, they are condemned. Yes, all honour to
Nietzsche, that he took such a serious view of the value and
significance of human culture. But at the same time
Nietzsche, as I have maintained in this book, tried to undermine and destroy the very foundations on which true
culture must rest. Man, for Nietzsche, has no roots in
eternity, in the Transcendent-Immanent Godhead—for
there is no God—and so the spiritual foundation of culture
is entirely wanting. Yet it was on a spiritual foundation
that our European culture was built up, and it is from lack
of recognition of that foundation that the storm has come
upon us, a storm that threatens to engulf the best of our
culture in the abyss of its Nihilism.

In the pages of this book I have tried to represent
Nietzsche's thought fairly and candidly, as it appears to
me—for misrepresentation and vituperation are no help
at all in the study of a philosopher—but I willingly admit
that the book is a criticism of Nietzsche's position and, in
regard to the profound and ultimate issues, an adverse
criticism, for the philosophy of Nietzsche emphatically does
not present us with any way of salvation from our present
difficulties. But at the same time, I am by no means without
respect and sympathy for Nietzsche as a man, and I regard
his thought as in many ways a challenge to modern man, a
challenge above all to the Christian. I cannot look on the
philosophy of Nietzsche as the worthless mouthings of a
neurotic: on the contrary, it is my opinion that we must
come to grips with the thought of Nietzsche and must rise
above it, incorporating all the good that it may have to
offer on the way. It is an expression of a searching and
earnest soul, a poet and master of the German language,
and has by no means lost its relevance to the condition of
Europe since the death of its author. Rather has its
importance increased, and the issues involved stand up
clearly to-day for all thinking men and women to see.

At the same time, although one sympathizes with the
personal tragedy of Nietzsche's life, although one respects
to a certain extent the vigour and courage with which he
devoted himself to what he tried to regard as his 'mission',

although one recognizes his natural good qualities and regrets the squandering of so much talent and energy on false ends, one is in duty bound to point out, that Nietzsche shut his eyes to the light, deliberately rejecting God and Christianity, and so meriting the severest moral censure. We do not presume of course to pretend to know what went on in his soul at the last—God can act in a soul even when no external sign of interior conversion is normally possible—but the fact remains, and must be clearly stated, that during the period of his literary activity Friedrich Nietzsche chose darkness rather than light. It is not as though Nietzsche, momentarily overwhelmed, for example, by the sight of the world's suffering and man's sin, had undergone an atheistic 'phase': no, he deliberately cultivated, maintained and propagated atheism. We can only say, therefore, that he was—intellectually—a very wicked man. Catholic theologians are agreed that no man can remain in ignorance of God's existence for any length of time (we know that God gives sufficient grace for all men for their salvation), and St. Paul tells us that those who fail to recognize God are inexcusable. It is true that Nietzsche did not *aim* at robbing the *herd* of their religion, but in trying to 'set free' potential disciples from the 'shackles' of religion and morality he shows himself as a man who has said, 'Evil, be thou my Good'. In *Ecce Homo* Nietzsche declares, that his book *The Twilight of the Idols* is the most *wicked* of books, and in the same work he says, 'I am horribly frightened that one day I shall be pronounced "holy"—I refuse to be a saint; I would rather be a clown'. He claimed to be wicked, and he was correct—he *was* wicked. His campaign against Christianity and universal morality bear witness to the fact: in the latter respect he falls far short of a great pagan philosopher like Plato, who insisted on the absolute and universal character of moral values.

Nowadays, when there is a widespread tendency to equate virtue and religion exclusively with sincerity and kindness in dealing with other men and with freedom from the grosser exhibitions of lust, some may point triumphantly to Nietzsche's private life and say: 'Here is a good and moral man'—as if intellectual opinions did not matter. But they do matter, and wickedness in the intellectual sphere is worse than, for example, sexual sin, since, while the latter is rendered all the easier by the desires of the flesh which are common to man, intellectual wickedness argues a still more deliberate and clear-sighted sin against the light, especially in a man who had a Christian and pious upbringing. We cannot, therefore, regard Nietzsche as an atheistic 'saint': he was not a saint at all but a wicked man. If he was not licentious in the ordinary sense, that is certainly to his credit; but to fight deliberately against God is a worse sin, and more deeply-rooted in the soul, than the common vices into which men fall through human frailty.

If during the course of this book we seem to give a kindlier view of Nietzsche, that is not because we wish to be understood as retracting what we have just said. Nietzsche had many good qualities, and with these we can sympathize: he said many true things, and these we can commend: he suffered greatly, and we can feel for him in his sufferings: he had an ideal of culture and an ideal for man, and these we can, to a greater or less degree, honour and respect: but all that cannot alter the fact that he deliberately set himself against Him Who is the Way, the Truth and the Life. I ask readers of this book to remember the fact, and not to think that the author is condoning the sin of a man who was, in the literal sense, an *Antichrist*.

In the concluding chapter I have set Henri Bergson over against Friedrich Nietzsche. This I have done, not because I wish to subscribe to all that Bergson says, but because Nietzsche and Bergson both proclaimed a philosophy of life and both gave prominence to the 'higher man', though Bergson fully recognized the spiritual foundation of the universe and the spiritual character of true culture, and is said by some to have finally sealed this recognition by the reception of sacramental baptism.[1] Bergson, then, may be regarded as in many ways affording the most remarkable

---

[1] It has, however, also been asserted, that Bergson, for certain reasons, refrained from receiving sacramental baptism. At the moment the facts do not seem to be known with certainty—in this country at least.

modern solution of the Nietzschean problems, and as showing that we have to *surpass* Nietzsche by admitting the Transcendent and Supernatural, and not surrender to Nietzsche by riveting our attention on *Dasein* in the sense of Martin Heidegger.

Georg Brandes, in his lectures on Nietzsche, said that 'Little as he feels himself a German, he nevertheless continues the metaphysical and intuitive tradition of German philosophy, and has the German thinker's profound dislike of any utilitarian point of view'.[1] This is true: Nietzsche certainly stands in the line of the great German philosophers. He owed a great deal to the thought of the celebrated Pessimist, Arthur Schopenhauer, and shared in the latter's reaction to that remarkable development of dialectical metaphysics, which, taking its point of departure in Kant's *Critique of the Pure Reason*, culminated in the gigantic rationalistic and optimistic system of Hegel. But while, owing much to Schopenhauer, Nietzsche's thought wrestled with that of Schopenhauer and overthrew it, passing to a real *Lebensphilosophie*. But, as I have argued in the following pages, Nietzsche offers no real substitute for pessimism, in spite of all claims to the contrary: he never *could* overcome metaphysical pessimism, for his philosophy, like that of Schopenhauer, is atheistic. This is his πρῶτον ψεῦδος.

In attempting a criticism of Nietzsche from the Christian standpoint, while at the same time feeling that there is much of value in Nietzsche's philosophy and that his ideas on culture demand a really serious treatment, I realize that a more lengthy discussion would please some of my readers. Possibly, at some future time, I—or someone, who writes from the same standpoint, but is possessed of a greater competence than I am—may be able to attempt a more adequate, profound, and far-reaching treatment of Nietzsche, at once sympathetic, critical, and positive.

I express my gratitude to the Editor of the English translation of the works of Nietzsche, Dr. Oscar Levy, and to the publishers, Messrs. George Allen and Unwin, Ltd., for their kind and generous permission to include quotations from

[1] *Friedrich Nietzsche*. Trans. Chater. (Heinemann, 1914.) p. 52.

that translation in my book. Also to Messrs. Macmillan and Co., Ltd., for kind permission to quote from the English translation of Bergson's *Two Sources*, by R. Ashley Audra and Cloudesley Brereton, with the assistance of W. Horsfall Carter, and to Messrs. T. Werner Laurie, Ltd., and Dr. O. Levy, for permission to quote the description of Nietzsche's death from *Nietzsche* by J. M. Kennedy.

I may mention, that in giving references to the English translation of the works of Nietzsche, I have given the reference according to the page in the case of the non-aphoristic books, or where this course seemed to be preferable, while in the case of most of the aphoristic books, I have referred to the number of the aphorism, since several aphorisms are often found on one page.

Finally, it should be observed, that this book is in no way designed as an introduction for Christians to the works of Nietzsche. It is very far from the author's thought to suggest, that convinced Christians would do well to read such books as *Antichrist*—far from it. At the same time, an author who set out to depict Nietzsche in the blackest terms and to falsify his views or misinterpret them 'in deterius' could hardly hope to gain a sympathetic hearing, or even serious consideration, from those already acquainted with Nietzsche's writings. The author's aim is not to 'whitewash' but to depict the lights and shadows as honesty would seem to require.

(Heythrop, 1942)   *Frederick C. Copleston*

CHAPTER I

LIFE OF NIETZSCHE

ON the 15th October, 1844, a first child was born to the Lutheran pastor of Röcken in Prussian Saxony, and was given the names of Friedrich Wilhelm, in honour of Friedrich Wilhelm IV, King of Prussia, whose birthday fell on 15th October and who was the royal patron of pastor Nietzsche. Thus Friedrich Nietzsche, later to be known as a determined enemy of Christianity, spent his first years in a Christian and clerical home. His mother's father and grandfather had also been clergymen, and in his youth Nietzsche hoped to become a clergyman himself. His idealistic and poetic soul could not but be influenced by the religious atmosphere of his childhood, the service and music of the village church, the example of his father, and even in later years he retained a respect for genuine Christianity: we learn that he always discouraged convinced Christians from reading his books.[1] Once, when Nietzsche was engaged on the composition of *Zarathustra*, a young lady asked him if he had been to church that day, Sunday, and Nietzsche replied politely, 'To-day, no'. To his friend Lanzky he explained afterwards, 'If I had troubled that girl's mind, I should be horrified.' And do we not read in the second part of *Zarathustra*, 'Here are priests: but although they are mine enemies, pass them quietly and with sleeping swords! Even among them there are heroes; many of them have suffered too much—so they want to make others suffer. Bad enemies are they: nothing is more revengeful than their meekness. And readily doth he soil himself who toucheth them. But my blood is related to theirs: and I want withal to see my blood honoured in theirs'.[2] Early influences cannot be easily obliterated, and

---

[1] This respect for genuine Christians remained, but it cannot be denied, that his works contain much that is blasphemous and that is most repugnant to the Christian reader.

[2] pp. 105–6.

1

it may well be that Nietzsche's later ferocious attack on Christianity masked a feeling, half-formed and constantly repressed, that he was being unjust to the religion of his upbringing, perhaps even that it was he himself, and not the Christian, who was mistaken and misled. The dark years of madness that came upon him in the final period of his life may well have been due in part to the constant tension involved in denying and attacking a Faith which he felt to be confronting him with a claim that brooked no denial.

Nietzsche's father died in 1849, after a period of mental aberration brought on by a violent fall, and his mother removed to the town of Naumburg. Here Nietzsche lived with his mother, his sister, a grandmother and two aunts, a very feminine society for a young boy. He was a grave, introspective child, 'the little pastor', as his companions at school nicknamed him. There is an oft-quoted story which tells how, on one day of heavy rain, his mother looked out of the window to watch her son returning from school, and saw him walking along sedately though without overcoat or umbrella. In answer to her expostulations he replied that according to the school regulations, the boys were not to run in the streets. It was at Naumburg that music began to play a real part in his life, and it was at an early age that he began himself to compose motets and poems. As a grown man he became one of the masters of German literature and music always meant a great deal to him. Indeed his genius is sometimes said to lie rather in his poetic, literary and imaginative gifts than in the content of his philosophy. The latter does not contain the great message to mankind, which Nietzsche fondly ascribed to it, but as a German writer he cannot die.

In 1854 Nietzsche entered the Gymnasium at Naumburg, but in 1858 Frau Nietzsche was offered a scholarship for her son at the famous school of Pforta, five miles from Naumburg. The original Cistercian foundation had given place, at the Reformation, to a Lutheran boarding-school, and it was here that Nietzsche passed six years of his life, at the school which had given to the world men like Novalis, the Schlegels, and the patriot-philosopher Fichte, whose stirring addresses to the German people at Berlin, during the period of the Napoleonic domination, did much to keep alive the spirit of patriotism in a time of national humiliation. Nietzsche was not particularly happy during his first years at Pforta: the discipline was very strict and he found the routine irksome: but he worked hard, and he certainly enjoyed his year as a *Primaner*. He read Schiller, Hölderlin and Byron, of whom he preferred Hölderlin, and under the influence of his reading, as also under that of one or two of the masters who expounded higher criticism, he began to move away from Christianity. But the alienation was certainly not completed at Pforta. 'Can it be that, armed solely with the results of a boy's reflections, any one will venture to destroy the authority of two thousand years, guaranteed as it is by the deepest thinkers of all the centuries?' The final break came only later, but it was at Pforta that the estrangement began.

Nietzsche's leaving certificate asserted his deficiency in mathematics, while declaring him to be good at Greek, brilliant in Scripture, German and Latin. It was naturally in the period of his school days that his interest in and admiration for Greek culture were aroused. His favourite classical authors at that time were Plato and Aeschylus. The composition of poems and music was a delight to Nietzsche, and he and his friends founded a literary society which they named *Germania*. In the last year at Pforta Nietzsche enjoyed the easier discipline of the senior boys, and found stimulus in the *Germania* society and the company of his friends, in intercourse with the professors and in his own literary work.[1] It was then with sincerity that at the leaving ceremony Nietzsche expressed his indebtedness and gratitude to God, to the king, to his masters and comrades. In September, 1864, Nietzsche left Pforta.

At Pforta Nietzsche's particular friends were Gersdorff and Paul Deussen, the latter of whom was to become a professor at the University of Kiel. These two always

---

[1] The subject of his Latin essay for the leaving examination was Theognis, the aristocratic poet.

remained his friends. Friendship always meant a great deal to Nietzsche, and he has hymned its praises in stirring words. The great friendship of his life, which led to so sad an estrangement, was the friendship with Richard Wagner, when Nietzsche was professor at Bâle. The desire for friendship, the need to love and be loved, to be on intimate terms of understanding, remained ever strong in Nietzsche, and the increasing loneliness of his later years was contributory to the final breakdown. True, he was largely responsible himself for the loss of his friends—but that does not alter the fact that he longed for friendship and that loneliness was to him a terrible burden. Towards the end he wrote to his sister: 'A profound man needs friends, unless indeed he has a God. And I have neither God nor friend! Ah, my sister, those whom you call by this name, once they were friends—but now?'

However, when Nietzsche went to Bonn in October, 1864, in the company of his friend Paul Deussen and a cousin of the latter—happy, carefree students, riding through the Rhineland, singing beneath the windows—the black clouds of his tragic future were hidden from him. 'I arrived at Bonn with the proud sense of an inexhaustibly rich future before me'. Nietzsche joined, as was customary, one of the student-associations, throwing himself at first into the gay rollicking life of his companions—he even fought a duel—but he soon became disgusted with their ways, particularly with the heavy drinking. After an unsuccessful attempt to win over his companions to his own ideals, he broke with the association and withdrew from society. (Professor Karl Jaspers points out the importance of this incident. Nietzsche's companions naturally ascribed his withdrawal to pride or lack of 'camaraderie', but in reality he was beginning to feel the exceptional character of his 'vocation', without however yet realizing what form this 'vocation' was to take. The 'Entweder-Oder' is beginning to press upon him, though in an as yet undefined form.) At first he had studied both theology and philology, but after a time gave up the former study. 'If you wish to become a strong man', advised his favourite professor, Ritschl, 'acquire a speciality'.

Accordingly when Ritschl went as professor to Leipzig, Nietzsche made up his mind to leave Bonn, where he was no longer happy, and to follow Ritschl to Leipzig.

It appears that Nietzsche, while at Bonn, remained attached in some degree to Christianity. When Deussen suggested that prayer has no real value and that the confidence it imparts is but illusory, Nietzsche replied, 'that is one of the asininities of Feuerbach'. Again, when Deussen spoke approvingly of the *Life of Jesus* by Strauss, Nietzsche remarked, 'If you sacrifice Jesus, you must also sacrifice God'. But he felt all the torment and turmoil of doubt, as is evident from a letter to his sister, who was a believing Christian. '. . . What is it we are seeking? Rest and Happiness? No, nothing but Truth, however evil and terrible it may be. . . So are the ways of men marked out; if you desire peace of soul and happiness, believe; if you would be a disciple of Truth, enquire . . .' When he wrote this letter he had already declined to accompany his mother and sister to the Lutheran Communion service in the Easter vacation of 1865.

In the autumn of 1865 Nietzsche went to Leipzig, and continued to study philology under Ritschl and other professors. It was at Leipzig that he came across Arthur Schopenhauer's *World as Will and Idea*. Schopenhauer's picture of the world as the manifestation of blind Will, together with the essential position accorded to æsthetic experience in his philosophy and the metaphysical significance ascribed to music in particular, spoke to Nietzsche's soul in compelling tones. He was attracted, he says, by Schopenhauer's atheism and regretted that he had never had the opportunity of meeting the philosopher personally. (Schopenhauer died in 1860.) The separation with Christianity was thus completed at Leipzig, but the violent antagonism thereto was a later feature in Nietzsche's development. Schopenhauer was a master of language, and even a convinced Christian can understand the effect that his masterpiece might well produce on a temperament like that of Nietzsche, especially when he had already felt the torment of doubt and had become estranged from the religion of his fathers. But, as already remarked, one cannot feel certain that Nietzsche's separation from Christianity was ever so complete as he himself imagined: the very violence of his later hostility may have been an experience of his inner tension. And indeed, even in 1881, Nietzsche wrote to Peter Gast: 'Whatever I may happen to say of Christianity, I cannot forget that I owe to it the best experiences of my spiritual life; and I hope never to be ungrateful to it at the bottom of my heart'.

Nietzsche was happy at Leipzig: philology was less irksome to him, and he became the favourite pupil of professor Ritschl, who realized his great ability. In 1866 Nietzsche wrote: 'Three things are my consolations. Rare consolations! My Schopenhauer, the music of Schumann, and lastly solitary walks'. He was working up his *Theognidea* for the *Rheinisches Museum*, studied the sources of Diogenes Laërtius and conceived the desire of writing, of presenting the results of his studies, not in the inartistic way common among German scholars, but in an harmonious and beautiful form. 'The categorical imperative, "Thou shalt write, it is necessary that thou writest", has awakened me'. His joy was full when he met Erwin Rohde, a fellow-student at the University. Deussen was at Tübingen, Gersdorff at Berlin; but now Nietzsche formed an intimate friendship with a man whom he admired and liked from their first meeting, and who could be to him not merely a correspondent, but a daily companion. 'I experience for the first time the pleasure of a friendship founded on a moral and philosophic groundwork'. In August of 1866 Nietzsche and Rohde tramped the Bohemian forest country together and dreamed of revitalizing the Greek genius, of presenting it, not in the cut-and-dried manner of philological scholarship, but in such a way that men could feel the beauty and life of the Greek culture. Nietzsche's friendship with Rohde lasted many years and it was Rohde who was to leap to his friend's defence against the attack of Wilamowitz-Moellendorff consequent on the publication of Nietzsche's *Birth of Tragedy*. Indeed, next to Wagner, Rohde was the friend whom Nietzsche loved most. Yet this friendship was to become impaired in later years when Rohde, then professor at Leipzig, was a philologist of European reputation.

This happy life of study and friendship at Leipzig was broken by the fact of Nietzsche's being summoned to do his military service in 1867. He had been hitherto exempted on account of his bad eyesight, but in 1867 the Prussian army was in great need of men, and Nietzsche was enrolled in an artillery regiment. He was in barracks at Naumburg and became known as a good rider. 'In the barracks one learns to know one's nature, to know what is best to give among strange men, the greater part of whom are very rough.' However, a fall from his horse resulted in a dangerous injury and Nietzsche, after having been laid up for some time, returned to his studies at Leipzig. It was at this period that he came to know the music of Wagner. He was impressed by *Tristan* and enthusiastic over the *Meistersinger*. 'Last night, at the concert, the overture to the *Meistersinger* caused me so lasting a thrill that it was long since I had felt anything like it'. On the subject of the relation of Wagner's production to Schopenhauer's philosophy I touch briefly in the essay on *Nietzsche and Schopenhauer*. Nietzsche had the happiness of a personal meeting with Richard Wagner at the house of the latter's sister, Frau Brockhaus, and was seized with admiration for his new-found friend. The friendship thus begun developed into one of the greatest joys of Nietzsche's life : it was also to become, for him, a source of bitter pain and of disappointment.

To Nietzsche's astonishment Ritschl asked him one day if he would like to be appointed a Professor at Bâle. The essays, which Nietzsche had published in the *Rheinisches Museum*, had prompted the University authorities of Bâle to write to Professor Ritschl asking if Herr Friedrich Nietzsche could be safely entrusted with the Chair of Philology. To this letter Ritschl replied that Nietzsche was a young man possessed of the ability to do anything he chose to do. Nietzsche was disappointed not to be able to make his projected stay in Paris with Erwin Rohde, but he naturally accepted the very flattering invitation from Bâle, and the authorities at Leipzig conferred on him his final degree without examination, not liking to examine a fellow professor. In a letter to Gersdorff Nietzsche bids farewell to the golden time of free and unfettered activity, and expresses his desire to be more than a professional philistine, 'a pedagogue to honest savants'. 'Since we must endure life, let us at least endeavour so to use it as to give it some worth in the eyes of others when we are happily delivered from it'.

Thus at the age of twenty-four Nietzsche became a University professor. As Mr. Knight says: 'At heart he remains a teacher for the rest of his twenty years of active life. In the first decade he is partly a philologist and partly a philosopher: in the second he is purely a philosopher. There then remain another eleven years during which he is hopelessly and paralytically insane'.[1] On 28th May, 1869, Nietzsche delivered his inaugural lecture on *Homer and Classical Philology*. He began with only eight students, but taught Greek to the top form of the chief Gymnasium at Bâle in addition to his University work. In *Ecce Homo* he tells us that 'during the seven years in which I taught Greek to the sixth form of the College at Bâle, I never had occasion to administer a punishment; the laziest youths were diligent in my class'.[2] Nietzsche's work gave great satisfaction, and his early lectures are full of interest, expressed in a manner far removed from that of dry-as-dust scholarship. One can only echo the words that were later uttered by his mother: 'Oh, Fritz, Fritz, if only you had kept to your Greeks!'

At first Nietzsche felt somewhat lonely among the reserved people of Bâle; but Richard Wagner had a house not far distant, and the delights of a growing intimacy with the master and his gifted wife, Cosima, dispelled all clouds. The villa of Tribschen on the lake of Constance became a place of refuge and consolation to him. 'Wagner realizes all our desires: a rich, great, and magnificent spirit, an energetic character, an enchanting man, worthy of all love, ardent for all knowledge'. Nietzsche wrote to Rohde at Rome, that he too had his Italy. 'My Italy is called Tribschen, and I

[1] *Aspects of the Life and Work of Nietzsche*, A. H. J. Knight, Camb. Univ. Press (1933), p. 16.
[2] p. 16.

already feel as if it were my home'. In 1869 he spent Christmas with Wagner and his family, appreciating ever more the privilege of intimacy with the Master, and eager to make the work of Wagner known and valued in Germany. But when the Franco-Prussian war broke out Nietzsche resolved to ask permission from the University authorities (he had become a Swiss citizen) to serve in the German army in the ambulance corps. After a short course of training Nietzsche was sent to the front; but his service did not last very long, since he contracted dysentery and diphtheria from a convoy of sick soldiers whom he was accompanying from France to Carlsruhe. After an insufficient period of convalescence he returned to Bâle in order to take up, once more, his professional duties.

When Nietzsche set out for the war he was stirred by patriotic ardour, filled with the vision of the splendour, heroism, and self-sacrifice of war. But the result of the war, the German victory over France, made him anxious and apprehensive: he feared that 'we shall pay for our marvellous national victories at a price to which I, for my part, will never consent'. Nietzsche feared that the national aggrandisement of Germany might lead to her vulgarization, to a loss of true culture. The Prussia of Bismarck and Moltke was the great military power, and in Nietzsche's opinion 'modern Prussia is a Power highly dangerous to culture'. 'Be careful to free yourself from this fatal Prussia, with its repugnance to culture!' he writes to Rohde; and he applauded the words of his colleague at Bâle, Jacob Burckhardt, who exhorted his students not to take military triumph and the expansion of a State for true greatness. 'How many nations have been powerful', declared Burckhardt, 'who are forgotten and merit their oblivion! . . . Some unknown genius leaves us Notre Dame de Paris; Goethe gives us his Faust; Newton his law of the Solar System. This is greatness, and this alone'. Nietzsche even contemplated the formation of a 'cloister', a kind of seminary or monastery of culture, where he and his friends should live a life of thought and art. Rohde objected that they had not the necessary funds, and that in any case he personally did not feel a taste for such a cloistered life. The project was abandoned.

Nietzsche's illness, consequent on the war, had left a legacy of neuralgia, insomnia, eye-trouble and indigestion, and he had to go to Lugano to recuperate. (He chanced to meet Mazzini on the way.) At Lugano he spent two happy months and then returned to Bâle, where he resumed work upon the manuscript of *The Birth of Tragedy*. This work is an analysis of Greek culture in which Nietzsche contrasts Greek culture before Socrates—'Dionysian', strong and grand—with Greek culture after Socrates—rationalistic, anæmic and feeble. Applying his ideas to Germany, Nietzsche declared that the culture of his time bore only too strong a resemblance to the second period of Greek culture: it could only be saved if it came to be reformed by the spirit of Wagner. The book, though written as a scientific work on Greek culture, was thus made into an apology for Wagner through the introduction of extraneous matter, inspired by Nietzsche's admiration for, and loyalty to, Wagner. Nietzsche experienced some difficulty in finding a publisher, but at length the book was brought out by Wagner's own publisher, at the end of 1871, with the title *The Birth of Tragedy from the Spirit of Music*, the sub-title *Hellenism and Pessimism* being added to the second edition in 1885. It is one of the few well-constructed works of Nietzsche.

Wagner naturally received *The Birth of Tragedy* with enthusiasm, and wrote to Nietzsche that he had never read a finer book. The author had expected his 'centaur' to be successful, but in point of fact it was received by the philologists, even by Ritschl, with silence, or in some cases open hostility. Wilamowitz-Moellendorf, then a young man, wrote an abusive pamphlet against the book, and though the faithful Rohde came to his friend's defence with a counter-pamphlet, Nietzsche lost credit as a serious classical scholar. While these early works of Nietzsche (for example his lectures on *The Future of our Educational Institutions*) certainly contained valuable matter on the spirit of antiquity and the place and function of classical education, his failure to obtain recognition for his ideas was practically universal and he felt the unexpected disappointment very keenly. To this disappointment was added that of Wagner's change of residence to Bayreuth. Gone were the happy days at Tribschen and, when in later years, Nietzsche looked back to his friendship with Wagner, it was to those days that he returned in spirit. In *Ecce Homo*, written in 1888, Nietzsche expresses himself on the greatest consolation of his life, his intimate relationship with Richard Wagner. 'All my other relationships with men I treat quite lightly; but I would not have the days I spent at Tribschen—those days of confidence, of cheerfulness, of sublime flashes, and of profound moments —blotted from my life at any price. I know not what Wagner may have been for others; but no cloud ever darkened *our* sky' (p. 41).

It is in reference to this period that Mähly speaks of Nietzsche's friendliness and the sympathy felt for him by his colleagues; and Eucken remarks on Nietzsche's kind manner towards the *Doktoranden*, friendly and considerate, not excited or irritable.

In the period 1873-6 there came from Nietzsche's pen the four essays, which he called *Thoughts out of Season*. The first of these, *David Strauss, the Confessor and Writer*, was an exposure of German culture-philistinism. Public opinion, thought Nietzsche, attributed the victory over France, not only to German military talent, but also to German culture —a pernicious and deplorable error, which 'threatens to convert our victory into a signal defeat'. As a typical adherent of this pseudo-culture Nietzsche took David Strauss —'a genuine example of the *satisfait* in regard to our scholastic institutions, and a typical Philistine'. He examines Strauss' book, *The Old Faith and the New*, and subjects it and its author to a powerful and pungent criticism. Nietzsche says much that is to the point, but one can well sympathize with the astonishment of Strauss at being attacked so fiercely by a stranger. The second essay was on *The Use and Abuse of History*, in which Nietzsche inveighs against the idolization of historic learning. 'We would serve history only so far as it serves life'. In the third essay, *Schopenhauer as Educator*, the great

Pessimist is held up as the philosopher *par excellence* in contrast to the senile professional philosophers of the Universities. The fourth essay, *Richard Wagner in Bayreuth*, is a eulogy of Wagner, in which the art of Wagner is represented as a re-birth of the art of Greece.

Richard Wagner in Bayreuth was published in 1876, but as a matter of fact Nietzsche and Wagner had already had misunderstandings and had begun to drift apart. There can hardly be any doubt that Nietzsche was justified in thinking that Wagner regarded him as a tool and wanted him to subordinate his interests to the propagation of Wagnerism. Nietzsche had indeed contributed as much as he could both by pen and money to the success of the Bayreuth venture, the idea of the national theatre; and he might have continued to work for it if he had not begun to feel that he was mistaken in thinking Wagner's art to be the rebirth of the great art of Greece. He came to feel that his ideal Wagner was not the real Wagner, and the publication of *Parsifal* completed the separation. Wagner had gone over to Christianity. 'Richard Wagner, apparently the conquering hero, actually a despairing decadent who had become rotten, suddenly sank down, helpless and broken, before the Christian Cross'.[1] Nietzsche's disgust at Wagner's *lapse* into Christianity, as also his extreme concern at Romundt's decision to become a Catholic priest, shows how inimical he had become to that religion, which he regarded as the antithesis of the Greek genius. As Mr. Knight observes: '. . . probably the driving-force behind the whole Wagner episode was Nietzsche's love of Greece'.[2]

With Nietzsche's separation from Wagner began the second period of his work, when he is less of a poet and more of a philosopher, where he prefers Socrates to the pre-Socratics and questions all accepted opinions. Later he was to return to anti-Socratism. This second period, the *Apollonian*, as contrasted with the previous *Dionysian* period, saw the composition of *Human, All-too-Human*, *The Dawn of Day*, and *Joyful Wisdom*. Nietzsche's wretched

---

[1] Pref. to 2nd vol. of *Human, All-too-Human*, 1886.
[2] *Aspects of the Life and Work of Nietzsche*, p. 30.

health, largely due to the state of his eyesight, forced him to ask for a year's leave from Bâle, and he went to Naples, where he stayed with Fräulein von Meysenbug, in the company of Alfred Brenner and Dr. Paul Rée, a Jew. Richard Wagner was staying at Sorrento, after the triumph at Bayreuth and, disliking Jews, counselled Nietzsche against Rée. Nietzsche took no notice. Dr. Rée read aloud to the other three, since both Nietzsche and his hostess were short-sighted, while Brenner's lungs were affected. Fräulein von Meysenbug speaks of their happy circle: 'Nietzsche was indeed the soul of sweetness and kindliness! How well his good and amiable nature counterbalanced his destructive intelligence! How well he knew how to be gay, and to laugh with a good heart at the jokes which often came to disturb the serious atmosphere of our little circle'. From Naples Nietzsche went to Rosenlaui to take the cure, and then returned to Bâle.

During his year of leave from his professional duties Nietzsche had been working at the composition of *Human, All-too-Human*. The work is not a connected whole, like the *Birth of Tragedy*, but a collection of aphorisms or detached thoughts grouped together under certain leading ideas, thoughts which occurred to him from time to time. But though *Human, All-too-Human* is disconnected in form, it represents, as a whole, the second period of Nietzsche's development, the ascendency of science over poetry, the placing of Socrates above Aeschylus. 'If all goes well, the time will come when in order to advance themselves on the path of moral reason, men will rather take up the *Memorabilia* of Socrates than the Bible, and when Montaigne and Horace will be used as pioneers and guides for the understanding of Socrates, the simplest and most enduring of interpretative sages'.[1] Nietzsche rejects his former opinion. As Daniel Halévy has said: 'Pereat veritas, fiat vita!—he had once written. Now he writes, 'Pereat vita, fiat veritas'. The first volume of the work was published in 1878, and Nietzsche sent a copy to Richard Wagner, from whom he had himself received a copy of *Parsifal*. Neither acknowledged the work of the other: the separation of their

[1] *Human, All-too-Human*, II, 2, 86.

ways was now only too apparent. The book met with adverse judgment and was unacceptable, even to Erwin Rohde.

(It is often said—and with ample justification—that Nietzsche's development falls into three successive phases. First comes the period in which the *geniuses*, men like Wagner and Schopenhauer, are held up to honour—the period of *The Birth of Tragedy* and *Thoughts out of Season*: secondly, there is the period of ice-cold questioning, of the *Wissenschaftsideal*, detached, critical, doubting, the Socratic period, the period represented, for instance, by *Human, All-too-Human*: thirdly, there is the period in which Nietzsche comes to the consciousness of his own thought, the period in which he is the independent philosopher, the period of *Zarathustra, Beyond Good and Evil, The Genealogy of Morals*, etc.

But there are two qualifications which should be born in mind. The first is this, that Nietzsche's third period is not a static, rounded-off and clearly-articulated whole in which he presents a defined and already-elaborated philosophy of life, but is itself a period of growth. He himself speaks of *Zarathustra* as a *Vorhalle*, and though his later works may represent his autumnal season, his *Erntezeit*, yet he was always feeling his way, always *ein Werdender*, always striving to express an ill-defined ideal, too rich to be pinned down and clearly delineated in words. The second qualification to be remembered is that there exists a certain inner community between the three periods which Nietzsche himself recognized. Did he not say that in his earlier presentation of Schopenhauer and Wagner it was himself that he was really presenting, whom he was reading into them? Even if we allow that Nietzsche tends to read his later thought back into his earlier, there is, I consider, much truth in his assertion; and it could be substantiated by quotations from earlier works and essays which hint—sometimes very obviously—at ideas that we have learnt to associate with the third period of Nietzsche's development, that of his independent philosophizing.)

Nietzsche's health grew worse, and the state of his eyes, stomach and head compelled him to resign his chair at Bâle:

he was granted a pension by the authorities of the University in consideration for his past services. Nietzsche went to the Engadine, and there recovered sufficiently to enable him to work at the second part of *Human, All-too-Human*, which appeared in 1879. But his health grew worse again, and he wrote to Peter Gast (Heinrich Köselitz) of his expectation of death—'I feel like a very old man'. He spent the winter with his mother and sister at Naumburg, a winter of suffering, somewhat alleviated by Rohde's appreciation of *The Wanderer and his Shadow*. In a letter to Fräulein von Meysenbug, written in the expectation of death, Nietzsche speaks of the Wagners. 'I think of him with a lasting gratitude, for I owe him some of the strongest incitements towards spiritual liberty. Madame Wagner, as you know, is the most sympathetic woman whom I have met. But our relations are ended, and assuredly I am not the man to resume them. It is too late'. But Nietzsche lived, and in the spring of 1880 he went to Venice with Peter Gast. The latter played Nietzsche his favourite music—Chopin at that time—walked with him and acted as his secretary. In July Nietzsche was at Marienbad, in September at Naumburg, in October back again in Italy. He lodged at Genoa, where he lived very frugally, so that the neighbours called him *Il Santo*. In the morning he would go out to a rock near the sea and lie there 'motionless as a lizard, with nothing before me but the sea and the pure sky'. In the *Dawn of Day* he describes the impression made on him: 'Here is the sea, here may we forget the town. It is true that its bells are still ringing the Angelus—that solemn and foolish yet sweet sound at the junction between day and night,—but one moment more! Now all is silent. Yonder lies the ocean, pale and brilliant; it cannot speak. The sky is glistening with eternal mute evening hues, red, yellow, and green: it cannot speak. The small cliffs and rocks which stretch out into the sea as if each one of them were endeavouring to find the loneliest spot—they too are dumb. Beautiful and awful indeed is this vast silence which so suddenly overcomes us and makes our hearts swell'.[1]

[1] *Dawn of Day*, aph. 423.

The *Dawn of Day* appeared in July, 1881. This book shows hostility towards Christianity, and in *Ecce Homo* Nietzsche says of it: 'With this book I open my campaign against morality', and 'With *The Dawn of Day* I first engaged in a struggle against the morality of self-renunciation'.[1] He again failed to win recognition, and Rohde neither acknowledged the receipt of the work, nor answered Nietzsche's subsequent letter.

It was at this period that the idea of the *Eternal Recurrence* came to Nietzsche. When staying at Sils-Maria the thought occurred to him, as he sat at the foot of a rock near Surlei, that every event necessarily occurs again. Time is infinite, and there must be necessary periodic cycles in which all that has been is repeated over again. This process continues to infinity. Nietzsche seems to have thought that this was an entirely novel idea, a discovery on his part, whereas in point of fact it was by no means new, but had been familiar to Greek thinkers. It is, of course, a false notion, but it is easy to understand how those who accept it would find it somewhat depressing. Nietzsche, too, found it depressing, but he recovered his spirits at Genoa in the autumn of 1881. The weather was mild and Nietzsche's joy was full when he discovered Bizet's *Carmen*. 'It is like a story of Merimée's, clear, powerful, sometimes touching. . . . I almost think that *Carmen* is the best opera which exists'. The fruit of his new-found joy was *Joyful Wisdom*, which appeared in September, 1882. (A fifth part was added in 1886.) The fourth part is dedicated to the memory of the cloudless month of January, 1882, which Nietzsche had spent at Genoa. Nietzsche's good spirits appear in the *Dancing Song to the Mistral*, included in *Joyful Wisdom*:—

'Dance, oh! dance on all the edges,
Wave-crests, cliffs and mountain ledges,
    Ever finding dances new!
Let our knowledge be our gladness,
Let our art be sport and madness,
    All that's joyful shall be true!

[1] *Ecce Homo*, pp. 91 and 95.

Sweep away all sad grimaces,
Whirl the dust into the faces
    Of the dismal sick and cold !
Hunt them from our breezy places,
Not for them the mind that braces,
    But for men of visage bold'.[1]

From Genoa Nietzsche went to Messina; but the sirocco at the end of April drove him away; and he stopped in Rome at the earnest request of Fräulein von Meysenbug. This good lady had made the acquaintance of a Russian girl, Lou Salomé, who was travelling in Europe with her mother. She gave Lou Salomé Nietzsche's works to read and thought that she would be just the wife for Nietzsche. In 1875 Nietzsche had proposed to a charming young Dutch lady, but had been refused: the affair with Lou Salomé was to have no better success. But Wagner was probably right when, in earlier years, he had advised Nietzsche to marry. If Nietzsche had found a wife who could understand and sympathize with him, it might have made a very great difference to the course of his life. Nietzsche seems to have fallen in love with Lou Salomé, and, according to her account, he even said to her, after recounting the story of his life: 'Yes, my adventures began in this manner. They are not ended. Where will they lead me ? Whither shall I adventure again ? Should I not come back to the faith ? To some new belief ?'—adding 'In any case a return to the past is more likely than immobility'. Miss Salomé refused Nietzsche's offer of marriage, but expressed her desire to remain his friend and disciple. They met in Germany and Nietzsche initiated her into his thoughts, but he evidently expected an unconditional assent to his philosophy and Lou Salomé was not prepared to give such an assent. Eventually Nietzsche came to think that Paul Rée and Lou Salomé were leagued against him. Nietzsche's sister did not like the latter and encouraged her brother to suspicion. In the end Nietzsche lost the friendship of both the Russian girl and Dr. Rée. It is difficult to make out exactly what happened

---

[1] Strophes 6 and 9, *Joyful Wisdom*, pp. 369–370.

as the account of Elisabeth Nietzsche and of Lou Salomé herself differ; but it is at least clear that a painful situation was created which Nietzsche was unable to resolve. He was not made to deal with such difficulties. He complained to the Overbecks at Bâle that he had been betrayed by everyone and declared: 'To-day I enter into a complete solitude'.

Lou Salomé comments on the note of hiddenness in Nietzsche's appearance, an impression of silent loneliness: he bore the stamp of one standing apart from the throng, of one who stands alone. His large eyes appeared to her as guardians of his inner treasure. They seemed to look within and at the same time into the distance. In the course of a lively conversation his eyes lit up, but if Nietzsche was in melancholy mood, they betrayed his inner loneliness, as though they looked out from secret depths. In ordinary life he was a man of great politeness and even mildness, and he was always careful of the tidiness of his appearance and clothes, but this outward ordinariness was a mask that covered a soul which came from the wilderness and the mountain. Portraits of Nietzsche can give but an inadequate idea of the impression he made on those who knew him— this lonely solitary soul that lived in the depths of his own vision.

Nietzsche went to Genoa and then to the bay of Rapallo where he spent the winter of 1882–3. The weather was poor and Nietzsche was not comfortable, yet 'it was during the winter and in this discomfort that my noble *Zarathustra* was born'. The thought of *Zarathustra* had occurred to Nietzsche at Sils-Maria: he would use this Persian figure as a means of expressing his thought. But by the time that Nietzsche came to write the first part of *Zarathustra* Nietzsche's development had begun. This is characterized by his insistence on the ideal of aristocracy, as centreing round the conception of the Superman. The first part of *Zarathustra* was written in ten days and published in May, 1883. The doctrine of the Eternal Recurrence does not appear in this part, but Nietzsche teaches the doctrine of the Superman through the lips of Zarathustra. 'Lo, I teach you the Superman! The Superman is the meaning of the earth.'

God is dead, and all those who cling to supernatural hopes are condemned as contemners of the earth, as poisoners of life. As man surpasses the ape so is man himself to be surpassed by Superman, the finest flower of the human race. 'Man is a rope stretched between the animal and the Superman—a rope over an abyss'. The Superman is the aristocrat of culture, strong in mind, strong in body, who has freed himself from Schopenhauer's pessimism. Modern man has no goal or goals: Nietzsche gives him an ideal, the Superman. Man is to save himself by this glorification and ennoblement of his own species, not by recourse to the Saviour, Christ. Thus does Nietzsche answer *Parsifal*.

The second part of *Zarathustra* was written in Switzerland between 26th June and 6th July of the same year, 1883. In the autumn Nietzsche went to Germany, where he stayed at Naumburg with his mother and sister. He was not happy there for his sister wished to marry a Herr Förster, an anti-Semite, who planned a colonial enterprise in Paraguay. Neither mother nor brother were prepared to lose Elisabeth: moreover Nietzsche hated and despised anti-Semitism. His sister was resolved to marry Förster and accompany him when he went to Paraguay—as indeed she did. Nietzsche left Naumburg in the late autumn, and after various wanderings arrived at Nice. There he wrote the third part of *Zarathustra*, again in about ten days: it was published early in 1884. In this part Nietzsche announces the doctrine of the Eternal Recurrence, which is supposed to be a counterblast to man's paralysing sense of guilt. One might be tempted to think that the doctrine of the Eternal Recurrence and of the Superman are incompatible; but in Nietzsche's eyes this was not so. Man must practise a heroic yea-saying to life, must so live that he will desire and affirm the eternal repetition of his actions. In this part appears the important chapter on *The Old and New Tables*. The old morality, the table of weariness and slothfulness that must hinder the coming of the *noble*, the new aristocracy, must be broken up. 'Break up, break, I pray you, the good and just!' In place of the old morality Nietzsche offers a new table, the morality of the strong and free, of the creative spirit, expressing the Will to Power. 'This new table, O my brethren, put I up over you. Become hard!'

Towards the end of April, 1884, Nietzsche arrived in Venice, where Peter Gast was staying. In June he went to Switzerland, and there, in August, he was visited by Baron Heinrich von Stein, a young man of twenty-six, who had published a little volume some years previously, *The Ideal of Materialism, Lyrical Philosophy*. Von Stein was a disciple of Wagner, and it is possible that Cosima Wagner—Richard Wagner was dead—hoped that von Stein would be an intermediary with Nietzsche, who had not yet published his attack on Wagner. In any case von Stein wished Nietzsche to go to Bayreuth in order to hear *Parsifal*. Nietzsche thought that he had found in Heinrich von Stein a kindred spirit who had some understanding for *Zarathustra*. He was very pleased that his visitor had come to see him and not merely for the sake of the Engadine, and von Stein, who stayed three days, was greatly impressed by Nietzsche. But Nietzsche's confidence that he had at last found a disciple was dispelled by the early death of von Stein, an event which caused him the bitterest disappointment.

Nietzsche met his sister at Zürich. She was by now Frau Förster, and her brother, wasting no time in reproaches, made himself very pleasant. His sister wrote of him that 'he is bright and charming; we have been together for six weeks, talking, laughing over everything'. At Zürich Nietzsche was engaged on the fourth part of *Zarathustra*, which he continued at Mentone and then at Nice. It was published early in 1885, but only forty copies at Nietzsche's own expense. He could find only seven people to whom he could send a copy—an indication of his increasing isolation and loneliness. Nietzsche's most famous work was then completed, but it met with no recognition. It is prophetic and poetic in tone, and is by no means always easy to interpret; but whatever the worth of its thought-content, it manifests the literary ability of its author. Nietzsche thought of continuing the book, adding another or even other parts, but he never did so. He decided to abandon the lyrical style: 'Henceforth I shall speak, and not Zarathustra'.

In the fourth part of *Zarathustra* Nietzsche makes it clear that he was writing for disciples, for superior men. It was his great grief that he failed to attach to himself some disciples. As we have seen, Heinrich von Stein had inspired hopes in Nietzsche, but von Stein was young and had not yet surrendered himself entirely to Nietzsche: in any case he died an early death. At Nice Nietzsche was joined by a German intellectual, Paul Lanzky, who had read *Zarathustra*, and who had written on the work in a Leipzig periodical and in the *Rivista Europea* of Florence. He addressed Nietzsche as 'Master'. 'You are the first to call me by that name', said Nietzsche with a smile. Lanzky had come to meet a prophet and he was astonished to find an affable and simple man. Indeed, one can say in general that a reading of Nietzsche's works would scarcely give an idea of what the author was like in personal intercourse. 'What a mistaken idea of you one gathers from your books', remarked Lanzky. It is indeed the great tragedy of Nietzsche's life that he came to regard himself as a man with the mission of trans-valuating all values. And did he always believe in that mission from the bottom of his heart?

In April and May of 1885 Nietzsche was in Venice, in June in the Engadine. He met his sister at Naumburg, before she set out for South America in order to join her husband. Elisabeth Nietzsche urged her brother, as she had done before, to return to a university; but Nietzsche replied: 'Young men are so stupid! and professors still more stupid! Besides, all the German universities repel me'. His sister suggested Zürich, but Nietzsche answered that Venice was the only town he could tolerate. From Naumburg he went again, via Munich, to Florence where Lanzky introduced him to the astronomer Leberecht Tempel. After their interview Nietzsche remarked characteristically to Lanzky: 'I wish that this man had never known my books. He is too sensible, too good. I shall harm him'. From Florence he went to Nice. There he put together some notes in the form of a new book, *Beyond Good and Evil, Prelude to a Philosophy of the Future*. As its title indicates, this work was meant to be a prologue to a 'magnum opus', on which Nietzsche was then engaged. This great systematic work was never completed; but the notes collected by Nietzsche for his projected chief work were published posthumously as *The Will to Power*. *Beyond Good and Evil* was published, at Nietzsche's expense, in 1885. In this collection of aphorisms appears Nietzsche's desire for a United Europe as contrasted with a nationalism that threatened to be the ruin of European culture.

In the spring of 1886 Nietzsche stayed in Venice, but his friend Peter Gast was absent in Germany, trying to get his opera, *The Lion of Venice*, accepted by a theatre. Both men were poor and Nietzsche, sympathizing with his friend's distress, offered to help him: 'Let us share my purse, let us share the little that I have'. Wishing to interview his publishers, Nietzsche went to Germany. Here he visited Rohde at Leipzig, where the friend of his youth had been appointed professor. It was an unhappy meeting for both of them. Nietzsche found himself received by his old friend without enthusiasm, and he had to listen to Rodhe's complaints concerning his colleagues, students and the climate of Leipzig. In *Ecce Homo*, when speaking of the influence of climate on intellectual ability and activity, Nietzsche says: 'I have a certain case in mind in which a man of remarkable intellect and independent spirit became a narrow, craven specialist and a grumpy old crank, simply owing to a lack of subtlety in his instinct for climate'.[1] Rohde on his side found Nietzsche strange. 'All his person was marked with an indescribable strangeness, and it disgusted me. There was about him something that I had never known, and of the Nietzsche whom I had known many features were effaced. He seemed to have come from an uninhabited land'. In other words the two friends had grown apart in the course of time—not such a very unusual event, after all—and this painful meeting at Leipzig made the fact clear, though the final estrangement came later.

[1] p. 34.

Nietzsche went to Leipzig, but he was not happy with his mother, since she read his books in spite of Nietzsche's exhortations to the contrary and was very distressed by their anti-Christian spirit. He went on to the Engadine, where he was liked and esteemed by his fellow-guests at the hotel —he was a vivacious table companion—but chance acquaintanceship could not fill the place of an intimate friendship. It was at this time that he wrote to his sister these words: 'A *profound* man needs friends, unless he has a God. And I have neither God nor friend'. He laboured at his projected work, *The Will to Power, an essay towards a Transvaluation of all Values*, but soon removed to Ruta, near Rapallo, where he prepared second editions of *The Birth of Tragedy*, *The Dawn of Day*, and *Joyful Wisdom*, adding new prefaces for the two last books. At Ruta Nietzsche received some consolation, since a letter arrived from Hippolyte Taine, appreciating *Beyond Good and Evil*, and Paul Lanzky came to join him. But Nietzsche did not stop there long: the restless man moved on alone to Nice, saying that he needed light and air. At Nice he read Baudelaire, Paul Bourget, Maupassant, and other French authors, taking an interest also in the works of Dostoievsky. He heard the prelude to *Parsifal* at a concert in Monte Carlo and wrote to Peter Gast: 'I loved Wagner, I still love him'. In March, 1887, he experienced the earthquake at Nice and his calm demeanour was remarked on.

Nietzsche's health was in poor condition, and it was not improved by a quarrel with Rohde. Writing to the latter Nietzsche asserted that Taine, Burckhardt, 'and even you are not old enough for me'. Rohde, who was already a famous scholar, was not unnaturally annoyed, and he wrote a strong letter to Nietzsche, which he afterwards regretted. Nietzsche went to Switzerland for medical treatment and while there he was struck by a fresh blow, the death of Heinrich von Stein at the age of thirty. 'This has put me out of my senses; I truly loved him. I always thought that he was reserved for me some day'. So wrote Nietzsche to Peter Gast. In spite of his depression, however, he composed *A Genealogy of Morals* in some fifteen days. This book was an answer to a Swiss critic's attack on *Beyond Good and Evil* and appeared later in 1887. After visiting Peter Gast at Venice, he returned to Nice in October, and while he was there, occurred the final estrangement from Erwin Rohde. Nietzsche reproached Rohde for his criticism of Taine, but the last words of his letter might well have moved his friend—'I have forty-three years behind me and am alone as if I were a child'. Nevertheless this letter marked the end of his friendship with Rohde, though Nietzsche's isolation was somewhat alleviated by a very appreciative letter from the celebrated Danish critic, Georg Brandes, who later delivered a course of lectures on Nietzsche's doctrine at Copenhagen.

Nietzsche longed for real friends who could understand him, and to whom he could communicate his inmost thoughts: in the course of time, as the conviction of his own *mission* grew upon him, he came to long more and more for *disciples*. The problem of Nietzsche's longing for intimate friendship and of his failure to find it or keep it would deserve a special treatment, and can only be briefly alluded to in a short sketch of his life. The question is a complicated one, and there are several factors to be born in mind. First, Nietzsche seems to have found a difficulty in loving his friends as they were: he measured them by absolute standards and found them wanting. Secondly, he desired them to subordinate themselves to his own *mission* —and yet it was precisely this *mission*, Nietzsche's inmost convictions, that so often repelled—and so in a sense was loving *himself* and not *them*.[1] Thirdly, he became ever more conscious of himself as an exception in his age, as one looking to the future, as concerned with the future man, and this conviction drove him more and more into solitariness. One may safely say that Nietzsche's *mission* or *vocation* drove him to loneliness, while at the same time he remained a human being, who longed for the warmth of intimate relationship with intellectual equals. This constant tension

---

[1] In other words Nietzsche himself cannot be acquitted of the charge which he brought against Wagner, though—as far as theory goes—he declared that he wanted independent disciples.

caused him great agony and suffering of soul—a tension recognized by Nietzsche himself.

But one should not forget that though Nietzsche failed to find those relationships which he desired, there were, to the last, kind and true souls ready to help and befriend him —his own mother and sister, Peter Gast, Professors Burckhardt and Overbeck. Nietzsche was not friendless in the superficial sense; but he became friendless in a deeper sense, for he could enjoy no real and full communication of thought and soul even with men like Overbeck and Burckhardt, whom he respected and admired. The lonely wanderer could enjoy from time to time the amenities of surface friendship (I do not, of course, mean to imply that Overbeck, etc., were insincere), but the inner loneliness grew, and the void that first Rohde, and then—more especially—Richard Wagner had given promise of filling, became a yawning abyss.[1]

Nietzsche was by now in a state of extreme mental tension and distress, brought on largely by lack of recognition and loneliness, and by that insomnia for which he was accustomed to take drugs, particularly chloral. True, he had won two celebrated readers outside Germany, the Frenchman, Hippolyte Taine, and the Dane, Georg Brandes. But when Nietzsche, then at Turin, received a letter from Brandes in April, 1888, announcing the coming conferences at Copenhagen, it was probably too late. Leaving on one side the composition of his projected great work, Nietzsche composed a bitter attack on Wagner—*The Case of Wagner*. He seems to have felt some remorse over it, but a desire to attack and destroy—surely a prelude to his madness—drew him on. Already in February, 1888, he had written to Peter Gast that 'I am in a state of chronic irritability which allows me, in my better moments, a sort of revenge, not the finest sort— it takes the form of an excess of hardness'. After completing the attack on Wagner Nietzsche set out to attack ideas in *The Twilight of the Idols*, which was sufficient to prepare

---

[1] It is probably true to say that this solitariness and isolation contributed to warp his judgment. As he himself says, he had neither God nor friends, and this fact doubtless led to distortion of vision. The solitary does not *always* see more clearly.

people for the coming of the great work on the Will to Power. He then compiled what was to have been the first part of that work, *The Antichrist.*

These last works of Nietzsche are full of self-assertion and mental exaltation, as well as destructive in character—*The Antichrist* is a virulent attack on the Christian religion. The last months of 1888 were marked by a similar exaltation and hilarity in Nietzsche's soul: he praises everything in Turin and writes enthusiastically of the city to Peter Gast. But a premonition of the approaching disaster that was to follow on this exalted state, is discernible in his words; and incipient madness may surely also be recognized in his last work, *Ecce Homo*, a kind of autobiography. Nietzsche was certainly not yet mad in the full sense, but the triumphant self-assertion and bizarre atmosphere of *Ecce Homo* are definitely abnormal. 'Why I am so wise', 'Why I am so clever', 'Why I write such excellent books', 'Why I am a fatalist',—so Nietzsche heads his chapters. The book concludes with an affirmation of his absolute hostility to Christianity, to the *Vampirism* of Christian morality. 'Ecrasez l'infâme!' 'Have you understood me? *Dionysus* versus Christ'. So Nietzsche flung his final defiance at the Christ of his youth.

Brandes had obtained for Nietzsche a new reader, the Swede August Strindberg: Professor Deussen sent him 2,000 francs, the gift of an unknown donor, towards an edition of Nietzsche's works: a French lady offered him another thousand. But this late success was too late, and could not stave off the final catastrophe. Nietzsche prepared a new pamphlet for publication, *Nietzsche contra Wagner*, but no further work was to be written, for at the beginning of January, 1889, he went mad. Nietzsche wrote strange letters to his friends, to Burckhardt, Brandes, Peter Gast and others. To Burckhardt he declared that he was Ferdinand de Lesseps, the letter to Brandes he signed, 'the Crucified', he told people in Turin that he was God, and squandered his money. Burckhardt went to see the Overbecks, and Professor Overbeck at once left Bâle for Turin, where he found Nietzsche in a state of mental collapse. For a time Nietzsche was in a home, first at Bâle, and then at Jena: afterwards his mother took him into her house at Naumburg, and after her death his sister—who returned from Paraguay when her husband died—took him to a new house at Weimar, where they lived together.

There does not appear to have been any definite sign of madness, as a psychical condition, before 27th December, 1888, when Nietzsche wrote to Overbeck that he was working at a 'Promemoria' for the European courts with a view to an anti-German League. He wanted the 'Reich' to be encircled and provoked to a war of desperation. But as there is question of an organic disease of the brain, probably paralytic in character, there must have been a progressive organic deterioration before psychological insanity declared itself. At the time methods of investigation were not sufficiently advanced to admit of a clear and definite diagnosis, and though comparative studies, etc., may help in the formation of an opinion, it is unlikely that we can ever be absolutely certain of the precise character of Nietzsche's illness and still less disentangle its foregoing symptoms from those of other—perhaps independent—ailments or determine its influence on his literary productions. From the point of view of a purely historical study of Nietzsche, the man and his thought, these and allied questions are clearly of paramount interest and importance; but it may be as well to point out that for a study of his thought as expressed in his writings, with a view to estimating its objective value or truth in itself, the nature of the contributing causes of that thought is of considerably less importance. (Medical opinion is nowadays inclined to see in the association of motor paralysis with mental disturbances of the type that afflicted Nietzsche the syndrome characteristic of general paralysis of the insane.)

Nietzsche never recovered, but he could appreciate music and literature, and he impressed everyone by his patience, consideration and gentleness. When shown portraits of Wagner, he would say, 'I loved him'; and when his sister wept, as she sat by his side, he said: 'Lisbeth, why do you cry? Are we not happy?' He was able to enter into conversation with visitors, and was particularly delighted when Peter Gast came and played to him. Thus, in the period of his mental breakdown (brought on by his ill-health, the use of drugs to alleviate insomnia, his loneliness and isolation, his intense intellectual life and inward struggle—perhaps also by a half-formed doubt as to the reality of his mission) Nietzsche's inherent goodness of disposition manifested itself with natural ease. As one reads the story of these closing years of his life one can only grieve that such a man should have considered himself destined for such a mission. Nietzsche wrote a pamphlet *Nietzsche contra Wagner*: one might speak of the philosophy of Nietzsche as *Nietzsche contra Nietzsche*.[1]

On the 25th August, 1900, Friedrich Nietzsche died of pneumonia at Weimar. His sister describes the hour of his passing, preceded by a great thunderstorm, when she thought that he would depart amidst thunder and lightning. 'But he rallied again, recovered consciousness later in the evening, and tried to speak. I went into his room at two o'clock the following morning to give him a refreshing drink, and as I pulled the lamp-shade to one side so that he could see me, he cried joyfully: "Elisabeth!" which led me to think that the danger was over. He slept for several hours after this, which I thought would help his recovery. But his face changed more and more; his breathing became ever more difficult: the shadow of death fell over him. Again he opened those wonderful eyes of his. He moved uneasily, opened his mouth, and shut it again, as if he had something to say and hesitated to say it. And it seemed to those who stood around that his face slightly reddened thereat. Then a light shudder; a deep breath—and softly, silently, with one final majestic look, he closed his eyes for ever.

'Thus it happened that Zarathustra departed'.

Nietzsche was buried at Röcken, and Peter Gast, his faithful friend, pronounced a short eulogy at the graveside. The tragic and lonely spirit of Friedrich Nietzsche had gone

---

[1] It is only right to point out that the original narration of the last phase of Nietzsche's life was most probably coloured by sisterly affection. There seems to have been another side to the picture.

forth to its Maker, whom it had denied: who will be prepared to affirm that He who searches the hearts of all, may
not have given him at the last the grace to seek for mercy
where it is never sought in vain?

Chapter II

NIETZSCHE'S CULTURAL IDEAL

That Nietzsche was a great metaphysician cannot be reasonably maintained by anyone. He lacked the detachment
necessary for a true philosopher, and the power of sustained,
scientific and rational argument. It does not require a
profound knowledge of his works in order to realize that
he cannot be considered as one among men like Aristotle,
St. Thomas Aquinas, Leibniz, Kant, Hegel, Whitehead. He
made no real contribution to logic, ontology or theory of
knowledge. There is, of course, abundant evidence of
psychological insight in his writings, but it cannot be said
that Nietzsche was a scientific psychologist. His assertion
of the doctrine of the Eternal Recurrence cannot be said
to entitle him to the position of a speculative philosopher:
it was not a new 'discovery' on his part—in spite of his
apparent belief that this was so[1]—and in any case, however
much importance Nietzsche may attach to the doctrine in
Zarathustra, it was stated mainly in the interest of his
ethical ideas. Can Nietzsche justly be termed a moral
philosopher? If a moral philosopher be taken to mean a
man who presupposes or enunciates an absolute system of
ethics, then, of course, Nietzsche is not a moral philosopher
in this sense—he summons us 'Beyond Good and Evil'—
but if a moral philosopher be taken to include a man who
has a doctrine about morality and moral values, then he
certainly is a moral philosopher. We make this distinction
because it would be a great mistake to think that Nietzsche
was primarily concerned with scientific statement. The
scientific ethician is not so much concerned with making

[1] Nietzsche does, however, recognize Empedokles as a predecessor.

men better as with analysing the moral judgment, discerning its foundations, and so on. Nietzsche, however, is primarily concerned with the promotion of a new type of man; his moral philosophy is not scientific, analytic, and static, but is assertive, exhortatory, dynamic. He desires a trans-valuation of all values, with a view to the attainment of what he regards as true culture. He does not, therefore, like Aristotle, accept the normal moral judgments of mankind as the basis of a scientific ethic, but rejects those judgments and demands a new table of values in the service of a higher culture. Thus his 'moral philosophy' has not the calm atmosphere of that of Aristotle for instance, but appears in a prophetic and in some sense even *religious* garb. It is not for nothing that Nietzsche, in his most famous book, speaks through the lips of the Persian religious reformer Zarathustra or Zoroaster. Even in his moral philosophy, Nietzsche appears as an avenger and destroyer, as a prophet and a herald. Historic and psychological insight, imaginative and poetic élan, are placed at the service of a hatred of the old tables, the hitherto-accepted values—particularly Christian morality—and a flaming enthusiasm for a new cultural ideal, which Nietzsche imagined to be a continuation and development of Greek culture in its best period.

Nietzsche's treatment of morality falls therefore naturally into two complementary halves, his exposure and destruction of former and current values, and his assertion of and appeal for a new cultural ideal. It is this second aspect which we propose to consider first, leaving to another essay his criticism of morality, especially Christian morality. A certain repetition will thus be unavoidable, but that should not be surprising in dealing with Nietzsche, who does not hesitate to repeat himself over and over again. Moreover it is not illogical to take his positive cultural ideal for prior con-sideration, since it was with a view to the establishment and realization of this ideal that he criticized so bitterly the standards of the past. In the course of this exposition it will, I hope, become clear that there is much that is true and valuable in what Nietzsche says—how could it be other-wise in a man of his intellectual stature?—while at the same time there is much that is simply false, much that is one-sided and exaggerated and a good deal that is blasphemous. Nietzsche certainly had his virtues, but moderation was never one of them. The ideal of his first period of development was the Dionysian ideal, and this was also the ideal of his final period, when it reappeared in the developed philosophy of the Superman and the Will to Power. The middle or second period, the Socratic period, was supposed to be a return to *Positivism*, to clear and cold science, a sceptical, questioning and detached period; but in point of fact it was a temporary reaction, a step on the road to the further elaboration of the philosophy of Dionysos. Nietzsche asserts Dionysos against Christ; he also asserts Dionysos against Apollo—we might almost say, exaggeration against moderation. Nietzsche is a tragic poet, a man of blacks and whites, of sharp antitheses; but his talent as poet and dreamer is harnessed to a restless and powerful intellect, the one factor preventing him from being the painstaking and detached scholar, the other driving him on beyond the confines of art into the field of philosophy.

In his days as professor of philosophy at Bâle Nietzsche revolted against the traditional, *scholarly* view of the method and function of philosophy: 'philologia facta est quod philosophia fuit'. Just as he declared that historical study is of value only in so far as it is dedicated to the service of life, so he declares that philology is of value in function of its cultural background and philosophic aura. Science in other words must be not the closeted pedantry of the *Wissenschaftler*, but the promoter and servant of culture, of life. What then was Nietzsche's ideal of culture? And in asking this question one must not, of course, imagine that Nietzsche was a man devoid of all exact knowledge. He may have been—no doubt was—temperamentally unfitted for a life of exact scholarship, with all the careful, clear, and painstaking research and exact sifting of evidence involved; but we cannot forget that he received an excellent classical education at Pforta, and above all, at Bonn and Leipzig under Ritschl and other able professors. It was his published essays that prompted the authorities at Bâle to offer him the chair of philology at a remarkably early age, and Professor Ritschl had the highest hopes of the contribution that his gifted pupil would make to classical study. Nietzsche certainly had the necessary foundations and the necessary mental ability to become a scholar, though he equally certainly lacked the necessary temperament—or at all events, had he kept to philology, he would have found his temperament a great hindrance and would have had to fight a constant warfare against himself. Naturally one would not be prepared to affirm that Nietzsche *could* not have carried on this strife for self-mastery, or even that his temperament might not, if held in due control, have contributed to the value of his work and saved him from dry-as-dust pedantry; but, knowing what we do of Nietzsche's character, it is somewhat difficult to imagine him becoming an Erwin Rohde, still less a Wilamowitz-Moellendorff. *Post factum*, however, it is not as a classical philologist, but first and foremost as a master of the German language that he lives, and will live, and secondly as the poet-philosopher of culture.

Contemporary conceptions and ideals of culture found in Nietzsche a resolute and determined opponent. In the essay on David Strauss, Nietzsche defines culture. 'Culture is, before all things, the unity of artistic style, in every expression of the life of a people. Abundant knowledge and learning, however, are not essential to it, nor are they a sign of its existence; and, at a pinch, they might co-exist much more harmoniously with the very opposite of culture— with barbarity: that is to say, with a complete lack of style, or with a riotous jumble of all styles'. Culture, therefore, for Nietzsche, emphatically does not mean simply learning, science, *Wissenschaft*. *Culture* of the contemporary German variety, the culture which the Germans fondly imagined had triumphed in the Franco-Prussian War, is for him no real culture at all. It is not a style of living, not a harmonious artistic unity, but a riotous jumble of all styles. 'The German heaps up around him the forms, colours, products, and curiosities of all ages and zones, and thereby succeeds in producing that garish newness, as of a country fair, which his scholars then proceed to contemplate and to define as

"Modernism *per se*"; and there he remains, squatting peacefully, in the midst of this conflict of styles'.[1] The German, that is to say, constructs a sort of curiosity or bric-à-brac shop, taking an item out of this culture of the past and another item out of that culture: he jumbles them all up and imagines he is a cultured person. Add to this the pedantry of the scholar and you have a picture of German culture, which is no genuine and productive unity but a copy of other cultures, and no very skilful copy at that. The Germans imagined that their culture had triumphed over French culture. Not at all, said Nietzsche: German culture was dependent on Paris just as much after the war as before the war. 'Up to the present there has been no such thing as an original German culture'.

Now it is obvious that the German scholar was a man of deep and exact learning, painstaking in research and scientific in method: it is obvious, too, that the German culture which Nietzsche derides, included education, literary appreciation and standards, art and music. What then was the vital element which so-called men of culture in Germany left out, the omission of which made their culture not a real culture but a pseudo-culture? It was the essential vital element, self-possession, life, which means striving, the strenuous will. Life must dominate knowledge, and not knowledge life. 'Life is the higher, and the dominating power, for the knowledge that annihilated life would be itself annihilated too. Knowledge pre-supposes life'.[2] The Germans have knowledge—plenty of it—knowledge of the past, history; but the content of their knowledge is not unified under a vital form, it remains in their memories and brains. They know about culture, but they are not cultured, for they do not *live* culture: their knowledge is simply historical ruins and remains such, it does not subserve life. If it did, they would not be content to accumulate masses of information, but would endeavour to unify the content of knowledge in an *artistic style*, pushing on to an original form of German culture, a really natural, genuine, unified and creative form of life, when they would be truly self-

---

[1] *Thoughts out of Season*, i, p. 9.   [2] Ibid., ii, p. 96.

possessed and productive. As it is, form and content fall apart: the German has the content—'an enormous heap of indigestible knowledge—stones that occasionally rattle together in his body'—but not the form, since there is nothing external corresponding to the content of knowledge. He is like a man who eats without hunger or need, so that the food does not promote vigour of life: he is like the snake that has swallowed a rabbit whole and lies still in the sun, avoiding all movement not absolutely necessary. In brief, culture means *a way of life*, natural, original, creative, genuine, it does not mean historical knowledge. It may, of course, include historical knowledge, but this is not essential. 'A man can be very well educated without any history at all'. As the Germans have the knowledge without the way of life, the content without the form, their boasted culture is in reality not culture itself, but a knowledge *about* culture. Their historical sense makes them merely passive and retrospective instead of active, creative, forward-looking: they are a nation of followers, not a nation of *livers* of creative producers. This culture is a hollow sham, a battening on the past, a past which is undigested, without relation to life.

Nietzsche was certainly not without admiration for the German scholar of the best type, but the point he insisted on was this, that the scholar's knowledge remained mere knowledge of the past: it did not contribute to a present and creative way of life: it was dead, bookish, retrospective. 'For we moderns have nothing of our own. We only become worth notice by filling ourselves to overflowing with foreign customs, arts, philosophies, religions and sciences: we are wandering encyclopædias, as an ancient Greek who had strayed into our time would probably call us. But the only value of an encyclopædia lies in the inside, in the contents, not in what is written outside, in the binding or the wrapper. And so the whole of modern culture is essentially internal; the bookbinder prints something like this on the cover: "Manual of internal culture for external barbarians"'.[1] Modern man suffers from a weakened personality: he can

[1] *Thoughts out of Season*, ii, p. 33.

only know and remember: he cannot really assimilate valuable productions of past and present, since he is deficient in life and vigour. So it is that the Germans are a nation of 'followers', who have produced a merely Alexandrian culture, a culture of the encyclopædia, when they should be striving beyond and above this Alexandrian culture.

In *The Use and Abuse of History* Nietzsche speaks of the mission of youth 'that forms the first generation of fighters and dragon-slayers'. It is youth's mission 'to shake to their foundations the present corruptions of "health" and "culture", and erect hatred and scorn in the place of this rococo mass of ideas'. In accomplishing this work of destruction youth may appear uncultured, but the work of destruction is a necessary stage in the cure of modern humanity. 'At first they will be more ignorant than the "educated men" of the present: for they will have unlearnt much and have lost any desire even to discern what those educated men especially wish to know: in fact, their chief mark from the educated point of view will be just their want of science, their indifference and inaccessibility to all the good and famous things. But at the end of the cure they are men again and have ceased to be mere shadows of humanity'. But Nietzsche's ideal is very far from being destructive barbaric youth, the irresponsible déraciné blond beast. In the same essay he speaks of the 'plastic power' of a man or community or culture, and points out that 'the deeper the roots of a man's inner nature, the better will he take the past into himself; and the greatest and most powerful nature would be known by the absence of limits for the historical sense to overgrow and work harm. It would assimilate and digest the past, however foreign, and turn it to sap'. An excess of knowledge of the past, 'an excess of history', will make man flag and droop, but on the other hand, man must be able to turn the past to the uses of the present. 'If we could only learn better to study history as a means to life!'

Much of what Nietzsche says on this subject one can only endorse. Culture is not simply knowledge, it is much more than that: it must, if it is to deserve the title of a genuine culture, denote an harmonious, rich and unified way of life. A people that merely lived in the past would be an appendage to a former culture rather than a cultured people. Growth, life, creative production would be, when present, accidental factors, while static and retrospective elements would be the essential and dominant feature: the *Alexandrian* type of culture is backward- and not forward-looking. And in regard to the individual is it not true that we meet with men who may have a surprising abundance of knowledge, but who at the same time do not give us the impression of truly cultured personalities? Their memories are retrospective, they know much, but their 'culture' consists in a mass of items of information contained in the mind like a collection of sweets in a bottle. They are mines of information, walking encyclopædias, but not men in the highest sense of the cultured personality, for culture belongs to the whole man. On the other hand one meets men who may not, perhaps, be as learned as these walking encyclopædias, but give the impression of truly cultured personalities. They truly possess what they have learned— be it much or little—they have assimilated it into the living, unified, advancing wealth of their personality—with them it is the man, the delicacy of his mind, the refinement of his sensibilities, the creative power of his spirit, that strikes one, and not primarily the fund of information, of facts, which he can—and often does—pour forth at will. Such men are like the beautiful, vigorous and growing tree, assimilating nourishment, growing up into the air and sunlight, bearing blossom and rich fruit. How different are they from those other men who resemble heaps of stones piled up on one another without organic unity, lifeless, uncreative! To belittle learning and scholarship is very far from being our intention: like Nietzsche we are filled with admiration at the disinterested, exact, laborious and conscientious toil of the scholar, and willingly admit both that great learning as such is by no means incompatible with true culture—such an assertion would be foolish—as also that the type of man who professes to despise learning, and belittles the scholar, is a superficial and tiresome specimen, a 'pretentious loafer', who pronounces dogmatically on problems, the complexity and difficulty of which elude his powers of comprehension. The Philistine *tout court* is no more admirable than the 'Culture-Philistine'. No, all honour to the scholar and scientist. But we maintain with Nietzsche that learning alone is not enough, that learning alone does not make culture, whether in the individual or community, and that in order to form truly cultured men and women there is need of real *educators*. Far more can be gained from intercourse with a great and cultured personality than from the mere encyclopædia type, the merely learned professor or schoolmaster. As Nietzsche says so well in *The Twilight of the Idols*, 'Educators are needed who are themselves educated, superior and noble intellects, who can prove that they are thus qualified, that they are ripe and mellow products of culture at every moment of their lives, in word and in gesture'.[1] It is not the 'learned louts', the 'superior wet-nurses', whom we need in our educational establishments.

And may we not express agreement, or, at the very least, sympathy, with Nietzsche's protest against those who ascribe to education the function of training 'a vast crowd of young men, in the smallest amount of time possible, to become useful and exploitable servants of the state'. While not being prepared to assent without any reservation to his statements that 'Culture and the State are antagonists' and that 'All great periods of culture have been periods of political decline', we can agree with his contention that it is a cardinal mistake to suppose that development of the State and political aggrandizement are always, or often, accompanied by a development and growth in culture. The energy and strength expended 'in acquiring power, or in politics on a large scale, or in economy, or in universal commerce, or in parliamentarism, or in military interest', may well be accompanied by a decline in cultural standards and ideals. Who will be prepared to assert that the German Empire was more cultured than the German States? Nietzsche at least did not think so, and maintained that

[1] *Twilight of the Idols*, p. 55.

'At the very moment when Germany arose as a great power in the world of politics, France won new importance as a force in the world of culture'. He considered that though Germany won the Franco-Prussian War from the military viewpoint, it was France who won in the battle of culture. 'Germany is becoming ever more and more the Flat-land of Europe'. And it is clear to all observers that the political and military growth of Germany under Nazi domination to be the dominant Power in Europe, has been unaccompanied by a corresponding growth of culture—quite the reverse.

It may appear at first an inconsistency, that Nietzsche declares—that knowledge must serve life and then inveighs against a type of education that has as its ideal the practical one of producing useful citizens. For is this not to make knowledge subordinate to life? In a sense it is, but this is not Nietzsche's meaning. In *Schopenhauer as Educator* Nietzsche says that the self-interest of the civilized State requires the greatest possible breadth and universality of culture, and that it has the most effective weapons to carry out its wishes. Such a State 'generally implies, at the present time, the task of setting free the spiritual forces of a generation just so far as they may be of use to the existing institutions'.[1] But 'setting free' comes to mean in practice 'chaining up'. Education is made subservient to the self-interest of the State, i.e. to an alien aim. Similarly, the self-interest of business men, though needing the help of culture and helping her in return, demands a price, namely that the self-interest of business should prescribe the end and limits of culture. 'All education is detested that makes for loneliness, and has an aim above money-making, and requires a long time: men look askance on such serious education, as mere "refined egoism" or "immoral Epicureanism"'. 'The amount of education is determined by commercial interests'. (Indeed we not infrequently hear, to-day, a classical education defended or attacked as being, or not being, an asset in business, i.e. in money-making!) But this subordination of culture and education to alien interests, such as the self-interest of the State or commercial

[1] *Thoughts out of Season*, ii, p. 161.

interest, simply overlooks the true end of culture, the production of genius. 'The State may trumpet as it will its
services to culture, it merely helps culture in order to help
itself, and does not comprehend an aim that stands higher
than its own well-being or even existence. The business men
in their continual demand for education merely wish for—
business'.[1] The State, business, etc., certainly help culture
to some degree, but they are blind to what Nietzsche
considers the true aim of culture, the production of
genius.

The production of genius is, thus, for Nietzsche, the aim
of culture, and this is the aim of life. Life has no aim fixed
for it, given it, in the teleological sense—such a conception
would be impossible in Nietzsche's atheistic philosophy—
but we have to give it an aim, the production of the finest
flower of the human race, the genius, the truly noble and
original mind, the real man of culture—described in
Nietzsche's later thought as the *Übermensch* or Superman.
True culture is, therefore, essentially aristocratic: it renders
possible, favours, and promotes the growth of 'free spirits',
the true aristocrats of the mind. In his essay on *The Greek
State* (1871) Nietzsche insists on the aristocratic basis of
culture. 'In order that there may be a broad, deep, and
fruitful soil for the development of art, the enormous
majority must, in the service of a minority, be slavishly
subjected to life's struggle, to a *greater* degree than their
own wants necessitate. At their cost, through the surplus
of their labour, that privileged class is to be relieved from
the struggle for existence, in order to create and to satisfy
a new world of want'. He does not hesitate to affirm that
'*slavery is of the* essence of Culture'. In *Human, All-too-
Human*, this same idea appears. 'A higher culture can only
originate where there are two distinct castes of society:
that of the working class, and that of the leisured class who
are capable of true leisure; or, more strongly expressed, the
caste of compulsory labour, and the caste of free labour'.[2]
It was one of Nietzsche's main charges against the Culture-

---

[1] *Thoughts out of Season*, ii, p. 173.
[2] *Human, All-too-Human*, i, aph. 439.

Philistine, that 'he is a negative creature', that he is a barrier in the way of all powerful men and creators, . . . the fetters of those who would run towards lofty goals, the poisonous mist that chokes all germinating hopes, the scorching sand to all those German thinkers who seek for, and thirst after, a new life'.[1] The Culture-Philistine does not look with favour on seeking—on the contrary, he hates it. The aristocratic, free, and noble spirit, the seeker and discoverer, who goes forward on new paths, is the *bête noire* of the Culture-Philistines, who worship the past and cling to established norms, who regard themselves as constituting the stable and established building of culture.

That what Nietzsche says contains truth, cannot be denied. An education, for instance, that aimed simply and solely at producing efficient civil servants and citizens, would hardly promote a very high level of culture. We could say the same, with greater emphasis, of an education that aimed at producing efficient business men. It is one of the glories of the Greeks that they turned practical calculation into the science of mathematics, and it would be a sad day for culture when pure mathematics were entirely discarded in the exclusive favour of applied mathematics. The poet-laureate doubtless serves a useful function, but if the function of the poet were merely that of providing fun for the multitude or refined sentiments for the more educated, we could bid farewell to the Shelleys and Keats, the Leopardis and Hölderlins. And if music is to serve the interests of business or even of the State, intolerable fetters would be placed on the spirit of a Beethoven. And what of philosophy? In Soviet Russia philosophy serves the State, and what is the philosophic value of the stale and wearisome repetition of Marxist dogma? True culture may, indeed will, benefit the State; but if culture is entirely subordinated to the practical self-interest of the State, it will certainly not benefit culture, nor in the long run the State itself. The State is a value, but it does not exhaust the field of values; nor is it even the dominant value.

Again, it is perfectly true that culture progresses largely

[1] *Thoughts out of Season*, i, p. 13.

—though by no means exclusively—through the work of outstanding men of genius, and that the actual representatives
of 'culture' have sometimes misunderstood and hindered
the work of free and creative spirits. Greek Tragedy could
not have arisen without the genius of Æschylus and
Sophocles or Russian literature without Pushkin, Tolstoy,
Dostoievsky, etc. And how could the artistic possibilities
of the German language have unfolded themselves apart
from the literary genius of men like Goethe and Nietzsche
himself? That is of course a truism, and is obvious enough
in retrospect. But it is not always so obvious in reference to
present and future. Cézanne, as everybody knows, met with
scant appreciation in his lifetime, and it is hardly likely that
'Academy Art' will, of itself, deepen and extend our culture.
For growth in culture new geniuses, original talents, will be
necessary, and in a certain sense contemporary culture has
as its function to render possible the development and fruitful growth of such outstanding men, and not to stifle, fetter
and hinder them, or drive them to discouragement and even
despair. The Chattertons and Hölderlins are a standing
rebuke to the self-satisfied, self-appointed representatives of
culture, to the Culture-Philistines.

There is truth, then, in what Nietzsche has to say of the
'aristocratic' basis of culture; but there is also much that
is exaggerated and false. Culture exists for the development
of the powers of man, not for the glory of a few men, or even
of all men, but for the glory of God. We do not mean to
suggest that all features of culture must have a directly
religious and supernatural reference—for that would imply
that God is the Creator, not of spirit and matter, but of
spirit only—but we insist that God is glorified in the true
and harmonious development of *all* the powers of man, and
that this divine glorification is the ultimate end of culture.
God is glorified in the genius—in the Shakespeares and
Beethovens and Michelangelos—and He is glorified when
humble men and women partake, according to their abilities,
in the cultural wealth of the human race. He is not glorified
in the fettering of man's talents, in the smugness of the
Culture-Philistine, in the stifling of the outstanding men,

whose talents He has created; for the world is the external manifestation of God, and He is manifested in the works of beauty created by the genius as in the sublimity of the mountains and the glory of the stars. But to make human culture, even its most outstanding geniuses, an absolute, an end of itself, is to falsify the function of culture and in the end to debase and ruin it. Man, mere man—even the *Superman*—cannot achieve true culture if he denies and rejects God and all transcendent values; he will not only omit to cultivate the highest functions of the human spirit, but will end by stunting and dwarfing all cultural activities. True Religion is not the enemy but the friend of culture, however individual religious people may have behaved and in spite of all one-sided, anti-cultural 'religions'.

Nietzsche makes *slavery* the basis of culture, demanding a dichotomy between the aristocracy of free and noble spirits and the ministering multitude. We are not of course to suppose that Nietzsche demanded a return to the Greek or Roman type of slavery; but in some jottings that he made when composing *The Dawn of Day* and which were published by his sister, Nietzsche maintains not only that some will always have to do the rough and dirty work that cannot be done by machinery, but that if these workmen have opportunity and leisure to partake in higher education, they will undergo disproportionate suffering through the contrast between their work and their leisure-hours and will wish to get rid of their work altogether and turn it over to others. Thus a sphere of non-culture is seen to be a necessary basis for the sphere of culture. But is Nietzsche's view altogether true? That a gifted artist should not be compelled to work in a factory or on the roads is clear enough; but owing to modern technical development there is no reason why—given a proper rationalization of industry—workmen should not remain workmen and at the same time have ample opportunities and leisure for cultural development. If it be objected that a general and mediocre level of culture will tend to stifle the work of the original and creative, this can equally well be said of the cultivated and educated milieu of any time. Culture can obviously not be confined to the geniuses—even if this be desirable (and of course Nietzsche never envisaged such a ridiculous proposition)—and it does not appear that the mere *number* of the less cultured, whether it be greater or smaller, will really affect the question of the stifling or non-stifling of geniuses. On the contrary, the general extension of education and culture may well help to promote the development of outstanding talent. One hears occasionally of men of remarkable natural ability, who from want of any opportunity for education, and from want of intellectual guidance and intercourse, have remained stunted, undeveloped and fruitless. The present writer was told by a German professor of an uneducated countryman who was given to perpetual brooding over the great problems of life (a *Grübler*) and who derived great help from being able to speak occasionally with a man of deep culture who understood him and could help. When, owing to certain circumstances, this intercourse was no longer possible, the unformed philosopher of nature was driven back into his own lonely isolation and in the end committed suicide. It is true that such a man might have been 'spoilt' by a stereotyped State education; but frequent intercourse with a man of real culture, who could understand and sympathize, help and encourage, might have led to the unfolding of remarkable talent.

Holding that culture exists only for the few, Nietzsche maintained, as we have seen, that the function of the many is to serve the few. Even if this were true, it might still be pointed out that the multitude will serve the few the more profitably if they—the multitude—are educated; and the more real culture—not mere information—they possess, the more will they be able to act as a seed-ground for geniuses. And, as a matter of fact, Nietzsche himself pretty well recognizes this fact. In his lectures *On the Future of our Educational Institutions* Nietzsche speaks of the 'incredibly small' number of really cultured people and remarks 'And even this number of really cultured people would not be possible if a prodigious multitude, from reasons opposed to their nature and only led on by an alluring illusion, did not devote themselves to education'. Again, 'Here lies the whole secret of culture—namely, that an innumerable host of men struggle to achieve it and work hard to that end, ostensibly in their own interests, whereas at bottom only in order that it may be possible for the few to attain it'. Nietzsche recognizes, therefore, that in order to render the production and development of genius possible, there must be a great number of people who strive after culture through education—and who doubtless think themselves cultured—but who never actually attain a deep and true culture. We agree, but would go further. In order to further the production and development of genius, it is necessary to extend education to all and to make culture in some degree possible to all, for it is only so—normally at least—that we can prevent the complete stultification of outstanding talent, when it is found in one whose social milieu gives him no opportunity for stimulus, development and personal guidance. If it is true that the extension of education and the fringe of culture would render possible the development, not of less, but of more 'free spirits', then Nietzsche's dichotomy between the sphere of non-culture and the sphere of culture—the 'slave' basis of culture—will have no justification.

We have already observed that if all men were possessed of a mediocre education, they might be thought to hinder the growth of genius, inasmuch as the multitude will resent the presence of the 'free spirit', the original, creative mind. He will be a reflection on themselves, and against his outstanding talent they will see reflected their own mediocrity. They will not appreciate and understand; but that will not prevent them from criticizing and attacking and from indulging in silent—or in open—persecution. This is, indeed, a very real danger, fallen human nature being what it is, but possibly the advantages of extended education will outweigh the dangers. For one thing, each individual man reflects God to some extent and should be able to glorify God by the development of what talents he possesses—the glory of God, and not the glory of geniuses being, as we have seen, the ultimate end of culture. Besides, could we not safeguard the rights of the genius and prevent what

Nietzsche calls the 'democratization' of genius by a system of cultural education, in which the youth who gives promise of outstanding talent will have ample stimulus and opportunity for natural growth and development without being formed into a preconceived mould or democratized to suit the demands either of the Culture-Philistine or the mediocre multitude? The danger will always remain in any case, but it can surely be lessened. It may be worth while to consider briefly what Nietzsche's idea of true cultural education is, as it is extremely likely that a man of his independent mind will have valuable suggestions to offer.

In his lectures *On the Future of our Educational Institutions* Nietzsche points out the dangers of specialization. Owing to the growth of science a man who wishes to attain any considerable degree of eminence must necessarily specialize in some particular branch, and the more science grows, the narrower becomes the limits in which specialization must be confined. The danger then arises that the specialist, although very learned in his own particular branch of science, may be to all intents and purposes an uneducated man in regard to matters outside his own branch. 'Thus, a specialist in science gets to resemble nothing so much as a factory workman who spends his whole life in turning one particular screw or handle on a certain instrument or machine, at which occupation he acquires the most consummate skill'. The result is that the general field of culture tends more and more to fall into the hands of Journalism. 'The newspaper actually steps into the place of culture' and 'the journalist, the servant of the moment, has stepped into the place of the genius'. Here Nietzsche mentions a very real danger, the ascendancy of journalism. Very many men and women read little beyond the newspaper and scarcely think at all: their opinions are formed for them by the Press, and the faculty of original thought is atrophied. Standardization and mediocrity result, which is often all the worse in that they masquerade under the appearance of independent and well-informed judgment. Even learning and scholarship must stoop to journalism, and we are offered history which disgusts by its facile superficiality and popular philosophy which presents us with hypotheses under the guise of facts, dogmatic assertions under the guise of science. This is the ruin of education, the death of culture, a debasing of the mind and a corruption of the human spirit.

Nietzsche lays great stress on the importance of the mother-tongue in education. 'Everybody speaks and writes German as thoroughly badly as it is possible to do in an age of newspaper German: that is why the growing youth who happens to be both noble and gifted has to be taken by force and put under the glass shade of good taste and of severe linguistic discipline. If this is not possible, I would prefer that in future Latin be spoken; for I am ashamed of a language so bungled and vitiated'. We might well take to heart what Nietzsche says of 'journalistic jargon' and we should do well to listen to his cry: 'Take your own language seriously! He who does not regard this matter as a sacred duty does not possess even the germ of a higher culture. From your attitude in this matter, from your treatment of your mother tongue, we can judge how highly or how lowly you esteem art, and to what extent you are related to it.' Nietzsche urges a real self-discipline in the mother-tongue, carried to such an extent that it becomes a habit of the mind, so that the young man acquires a 'physical loathing for the beloved and much-admired "elegance" of style of our newspaper manufacturers and novelists, and for the "ornate style" of our literary men'. If educational establishments serve merely to prepare the way for 'outrageous and irresponsible scribbling', making no serious attempt to discipline the pupils in speaking and writing the mother-tongue, they cannot be regarded as truly cultural institutions.

But if Nietzsche is insistent as to the importance of disciplinary training in the mother-tongue, he is equally insistent as to the evil of repressing individuality, of treating young men as if they were no longer young men. Subjects for essays are often set in schools, he points out, that demand real thought on the part of the pupil, while at the same time the boy has not as yet any really formed opinion on them. For instance, pupils may be told to criticize and compare poets, discuss historical figures and phases, treat of ethical matters, relate events connected with their own lives. It is perhaps the pupil's first individual creation: he feels the attraction and charm of this demand for self-reliance: he produces a composition that reflects his own awakening powers, his individual reaction to the problem: his mind has not, as yet, been formed into a mould, has not yet become stereotyped. What happens only too often? The teacher calls attention above all to any excess in form or thought— 'that is to say, to all that which, at their age, is essentially characteristic and individual. Their really independent traits which, in response to their very premature excitation, can manifest themselves only in awkwardness, crudeness, and grotesque features—in short, their individuality is reproved and rejected by the teacher in favour of an unoriginal decent average'. If the nature of the subject chosen for the composition was premature, it is only adding insult to injury to reprehend the individuality of the response to the premature excitation: rather should the teacher endeavour to understand the individual character of the pupil's mind and develop it. Moreover, as Nietzsche points out, though the teacher often tries to secure a decent and unoriginal uniformity, such uniform mediocrity is just the type of class-work calculated to bore the teacher inexpressibly.

The mother-tongue then should, according to Nietzsche, form the basis of education. 'Every so-called classical education can have but one natural starting-point—an artistic, earnest, and exact familiarity with the use of the mother-tongue'.[1] Through this familiarity with the mother-tongue the pupil will learn 'the secret of form'; he will acquire 'the power of discerning form and barbarity'. Then is the time to introduce him to the German classical writers, and it is 'by the wing-strokes of their past endeavours' that the pupil, who is to receive a 'classical' education, will be borne up 'to the land of yearning, to Greece'. Familiarity with the mother-tongue and a real appreciation of its best products is thus for Nietzsche an indispensable basis for

---

[1] *Future of our Educational Institutions*, pp. 60–1.

classical education in the sense of study of Greco-Roman—
particularly Greek—antiquity. But 'not a suspicion of this
possible relationship between our classics and classical
education seems to have pierced the antique walls of public
schools'.[1] On the contrary, the study of antiquity is begun
much too early, and is conducted by teachers who have no
real understanding of antiquity.

Nietzsche has a real sense of the value of the training in
the languages of antiquity—'the most wholesome feature
of our modern institutions is to be found in the earnestness
with which the Latin and Greek languages are studied over
a long course of years'—but his idea of a classical education
is of something much wider than a concentrated study of
linguistic form, and he insists more than once that the
attempt to introduce pupils to the study of antiquity is
generally made prematurely, at an age when they are
incapable of benefiting by it, with the result that they merely
become disgusted with the 'classics'. 'It would be much
more natural *per se* if our children were instructed in the
elements of geography, natural science, political economy,
and sociology, if they were gradually led to a consideration
of life itself, and if finally, but much later, the most note-
worthy events of the past were brought to their knowledge.
A knowledge of antiquity should be among the last subjects
which a student would take up'.[2] 'When we bring the
Greeks to the knowledge of our young students, we are
treating the latter as if they were well-informed and matured
men. . . . In the end we shall find that we can do nothing
for them beyond giving them isolated details. . . . My
belief is that we are forced to concern ourselves with
antiquity at a wrong period of our lives. At the end of the
twenties its meaning begins to dawn on one'.[3] Nietzsche
maintains that it is unpedagogical to introduce young
students to the ancients, since they cannot consciously
esteem them. First of all the student should be instructed
in what is necessary, i.e. in the sway of laws in nature, and

---

[1] *Future of our Educational Institutions*, p. 61.
[2] *We Philologists*, aph. 31.
[3] Ibid., aph. 74.

then in the 'laws of ordinary society'. When this has been done, the student will come to *feel* the need of history in order to ascertain how things have changed, in order to understand the changing element in things. 'To show how things may become other than what they are we may, for example, point to the Greeks. We need the Romans to show how things became what they were'.[1]

Nietzsche thus stresses the fact that knowledge of history, and of antiquity in particular, should be introduced at the point when a need for it has been awakened. In *The Dawn of Day* he says: 'Only think of this wasted youth, when we were inoculated clumsily and painfully with an imperfect knowledge of the Greeks and Romans as well as of their languages, contrary to the highest principles of all culture, which holds that we should not give food except to those who hunger for it!'[2] (The same criticism applies to other branches of education. 'Think of that period of our lives when we had mathematics and physics forced down our throats, instead of being first of all made acquainted with the despair of ignorance, instead of having our little daily life, our activities, and everything occurring in our houses, our workshops, in the sky, and in nature, split up into thousands of problems, painful, humiliating and irritating problems—and thus having our curiosity made acquainted with the fact that we first of all require a mathematical and mechanical knowledge before we can be allowed to rejoice in the absolute logic of this knowledge!')[3] Antiquity is too complex to be really appreciated by young students. 'Nothing becomes clearer to me year by year than the fact that the entire Greek and ancient mode of life, however simple and evident it must seem to our eyes, is in truth very difficult to understand, and even scarcely accessible, and that the customary ease with which we babble about the ancients is either giddy levity or the old hereditary conceit of our thoughtlessness. . . . And these are realms in which boys are allowed to roam about! Enough: we roamed about them in our childhood, and there we became seized with an

---

[1] *We Philologists*, aph. 182.   [2] *Dawn of Day*, aph. 195.
[3] Ibid.

almost ineradicable antipathy for all antiquity, the antipathy
arising from an intimacy which was apparently too great!'[1]

Music has an important function to fulfil in education, in
the task of producing the man of culture. As this chapter is
already long enough I will not attempt to treat of Nietzsche's
theory of music in itself, but simply mention one or two points
in Nietzsche's view of music's relation to culture. 'Music is, in
fact, not a universal language for all time, as is so often said
in its praise, but responds exactly to a particular period and
warmth of emotion which involves a quite definite, individual
culture, determined by time and place, as its inner law. The
music of Palestrina would be quite unintelligible to a Greek;
and again, what would the music of Rossini convey to
Palestrina? It may be that our most modern German music,
with all its pre-eminence and desire of pre-eminence, will
soon be no longer understood. For this music sprang from
a culture that is undergoing a rapid decay. . . .'[2] Secondly,
though music corresponds to a particular culture, it is a
late-comer in that culture. '. . . music is the last plant to
come up, arising in the autumn and fading-season of the
culture to which it belongs. . . . The eighteenth century—
that century of rhapsody, of broken ideals and transitory
happiness—only sang itself out in the music of Beethoven
and Rossini. A lover of sentimental similes might say that
all really important music was a swan-song'.[3] The same
thought is repeated in *The Will to Power* in the words,
'Music is the last breath of every culture'.[4] Thirdly, though
music is the last breath of a culture, it is also the herald of
a new culture. Caught in the grips of an outworn and
tyrannous culture men are governed by what Nietzsche
calls 'incorrect feeling'. 'Should they wish to speak, convention whispers their cue to them, and this makes them
forget what they originally intended to say; should they
desire to understand one another their comprehension is
maimed as though by a spell: they declare that to be their
joy which in reality is but their doom, and they proceed to
collaborate in wilfully bringing about their own damnation.

---

[1] *Dawn of Day*, aph. 195.   [2] *Human, All-too-Human*, ii, aph. 171.
[3] Ibid.   [4] *Will to Power*, i, aph. 92.

Thus they have become transformed into perfectly and absolutely different creatures, and reduced to the state of abject slaves of incorrect feeling'.[1] But when the strains of a master's music burst upon mankind thus sick and ill, the meaning of this music is '*correct feeling*, the enemy of all convention, of all artificial estrangement and misunderstandings between man and man: this music signifies a return to nature, and at the same time a purification and remodelling of it'.[2] Men are helped by music to break through the slavery of convention and fixed notions to a state of 'correct feeling', and the need for a new culture makes itself felt.

What we have hitherto said of Nietzsche's ideal of culture should at least make it plain that he was not a worshipper of the 'blond beast'. He believed wholeheartedly in the value of culture, and passionately desired the attainment of a higher and truer culture than the contemporary variety. But at the same time he rendered its attainment impossible by depriving it of its basis—an assertion which we will try to justify in a later chapter.

CHAPTER III

THE HISTORY OF CULTURE

NIETZSCHE'S treatment of Greek culture is of great importance, since it throws considerable light on his cultural ideal. Moreover it enables us to discern a greater consistency in his thought than is sometimes ascribed to him. That Nietzsche is only too frequently one-sided and exaggerated in his assertions cannot be denied; but his philosophy is very far from being a mere jumble of inconsistencies. Whether he first conceived the features of the true culture and then read them into early Greek culture, or whether he obtained his notion of true culture from a study of Antiquity, is a problem in itself: in either case this conception of true culture, its function and nature,

---

[1] *Thoughts out of Season*, i, p. 141.   [2] Ibid., p. 134.

as presented in his third period, is a consistent development of his conception of true culture in his first period, as he found it—or thought he found it—exemplified in the early culture of the Greeks. In the second period—beginning with *Human, All-too-Human,* and ending with *Joyful Wisdom*— Nietzsche turns his back on the early period, 'the Dionysian' period, and praises Socrates, so that to anyone who made no distinction between the periods of Nietzsche's thought, but tried to treat all his written work as forming one homogeneous philosophy of life, his thought would necessarily appear as riddled with inconsistencies. But if one treats Nietzsche according to his historical development and bears in mind the fact that in the course of that development there is a middle period, which is an interlude, a transitory period of reaction, a period in which Socrates is exalted instead of vilified, the apparent inconsistencies tend to disappear. The first period, that of the philosophy of Dionysus, reappears in the third period, the *Übermensch* period, or—to put it the other way round—the third period is found to have its roots in the first period. New and fuller conceptions certainly appear in the third period, but this period is nevertheless a development of the first period.

In Nietzsche's first period he extols the early Greek culture, the culture of the sixth century B.C. In so doing he departs from the notion, general in his time at least, that the greatest period of Greek culture was the Periclean period of Athenian greatness. As Bernard Bosanquet points out, owing to the Latin character of the Renaissance 'its direct contact with antiquity was on Italian soil, where the greatest works of Hellas, even if some had been transported there by purchasers or plunderers, were infinitely outnumbered by productions of a later age, and by copies freely multiplied, both from earlier and from later originals'.[1] For this, and for other reasons—e.g. the nature of their æsthetic criteria— the early art critics tended to regard a later rather than an earlier period of Greek art as the supreme period of achievement. Hirt, for example, regarded the fourth century as marking the summit attained by Greek sculpture. But,

[1] *History of Aesthetic,* p. 191.

apart from consideration of particular art-forms, it was but natural that the period after the Persian wars should be taken as the supreme period of Greek culture. The period which saw the adornment of Athens with marvellous works of sculpture, which witnessed the plays of Sophocles and the Athenian empire, was naturally accepted as marking the zenith of Greek greatness, and in Nietzsche's time Greek culture *par excellence* meant the fifth century B.C. This view was rejected by Nietzsche, who regarded—whether rightly or wrongly—the fifth century as a period of decadence when compared to the sixth.

Why did Nietzsche prefer the sixth century to the fifth? One reason is that he regarded the early period of Greek culture as the age of *great men*: it fulfils the primary requirement of a true culture, to be the means for the production of the genius, of the great man. Typical great men are the pre-Socratic philosophers, the aristocrats of the intellect. In his *Philosophy during the Tragic Age of the Greeks* (1873) Nietzsche says that 'Every nation is put to shame if one points out such a wonderfully idealized company of philosophers as that of the early Greek masters, Thales, Anaximander, Heraclitus, Parmenides, Anaxagoras, Empedocles, Democritus and Socrates. All those men are integral, entire and self-contained, and hewn out of one stone. Severe necessity exists between their thinking and their character. They are not bound by any convention, because at that time no professional class of philosophers and scholars existed. . . . Thus together they form what Schopenhauer, in opposition to the Republic of Scholars, has called a Republic of Geniuses; one giant calls to another across the arid intervals of ages, and, undisturbed by a wanton, noisy race of dwarfs creeping about them, the sublime intercourse of spirits continues'.[1] Thus the galaxy of pre-Platonic—not here pre-Socratic—philosophers is represented as a cluster of brilliant stars, of outstanding *men*, the geniuses of the early Greek culture.

The same thought is clearly stated in Nietzsche's *Criticism of Philosophy* in the *Will to Power*.[2] 'The real *philosophers*

[1] p. 79.   [2] *Will to Power*, i, aph. 437.

of Greece are those who came before Socrates (with Socrates something changes). They are all distinguished men, they take their stand away from the people and from usage; they have travelled; they are earnest to the point of sombreness, their eyes are calm, and they are not unacquainted with the business of state and diplomacy'. As a matter of fact, of course, one might well say that neither Plato nor Aristotle was 'unacquainted with the business of state and diplomacy'; but the point Nietzsche wishes to make is clear, whether he is right or wrong in his conception of the early philosophers of Greece. They are men, and not mere scholars; they are seekers and are not caught in the trammels and meshes of the Transcendent, as Plato was; they are aristocrats of the spirit, free and creative; they try to see the world as it is, and do not look at it through the golden mist of an idealistic morality; they are fundamentally honest; they are the justification of early Greek culture.

In his essay on *The Greek State* (1871) Nietzsche declares that 'In the case of many States, as, for example, in the Lycurgian constitution of Sparta, one can distinctly perceive the impress of that fundamental idea of the State, that of the creation of the military genius'. And he goes on to lay down the general principle that 'every human being, with his total activity, only has dignity in so far as he is a tool of *the* genius, consciously or unconsciously'. This thought of Nietzsche's earlier period was to be developed later in the conception of the *Superman*, the aim and highest point of culture, in contribution to whose production other men fulfil their true function. And in *Zarathustra*, the revelation of Superman, Nietzsche finds the will to power strong in the Greek soul, explaining the Greek genius. 'Always shalt thou be the foremost and prominent above others: no one shall thy jealous soul love, except a friend'—that made the soul of a Greek thrill: thereby he went his way to greatness'. 'The Greeks are interesting and quite disproportionately important', says Nietzsche, 'because they had such a host of great individuals'.[1]

---

[1] *We Philologists*, aph. 101.

If the early Greek philosophers represent the really great period of Greece, Socrates and Plato represent the decadence, or the beginning of the decadence of Greece: they betray the best tendencies of the Greek spirit and so are fundamentally anti-Hellenic. 'The apparition of Greek philosophers since the time of Socrates is a symptom of decadence; the anti-Hellenic instincts become paramount'.[1] In the early period of Greece the noble man, the free spirit, is the ideal, not the dialectician. *Instinct* and *Authority* are sufficient: 'there was no room for dialectics'. Socrates, however, introduced the dialectical spirit, and the dialectical spirit represents not only the revolt of reason against instinct, but also the triumph of the mob over the aristocrat. 'The dialectician's irony is a form of mob-revenge: the ferocity of the oppressed lies in the cold knife-cuts of the syllogism'. Nietzsche can therefore say that 'Socrates . . . was thus able to triumph over a more noble taste, the taste of *the noble*:—the mob gets the upper hand along with dialectics'. Early Greece is the age of instinct and the age of aristocracy, the age of the *Tyrants*: later Greece is the age of reason, of dialectics and of democracy. Instead of nobility, the aristocratic ideal, the concept is deified and is set up by Plato as the new ideal.

Nietzsche's great objection to Socrates and Plato—and here we come to the root of the matter—is their notion of an absolute morality. Denying the aristocratic ideal of instinct and the relativity of morals, they set up absolute standards of right and wrong, abiding concepts. They taught the immortality of the soul, the doctrine of the *Beyond*, the denial of the senses: they turned their back on the world and prepared the way for Christianity. In so far as the Sophists maintain the relativity of morals, Nietzsche praises them. 'The Sophists were *Greeks*: when Socrates and Plato adopted the cause of virtue and justice they were *Jews* or I know not what. *Grote's* tactics in the defence of the Sophists are false: he would like to raise them to the rank of men of honour and moralizers—but it was their honour not to indulge in any humbug with grand words and

---

[1] *Will to Power*, i, aph. 427.

virtues'. Plato and Socrates indulged in this 'humbug' :—
considering the pleasure of power as immoral, they had not
the courage to identify happiness with the will to power or to
regard virtue as a result of immorality, i.e. of the will to
power.

In declaring that Plato exalted reason over instinct, that
he taught the immortality of the soul and the abiding
character of transcendent values, Nietzsche was of course
right; but he was wrong in condemning Plato for these
beliefs. As Nietzsche made explicit profession of despising
dialectics, we naturally cannot expect him to meet, e.g.,
Plato's arguments against the Will to Power with counter-
arguments. Nietzsche states his case and fulminates against
his opponents, and that is that. We will treat in a separate
chapter of his objections to 'morality', and to Christian
morality in particular. But though we may not expect
Nietzsche to meet dialectic with dialectic, we can expect
him to be just—though in point of fact he is *not* just. Plato
believed in aristocracy: what is his philosopher-king but
the Aristocrat *par excellence*? He is certainly not the
incarnation of the Will to Power, but Plato gives excellent
reasons for rejecting the Will to Power 'morality'. And it is
really absurd of Nietzsche to speak of the philosophers he
disliked as 'Tartuffes' (did he not speak also of the
'Tartuffery of old Kant'?), because they spoke of virtue in
a Greek milieu, which permitted the Athenian treatment of
the Melians. 'Is it to be supposed that these small Greek
independent republics, so filled with rage and envy that
they would fain have devoured each other, were led by
principles of humanity and honesty?' No, it is certainly not
to be supposed; but if the implication is that one may not
lay down moral principles in a society that is often actuated
by immoral motives, then a great deal of what Nietzsche
says in the course of his writings had better have been left
unsaid. Nietzsche certainly denied an absolute morality,
but that denial did not prevent him from refusing to accept
mankind as it is and from affirming new ideals. Nietzsche's
attack on morality stands or falls according to the validity
or invalidity of his 'exposure' of morality: accusations of

Tartuffery, of turning one's back on life, etc., do not carry him very far.

The period of decadence, the period of rationalization, is reflected in the poems of Euripides—the tendency is discernible even in Sophocles. Hence Nietzsche ranked Æschylus above either of the later tragedians, and held that Greek tragedy degenerated after Æschylus. Euripides, says Nietzsche in *The Birth of Tragedy*, may be regarded 'as the poet of æsthetic Socratism', the supreme law of which is 'to be beautiful everything must be intelligible'. This principle of æsthetic Socratism is parallel to the Socratic proposition, 'only the knowing one is virtuous'. Æschylean tragedy, in which tragedy is already drama and not only the 'Dionysian' chorus, represents a fusion of Dionysian and Apollonian elements, of the Dionysian lyrics of the chorus on the one hand with the Apollonian dream-world of the scene on the other: Dionysos (Nietzsche regarded the tragic hero as originally Dionysos) speaks, not through 'forces', the lyrics of the chorus, but as an epic hero, the epic being typical of Apollonian art. In the tragedies of Æschylus the part of the chorus is still very important— and the musical lyricism of the chorus is of the essence of tragedy, 'which can be explained only as a manifestation and illustration of Dionysian states, as the visible symbolization of music, as the dream-world of Dionysian ecstasy'. Sophocles, however, limits considerably the sphere of the chorus, 'an important sign that the Dionysian basis of tragedy already begins to disintegrate with him'. Moreover, in Sophocles, there is much more of the conscious artist than in Æschylus and much less of the instinctive, 'ecstatic' genius.

An 'anti-Dionysian tendency' was therefore operative in tragedy before Socrates and Euripides, but it was the third great tragedian, who really rationalized tragedy. In Euripides and in the New Comedy 'optimistic dialectics drives *music* out of tragedy with the scourge of its syllogisms: that is, it destroys the essence of tragedy'. The chorus, which in Nietzsche's view, is the *cause* of tragedy, appears as something accidental: the Socratic maxim, that virtue is knowledge and that he who is virtuous is happy, reigns supreme:

the virtuous hero is a dialectician: the principle of 'poetic justice' is introduced, and the 'deus ex machina' is used to help it out. Thus the Euripidean tragedy, infected with Socratic optimism and dialectics, stands over against the Æschylo-Sophoclean tragedy. Sophocles indeed represents a step down from Æschylus, but Euripides is different from either of his two great predecessors: in the grip of optimistic dialectics he measured and 'corrected' all the elements of the dramas in accordance with the principles of æsthetic Socratism. The poetic deficiency and retrogression of Euripides in comparison with Sophocles is due to the former's rationalism and passion for intelligibility.

Nietzsche does not of course make the mistake of supposing that in Euripides there is no passion—in view of such a play as the 'Bacchae' a mistake of this description would be ridiculous—but he does not admit the passion of Euripides as a Dionysian element. 'Euripides is the actor with leaping heart, with hair standing on end; as Socratic thinker he designs the plan, as passionate actor he executes it. Neither in the designing nor in the execution is he an artist pure and simple. And so the Euripidean drama is a thing both cool and fiery, equally capable of freezing and burning; it is impossible for it to attain the Apollonian effect of the epos, while, on the other hand, it has severed itself as much as possible from Dionysian elements, and now, in order to act at all, it requires new stimulants, which can no longer lie within the sphere of the unique art-impulses, the Apollonian and the Dionysian. The stimulants are cool, paradoxical *thoughts*, in place of Apollonian intuitions— and fiery passions in place of Dionysian ecstasies; and in fact, thoughts and passion very realistically copied, and not at all steeped in the ether of art'.[1] Euripidean drama is therefore no longer characterized by that fusion of Dionysian and Apollonian elements which we witness in the Æschylo-Sophoclean tragedy, but primarily by the moralizing dialectic of Socrates, by optimistic rationalism.

Optimism versus Pessimism. It is in the light of this opposition that we can best understand what Nietzsche

----

[1] *Birth of Tragedy*, p. 97.

means by the philosophy of Dionysos, and unless we understand that, we cannot understand his reading of the Greek
spirit. In the *Birth of Tragedy* Nietzsche raises the question:
'What if the Greeks in the very wealth of their youth had
the will *to be* tragic and were pessimists? . . . And what if,
on the other hand and conversely, at the very time of their
dissolution and weakness, the Greeks became always more
optimistic, more superficial, more histrionic, also more
ardent for logic and the logicizing of the world—consequently
at the same time more 'cheerful' and more 'scientific'?[1] In
Nietzsche's opinion the Greeks were pessimistic, and their
pessimism is characteristic of their age of youthful greatness.
The later 'optimism' 'like democracy itself', is symptomatic
of declining vigour. Thus in the Notes for a continuation of
Philosophy in the Tragic Age of the Greeks (1873) Nietzsche
comments: 'Greek thought during the *tragic age is
pessimistic* or *artistically optimistic* . . . Deep distrust of
reality: nobody assumes a good god, who has made everything *optime*. . . . With Socrates *Optimism* begins, an
optimism no longer artistic, with teleology and faith in the
good god; faith in the enlightened good man. Dissolution
of the instincts'. Nietzsche does not mean that the Greeks
erected pessimism into an explicit clear-cut philosophy, but
that they had the feeling that life is terrible, inexplicable,
dangerous, that man is surrounded by hostile forces, that
optimism is an illusion—a feeling hinted at by their conception of ὕβρις—and by the sayings of poets, such as the
phrase of Theognis ὄλβιος οὐδεὶς ἀνθρώπων, ὁπόσους ἡέλιος
καθορᾷ.[2]
And does not even Sophocles declare?

μὴ Φῦναι τὸν ἅπαντα νικᾷ λόγον· τὸ δ᾽, ἐπεὶ Φανῇ,
βῆναι κεῖθεν ὅθενπερ ἥκει πολὺ δεύτερον ὡς τάχιστα.[3]

In the *Birth of Tragedy* Nietzsche writes: 'Depart not hence,
but hear rather what Greek folk-wisdom says of this same
life, which with such inexplicable cheerfulness spreads out
before thee. There is an ancient story that King Midas

[1] *Preface*, 1886.   [2] *Theognis*, 167–8.
[3] *Soph. 'Oed. Col.'* 1224–5.

hunted in the forest a long time for the wise *Silenus*, the companion of Dionysus, without capturing him. When at last he fell into his hands, the king asked what was best of all and most desirable for man. Fixed and immovable, the demon remained silent; till at last, forced by the king, he broke out with shrill laughter into these words: 'Oh, wretched race of a day, children of chance and misery, why do ye compel me to say to you what it were most expedient for you not to hear? What is best of all is for ever beyond your reach: not to be born, not to *be*, to be *nothing*. The second best for you, however, is soon to die'.[1]

In face of this fundamental pessimism two paths lie open. One is to create a dream-world, an artistically optimistic world—and this is the Apollonian way: the other is to face the real nature of the world and to affirm it, accept it, say 'yes' to it—this is the Dionysian way. The Apollonian culture is represented in the Olympian religion. 'To be able to live the Greeks had, from direst necessity, to create these gods. . . . How else would this so sensitive people, so vehement in its desires, so singularly qualified for *suffering*, have endured existence, if it had not been exhibited to them in their gods, surrounded with a higher glory? The same impulse which calls art into being, as the complement and consummation of existence, seducing to a continuation of life, caused also the Olympian world to arise'.[2] Homer is the poet of the Apollonian culture, and 'The Homeric "naïveté" can be comprehended only as the complete triumph of the Apollonian illusion'. The Apollonian way of meeting reality is thus the way of beauty, the way of illusion: a veil is spread over the horror beneath. 'The Greek knew and felt the terrors and horrors of existence: to be able to live at all, he had to interpose the shining dream-birth of the Olympian world between himself and them'. Schopenhauer quotes more than once the saying of Calderón, 'Pues el mayor delito del hombre es haber nacido': Nietzsche finds in the Greek a like pessimism as to the nature of the world, a pessimism which, in the Apollonian culture, is veiled by the illusion of the Olympian myth, beautiful and serene.

[1] *Birth of Tragedy*, p. 34.　　　　[2] Ibid., p. 35.

The other way in which the Greeks 'overcame' pessimism was by the Dionysian attitude. In the Appendix to the *Birth of Tragedy* Nietzsche tells us clearly what he means by 'Dionysian'. (In the *Birth of Tragedy* itself the conception is closely bound up with Schopenhauer's pessimistic metaphysic, a metaphysic which Nietzsche had long rejected by the time—1888—he came to write down the notes, which have been printed as an appendix to his early work.) In the Appendix he tells us that 'in the Dionysian symbol the utmost limit of affirmation is reached': in it there is 'a formula of *highest affirmation*, born of fullness and over-fullness, a yea-saying without reserve to suffering's self, to guilt's self, to all that is questionable and strange in existence itself'. The Dionysian attitude does not fail to recognize the suffering of existence: on the contrary a clear vision of the real character of the world is an essential foundation of the attitude. But does not the legendary Dionysos himself suffer and die? The Dionysian attitude recognizes the character of Life, non-teleological and godless; but, instead of turning away from life in hopeless pessimism, accepts life, says 'yes' to life, says 'yes'—in Nietzsche's developed thought—to the Eternal Recurrence of all things. It is the 'final, cheerfullest, exuberantly mad-and-merriest Yea to life'.

For this 'yea-saying' '*courage* is needed; and, as a condition thereof, a surplus of *strength*: for precisely in degree as courage *dares* to thrust forward, precisely according to the measure of strength, does one approach truth'. In treating of the Dionysian phenomenon in the historic Greek world (in *The Birth of Tragedy*) Nietzsche represents this courage and strength, necessary for a full and joyful acceptance, as drawn from intoxication and lyrical exaltation. 'It is either under the influence of the narcotic draught, of which the hymns of all primitive men and peoples tell us, or by the powerful approach of spring penetrating all nature with joy, that those Dionysian emotions awake, in the augmentation of which the subjective vanishes to complete self-forgetfulness'.[1] This Dionysian exaltation, eastern

[1] *Birth of Tragedy*, p. 26.

in origin, but tempered in its excesses by the Apollonian balance, tended to triumph in the soul of the Apollonian Greek. 'The muses of the arts of "appearance" paled before an art which, in its intoxication, spoke the truth, the wisdom of Silemus cried "Woe! woe!" against the cheerful Olympians. The individual, with all his boundaries and due proportions, went under in the self-oblivion of the Dionysian states and forgot the Apollonian precepts. The *Undueness* revealed itself as truth, contradiction the bliss born of pain, declared itself out of the heart of nature. And thus, wherever the Dionysian prevailed, the Apollonian was routed and annihilated'. (Though the Doric state and Doric art were 'a permanent war-camp of the Apollonians'.)

The phenomenon of intoxication is, of course, merely accidental to the ancient Dionysian worship; but the central thought of the Dionysian attitude—the fullest yea-saying to life *as it is*—was consistently maintained by Nietzsche, not only in his earlier works, but also in his developed philosophy. Thus in *Nietzsche contra Wagner* we read that 'there are two kinds of sufferers: those that suffer from *overflowing vitality*, who need Dionysian art and require a tragic insight into, and a tragic outlook upon, the phenomenon life—and there are those who suffer from *reduced* vitality'. The Dionysian man is 'the richest creature, brimming over with vitality'. (According to Nietzsche it is, above all, the Christian who suffers from 'reduced vitality'.) In *Also Sprach Zarathustra*, Zarathustra (i.e. Nietzsche) views the Eternal Recurrence (ch. 57) with disgust and loathing, as involving infinite repetitions of his own—i.e. Nietzsche's—none-too-happy life, but in the last chapter of the third part he utters his fullest Yes: 'Oh, how could I not be ardent for Eternity, and for the marriage-rings of rings— the ring of the return? Never yet have I found the woman by whom I should like to have children, unless it be this woman whom I love: for I love thee, O Eternity! *For I love thee, O Eternity!*' This is the Dionysian attitude: the Dionysian man, in the exuberance of his vitality, affirms life as it is, affirms it as the Will to Power, and affirms the Eternal Recurrence.

The Dionysian attitude is thus positive, one of the fullest affirmation and acceptance; and Nietzsche regarded it as a triumph over pessimism. Tragedy was for him the Greek triumph over pessimism, i.e. the pessimism of no-saying, of resignation. 'Tragedy is so far from proving anything in regard to the pessimism of the Greeks, as Schopenhauer maintains, that it ought rather to be considered as the categorical repudiation and *condemnation* thereof. The saying of Yes to life, including even its most strange and most terrible problems, the will to life rejoicing over its own inexhaustibleness in the sacrifice of its highest types—that is what I called Dionysian'.[1] If pessimism be taken as equivalent to no-saying, then of course the Dionysian attitude is not pessimistic: but if the atheistic *Weltanschauung* is—as it most certainly is—fundamentally pessimistic, then the Dionysian attitude, as depicted by Nietzsche, is no true triumph over pessimism.

In his treatment of Greek culture Nietzsche certainly advances opinions, the truth of which is at least very doubtful. Thus when he implies that Apollonian 'measure' kept Greek Dionysiasm from 'the horrible witches' draught of sensuality and cruelty', he is probably wrong. Moreover, his whole exaltation of early Greece at the expense of Periclean Athens (Athens brought in the reign of rationalism and speculation) is one-sided and exaggerated. The early Greek philosophies lead up to, and prepare the way for, the Platonic-Aristotelian philosophy, and, as an historian of philosophy, one cannot accept Nietzsche's condemnation of Socrates and Plato. The philosophy of Plato, whatever may be its faults, is an immense advance on the pre-Socratic cosmologies; and—from the personal point of view—what evidence is there to show that Plato was less of a *man* than e.g. Thales?[2]   After all, Thales theorized, and so did all the pre-Socratics. Yet in spite of exaggeration of this type, and in spite of historical mistakes, inaccuracies and arbitrary assumptions, Nietzsche's treatment of Greek culture is by

[1] *Twilight of the Idols*, pp. 119–120.
[2] In any case Plato is one of the greatest philosophers of all time, and those who, like Constantin Ritter, consider him *the* philosopher, are—whether right or not—by no means proposing an absurdity.

no means without value. For one thing he exposed the ridiculous notion that the Greeks were the optimistic, care-free, children of the sun, and insisted that the strange and terrible things of life were present there at the back of their minds, casting a sombre shadow over existence. This view has gained ground since, but Nietzsche deserves credit for having maintained it at a time when the opposite notion of the Greeks was current. Again, there is a great deal to be said for the contrast he draws between the Dionysian and Apollonian strain in Greek culture. And thirdly, we would doubtless agree with Nietzsche to a considerable extent in his judgment as to the comparative merits of the great tragedians. Who would be prepared to rank Euripides before Æschylus? Moreover, the view of Greek culture as an artistic unity, contrasted with modern ununified, curiosity-shop culture, is possessed of truth and value. As Nietzsche points out, the Greeks borrowed many elements of their culture from other peoples, but none the less they 'can do more than merely trim and adorn themselves with what they have borrowed, as did the Romans'.

In Greek life then, particularly in the earlier period, Nietzsche found an essentially aristocratic culture, the culture of the genius, and in the Dionysian attitude to life he found a full-blooded acceptance of life *as it is*. For him then Greek culture ever remained as the fine flower of the past, a past which he desired to be taken up and developed in the future. Greek culture might have produced greater fruit: but it was destroyed, first through the internecine wars of the States, and then through foreign conquest. Apart from the causes internal to culture itself, as those considered in connection with Socrates, politics were, in Nietzsche's eyes, the ruin of Greece. He does indeed speak highly of the Greek *polis*, but he also points out the danger of political life in Greece. Thus 'Sparta was the ruin of Athens in so far as she compelled Athens to turn her entire attention to politics and to act as a federal combination'.[1] Moreover, Nietzsche asserts that the influence of the Greek city was by no means always favourable to culture. In an

[1] *We Philologists*, aph. 123.

aphorism headed *The Development of the Mind feared by the State*, he says: 'The Greek *polis* was, like every organizing political power, exclusive and distrustful of the growth of culture; its powerful fundamental impulse seemed almost solely to have a paralysing and obstructive effect thereon. It did not want to let any history or any becoming have a place in culture; the education laid down in the State laws was meant to be obligatory on all generations to keep them at *one* stage of development. Plato also, later on, did not desire it to be otherwise in his ideal State. *In spite* of the *polis* culture developed itself in this manner; indirect— to be sure, and against its will, the *polis* furnished assistance because the ambition of individuals therein was stimulated to the utmost, so that, having once formed the path of intellectual development, they followed it to its farthest extremity. On the other hand, appeal should not be made to the panegyric of Pericles, for it is only a great optimistic dream about the alleged necessary connection between the Polis and Athenian culture; immediately before the night fell over Athens (the plague and the breakdown of tradition), Thucydides makes this culture flash up once more like a transfiguring afterglow, to efface the remembrance of the evil day that had preceded'.[1]

It is interesting to read Nietzsche's comment on the final political failure of Greece. 'The political failure of Greece is the greatest failure of culture; for it has given rise to the atrocious theory that culture cannot be pursued unless one is at the same time armed to the teeth'.[2] In spite of all his affirmation of the Will to Power, Nietzsche was of course under no illusion as to any necessary connection between military power and political supremacy on the one hand and cultural eminence on the other. One has only to read his remarks on the German Empire in relation to culture, in order to realize that fact. And when he spoke, as he did, of the bane that Athenian political supremacy was for the rest of Greece from the cultural point of view—an opinion however to which I should not care to subscribe without

[1] *Human, All-too-Human*, i, aph. 474.
[2] *We Philologists*, aph. 123.

considerable reservation—he may well have had in mind as a parallel the military victory of Germany in his own time. Did he not himself say that 'wherever Germany extends her sway, she *ruins* culture'?

Nietzsche naturally had not the same feeling for Rome that he had for Greece, though when it came to contrasting Greco-Roman culture with his *bête-noire*, Christianity, he left no doubt which he preferred. We have already seen how Nietzsche considered that the Romans, unlike the Greeks, were able only to 'trim and adorn themselves with what they borrowed'[1]—a probably apt criticism in regard to the Roman Empire, that magnificent and cosmopolitan hotchpotch—in spite of the political and judicial unity. Nietzsche distinguishes the 'purely productive period' of ancient culture—i.e. Greek, especially early Greek culture—from 'the entire Romano-Alexandrian culture', and declares that German resistance to antiquity 'is only justifiable in the case of the Romanized culture; for this culture, even at that time, was a falling-off from something more profound and noble'.[2] But though he will not admit Hellenic-Roman culture as the high-point of antiquity, Nietzsche asserts that Greece and Rome are complementary to one another. 'There are two kinds of geniuses: one which above all engenders and seeks to engender, and another which willingly lets itself be fructified and brings forth. And similarly, among the gifted nations, there are those on whom the woman's problem of pregnancy has devolved, and the secret task of forming, maturing, and perfecting—the Greeks, for instance, were a nation of this kind, and so are the French; and others which have to fructify and become the cause of new modes of life—like the Jews, the Romans, and, in all modesty be it asked: like the Germans?—nations tortured and enraptured by unknown fevers and irresistibly forced out of themselves, amorous and longing for foreign races (for such as 'let themselves be fructified'), and withal imperious, like everything conscious of being full of generative force, and consequently empowered 'by the grace of God'. These two kinds of

---

[1] *We Philologists*, aph. 117.   [2] Ibid., aph. 40–1.

geniuses seek each other like man and woman; but they also misunderstand each other—like man and woman'.[1]

Nietzsche recognizes, therefore, the genius of Rome, and in *The Genealogy of Morals* he speaks of the Romans as 'the strong and aristocratic; a nation stronger and more aristocratic has never existed in the world, has never even been dreamed of; every relic of them, every inscription enraptures, granted that one can divine *what* it is that writes the inscription'.[2] Moreover, when it comes to the question of style, Nietzsche definitely prefers the Romans to the Greeks. 'I am not indebted to the Greeks for anything like such strong impressions; and, to speak frankly, they cannot be to us what the Romans are. One cannot *learn* from the Greeks—their style is too strange, it is also too fluid to be imperative or to have the effect of a classic. Who would ever have learnt writing from a Greek! Who would ever have learned it without the Romans'![3]

The great enemy of Antiquity was—according to Nietzsche—Christianity. Christianity is hostile to life—it turns its back on life—and so it destroyed the ancient culture, precisely because it was through the ancient culture that life flourished. The Christian is a decadent and acts 'disintegratingly, poisonously and witheringly'—like a bloodsucker. 'Christianity was the vampire of the *imperium Romanum*—in a night it shattered the stupendous achievement of the Romans'.[4] The Roman Empire, 'the most magnificent form of organization, under difficult conditions, that has ever been achieved, and compared with which everything that preceded, and everything which followed it, is mere patchwork, gimcrackery, and dilettantism', was destroyed, 'until no two stones were left standing one on the other,—until even the Teutons and other clodhoppers were able to become master of it'.[5] The Roman organization was sufficiently firm to be able to resist corrupt

---

[1] *Beyond Good and Evil*, aph. 248.
[2] *Genealogy of Morals*, pp. 54–5.
[3] *Antichrist*, p. 113.
[4] Ibid., p. 222.
[5] Ibid., p. 221.

personalities, the bad emperors; 'but it was not sufficiently firm to resist the *corrupted* form of corruption, to resist the Christian'. The Christians destroyed the aristocratic organization of Rome, weakened the feeling of life, super-imposed their other-worldly religion, preached asceticism and a morality which drains life of its vigour and strength. Thus the whole labour of the ancient world was in vain. This labour had been preparatory inasmuch as the Greeks and Romans had laid 'all the prerequisites of a learned culture'—scientific method, 'the great and peerless art of reading well', natural science, mathematics, mechanics, etc. —which should have formed the substructure of a lasting building. But this work of preparation was denied, deprived of significance by the triumph of Christianity. *'All this in vain!* In one night it became merely a memory! The Greeks! The Romans! Instinctive nobility, instinctive taste, methodic research, the genius of organization and adminis-tration, faith, the *will* to the future of mankind, the *yea* to all things materialized in the *imperium Romanum*, become visible to all the senses, grand style no longer manifested in mere art, but in reality, in truth, in *life*.—And buried in a night, not by a natural catastrophe! Not stamped to death by Teutons and other heavy-footed vandals! But destroyed by crafty, stealthy, invisible anæmic vampires! Not con-quered—but only drained of blood! . . . The concealed lust of revenge, miserable envy, become *master*! Everything wretched, inwardly ailing, and full of ignoble feelings, the whole Ghetto-world of souls was in a trice *uppermost!*— One only needs to read any one of the Christian agitators— St. Augustine, for instance,—in order to realize, in order to *smell*, what filthy fellows came to the top in this move-ment. You would deceive yourselves utterly if you supposed that the leaders of the Christian agitation showed any lack of understanding:—Ah! they were shrewd, shrewd to the point of holiness were these dear old Fathers of the Church! What they lack is something quite different. Nature neglected them,—it forgot to give them a modest dowry of decent, of respectable and of *cleanly* interests. . . . Between ourselves, they are not even men. If Islam despises

Christianity, it is justified a thousand times over; for Islam presupposes men'.[1]

Nietzsche's views on Christianity will be discussed in the chapter on *Antichrist*; but it may be pointed out here that Nietzsche generally neglects the dark side of Roman civilization and the cankers which destroyed it from within. (Though he certainly does make explicit recognition of the dark side on occasion as when he says: 'If we think of Juvenal's Rome, of that poisonous toad with the eyes of Venus, we understand what it means to make the sign of the Cross before the world, we honour the silent Christian community and are grateful for its having stifled the Greco-Roman Empire'. But then he goes on to qualify this admission by declaring that 'To young and fresh barbarian nations, on the other hand, Christianity is a poison'.[2]) In his hatred of Christianity Nietzsche tends to neglect the fact that the Roman Empire, tending of itself to dissolution, would have passed away—Christianity or no Christianity. Moreover the exaltation of Greco-Roman culture above Christian culture depends for its validity on the justification of the denial of the transcendent and supernatural, on the negation of any life that is higher than natural life—for the Christians can be called 'enemies of life' only if the supernatural life is fiction and illusion. This Nietzsche presupposed: he never attempted to prove it. He could not. A true reading of history shows that Rome was indeed a preparation, but a preparation for Christianity, and that Christianity itself, so far from being a denial of life, represents a fresh irruption of life, of life from on high, which ennobles—without denying or destroying—the best in natural life.

Such being Nietzsche's view of Christianity, one would not expect him to look favourably on Christian medieval culture. He did, however, see some good points in it. Thus 'The Middle Ages present in the Church an institution with an absolutely universal aim, involving the whole of humanity —an aim, moreover, which—presumedly—concerned man's

---

[1] *Antichrist*, pp. 225–6.
[2] *Human, All-too-Human*, ii, aph. 224

highest interests; in comparison therewith the aims of the States and nations which modern history exhibits make a painful impression; they seem petty, base, material, and restricted in extent'.[1] He goes on indeed to say that this 'universal institution corresponded to feigned and fictitiously fostered needs, such as the need of salvation', and that the coming of future institutions will cast into oblivion 'that fantastic prototype, the Catholic Church'; but he does at least see something admirable in the universal character of the Church. Moreover, the Middle Ages were the period of great passions, manifesting a widening of the soul that can be observed neither in antiquity nor in the modern world. 'Never was the capacity of the soul greater or measured by larger standards'. Not seldom one person united in himself 'the physical, primeval sensuality of the barbarian races and the over-soulful, over-vigilant, over-brilliant eyes of Christian mystics'. If a man was seized by a passion, the fall was deeper than ever before. 'We modern men may be content to feel that we have suffered a loss here'.[2]

But if Nietzsche finds some points in the Middle Ages which admit of favourable comment, his final judgment on Medieval Christian culture is most certainly an adverse judgment. In his essay on *The Use and Abuse of History* Nietzsche speaks of the medieval *memento mori* and the 'hopelessness that Christianity bears in its heart towards all future ages of earthly existence'; and on another work he speaks of the weakening effect that the early Medieval Church had on the 'noble German'. 'In the early years of the Middle Ages, during which the Church was most distinctly and above all a menagerie, the most beautiful examples of the 'blond beast' were hunted down in all directions—the noble Germans, for instance, were 'improved'. But what did this 'improved' German, who had been lured to the monastery, look like after the process? He looked like a caricature of man, like an abortion: he had become a 'sinner', he was caged up, he had been imprisoned behind a host of appalling

---

[1] *Human, All-too-Human*, i, aph. 476.
[2] *The Wanderer and his Shadow*, aph. 222.

notions. He now lay there, sick, wretched, malevolent even toward himself: full of hate for the instincts of life, full of suspicion in regard to all that is still strong and happy. In short a 'Christian'. In physiological terms: in a fight with an animal, the only way of making it weak may be to make it sick. The Church understood this: it ruined man, it made him weak—but it laid claim to having "improved" him.'[1]

This is, indeed, Nietzsche's chief objection to Christianity, namely its weakening effect, its alleged no-saying attitude to life. It was in virtue of this characteristic that Christianity turned on the Moorish culture of Spain and trampled it to death, and that 'the Crusaders waged war upon something before which it would have been more seemly for them to grovel in the dust—a culture beside which even our Nine-teenth Century would seem very poor and very "senile". 'Christianity destroyed the harvest we might have reaped from the culture of antiquity, later it also destroyed our harvest of the culture of Islam. The wonderful Moorish world of Spanish culture, which in its essence is more closely related to *us*, and which appeals more to our sense and taste than Rome and Greece, was *trampled to death* (I do not say by what kind of feet), why?—because it owed its origin to noble, to manly instincts, because it said yea to life, even that life so full of the rare and refined luxuries of the Moors! . . .'[2]

Now, that the Moorish culture of Spain was from the material point of view a richer and more varied culture than that of contemporary Christian Europe—France and England for instance—is undeniable; but there are higher values than those of natural and material civilization. And is it not a pertinent question to ask whether the Christian conquest of the Moors was not in reality the victory of a vigorous, young, and growing culture over an over-ripe and decaying culture? Moorish culture at its best, at its period of toleration, of philosophy, and of science, was com-paratively short-lived: it was by no means exclusively due

[1] *Twilight of the Idols*, pp. 45–6.
[2] *Antichrist*, p. 226.

to Christianity that it perished. On the contrary the 'softer', more humane, enlightened, tolerant, and cultured elements—those elements which went to compose Moorish culture as Nietzsche understood it—tended to become submerged beneath the harsher, less cultured strains in the Mohammedan world; and just as Roman culture tended to self-destruction, so did Moorish culture. It became overripe, effete, and fell an easy prey to the narrow-minded strength of Mohammedan fanaticism. One has no wish to excuse all the doings of Christians in regard to the Moors; but it must be realized that the victory of Christianity was the victory of that culture which has supplied the foundation of all that is valuable in the culture of Europe. Moreover, the Christians appropriated a good deal of the Moorish heritage and further enhanced its value. We need only recall that it was mainly through Arabic sources that the Aristotelian metaphysics came to the Christian West. The thirteenth-century medieval culture was a period of intense intellectual activity—think of St. Bonaventure, St. Albert the Great, St. Thomas Aquinas, Dante—and it was in the Middle Ages, mainly under the influence of the Catholic Church, that Europe became a more or less unified and articulate cultural field. The spiritual and cultural values, for which we are fighting to-day, are an inheritance of that great medieval period of European civilization, even if not always recognized as such; and in challenging Christianity and the Catholic Church Nietzsche is challenging those very factors which have made European culture possible, those very factors, the denial of which leads, not to a higher culture but to Nihilism. If European culture does break down in the future, it will be because Christianity has not succeeded in permeating the whole political and social structure of Europe.

It is extremely doubtful if the Moorish culture of Spain, even if left to itself by Christianity, would have progressed or remained at the level it once attained; but in any case, when the Mohammedans attempted, not only to subjugate Spain, but also to cross the Pyrenees and subjugate Western Europe, they were a menace to the whole future of European civilization. For what was it that produced the unity of Europe? It was the common Faith, that common Faith that originated a fundamental community of outlook and of culture. It was the Church, under the leadership and guidance of the Papacy, the Church in whose sphere lay the departments of education, of social welfare, and to a large extent of art and literature, that preserved the Latin culture of the West, informed it by Christian ideals and brought to birth the specifically Christian and European civilization. If we want to see what the victory of 'vigorous' races over Christianity led to in practice, we have only to look at the Mongol invasion of Russia in the Middle Ages, which destroyed the young culture there in existence, separated Russia from Western cultural influence, and retarded the natural growth of Russia for centuries. If the Germanic tribes became a contributory factor in European civilization, it was not simply because they were 'young' or 'vigorous', but because these vigorous elements were Christianized. And if they have since become a menace to European culture it is largely because they were insufficiently subordinated to the Christian and Latin discipline.

Enlightened scholars of to-day refuse to admit that rigid dichotomy between the Middle Ages and the Modern Period, once so fashionable. They rather tend to emphasize the fact that the Renaissance, in many of its features, was prepared *within* the later Middle Ages. We cannot, therefore, join Nietzsche in regarding the Renaissance as essentially an attack on Christianity. In Nietzsche's opinion the Renaissance was an attack on Christianity, an attack in which the *noble* values were to have been set upon the throne, and through which Christianity would have been swept away. This attack showed every sign of succeeding —did not the Apostolic See itself succumb to Renaissance Humanism?—when Luther, the 'cursed monk', reinstated the Church by attacking it in the name of Christianity. Luther began the Reformation, and the Reformation occasioned the Counter-Reformation, and so the Renaissance failed. 'The Renaissance thus became an event without meaning, a great *in vain!*' Now this is quite untrue: the

Renaissance, as such, was by no means in vain: it had a permanent effect on Europe, and what there was in it of positive good was preserved. By the Protestant Reformation the religious unity of Europe was indeed destroyed; but the Italian Renaissance, together with later cultural, philosophic, and scientific movements, preserved and even tended to deepen an intellectual and cultural unity in Europe, so far as this was compatible with religious disunion. There *were*, of course, anti-Christian and exclusively humanistic strains in the Renaissance; but if these strains had been victorious and had not been defeated by the Church, so far from there having taken place a victory of culture, there would have occurred a victory for the forces which disintegrate culture—a victory which was happily delayed at any rate. Pure humanism inevitably ends in soulless barbarism and mechanical tyranny, for man is the subject of culture, and he is not truly man unless he is at the same time more-than-man. There is man anchored in the supernatural, and there is man decadent and degenerate, *deraciné* in the fullest sense: the purely 'natural' man is a fiction. *Entweder-Oder*, take your choice: there is no half-way house. It may seem, at a given period in history, as if there *is* a half-way house: but that is an illusion; if you posit the premisses, someone else at least will draw the conclusion. Pure humanists, anti-supernaturalists, have sown the wind—and we are reaping the whirlwind.

In regard to modern German culture we have already seen what was Nietzsche's opinion. German culture was no vital culture, no genuine and original creation, no artistic unity: it was a medley of different styles and was dependent on France, after, as before, the Franco-Prussian War. What then was Nietzsche's view of French culture? 'I believe only in French culture, and regard everything else in Europe which calls itself "culture" as a misunderstanding. I do not even take the German kind into consideration. . . . The few instances of higher culture which I have met in Germany were all French in their origin. The most striking example of this was Madame Cosima Wagner, by far the most decisive voice in matters of taste that I have ever heard'.[1] He speaks with approval of Molière, Corneille, Racine, Bourget, Guy de Maupassant, Stendhal, etc. And in *Nietzsche contra Wagner* we read: 'Even at the present day, France is still the refuge of the most intellectual and refined culture in Europe, it remains the high school of taste'. France is the land of intellectual refinement, of taste, of artists with a universal literary culture. Nietzsche finds 'three things, which the French can still boast of with pride as their heritage and possession, and as indelible tokens of their ancient intellectual superiority in Europe'. These are, first, 'the capacity for artistic emotion, for devotion to "form", for which the expression, *l'art pour l'art*, along with numerous others, has been invented'; secondly, 'their ancient, many-sided, "moralistic" culture, owing to which one finds on an average, even in the petty "romanciers" of the newspapers and chance "boulevardiers de Paris", a psychological sensitiveness and curiosity, of which, for example, one has no conception (to say nothing of the thing itself!) in Germany'; and thirdly, that 'in the French character there is a successful half-way synthesis of the North and the South, which makes them comprehend many things, and enjoins upon them other things, which an Englishman can never comprehend'.[2]

We have dwelt briefly on the past. What are Nietzsche's desires for the future? His hope for the future of culture lies, as ever, in the full-blooded affirmation of life as it is (i.e. as Nietzsche sees it) and in the production of the genius, the Superman. As a condition for the coming of Superman, the true aristocrat of culture, Nietzsche preaches a United Europe, a unified European culture—though at the same time he denies the indispensable foundation of European culture, the common supernatural Faith. If the countries of Europe are to be united, they must be united by something stable, permanent, guaranteed, transcendent of all differences and centrifugal factors, something which, while coming from without—or rather from above—will produce, if it is allowed to strike root, an harmonious development

---

[1] *Ecce Homo*, pp. 37–8.
[2] *Beyond Good and Evil*, aph. 254.

of culture, where legitimate varieties within a common framework are not condemned and stifled (as they are always bound to be stifled in an irreligious system—contrary to what some people imagine), but encouraged, harmonized, and enriched by their inclusion in a common whole and their submission to a common spiritual influence. This something can be none other than that which first produced European unity-in-difference, namely the Faith of the Catholic and Roman Church.

CHAPTER IV

THE SUPERMAN AND THE WILL TO POWER

THE aim of culture according to Nietzsche is the production of the genius; it is the genius, the great man, who gives meaning to life. To Nietzsche the notion that the aim of culture is to produce a multitude of mediocrities, was sickening and repugnant. The apologists of such a notion might appeal to the 'greater happiness of the greater number' principle, allying themselves with the Utilitarians. But the utilitarian principle is certainly ambiguous—for what is happiness? If happiness means a state of 'bourgeois' contentment, a state in which man—the average man—has every incitement to imitate the pig wallowing happily in the mire (and I am *not* speaking now of 'immorality'), one can only have sympathy with Nietzsche's loathing. Human life is a mysterious and in some ways a terrible thing (and we do not need a religious preacher to tell us that—witness Martin Heidegger), and cheap utilitarianism, which endeavours to suppress—or at least hide from view—the sublimities above and the abysses beneath, really aims at the degradation of human nature. The aim of culture is surely the ennoblement of human nature, the realization of its loftiest and profoundest potentialities, and in the concrete this must *include* the fullest realization of the greatest gifts where they are found, in the great men of history. Culture exists (we are speaking of its proximate end at present) not only for the production of mediocrities, but also for the production of the genius. In condemning a form of culture, which would result in the stunting of great personalities, in which the multitude, jealous and resentful, incapable of greatness itself and hating greatness in others, would prevent the growth of genius or persecute, ostracize and belittle the genius, Nietzsche voices the inner thoughts of all those who have a true reverence for human nature. If this sounds shocking to the democratic mind, let us ask the following question. Are you prepared, in the name of the multitude, to dispense with the saint, the great poet and artist, the man and woman of outstanding personality (even if you are prepared, when they are safely dead, to build the tombs of those whom your fathers have killed)? If so, then you stand under the condemnation of Nietzsche. If, however, you long for the coming of great men and women in the present and in the future, and are ready to recognize them and welcome them, then you are prepared to go part of the way with Nietzsche, however much you may dislike the name of the prophet of Superman.

But although, in sympathy and agreement with Nietzsche's condemnation of the low, mediocre and purely *bourgeois* ideal, we insist that a true conception of culture must find room for the finest flower of culture, the aristocracy of the spirit, we cannot agree that the *sole* aim of culture is the production of genius and that ordinary men and women are of value only in so far as they contribute to the production of genius. 'Humanity must work unceasingly for the production of solitary great men—this and nothing else is its task'. No, this is *not* true. Great men and women are indeed the finest flower of culture, and to deny them, theoretically or practically, is to fail in an understanding of the function of culture, but ordinary men and women, too, have their rights, and no man can be made a mere means to any other man, however great and however outstanding. For the function of culture, the realization of man's potentialities, spiritual and corporeal, social and individual, is ultimately the glory of God, the manifestation in varying degrees of the Infinite Divine Perfection. As the bird of paradise may be said to manifest the Divine Beauty less inadequately than the elephant, so certain men and women will manifest the Divine Perfection—holiness, wisdom, etc. —better than others, according to the dispensation of God's Providence—but all men and women are in some degree a manifestation of God, and the lower grades, if one may so speak, have a direct relation to God, the divine Exemplar, and not merely indirect—through outstanding personalities. Indeed, when looked at in relation to God Himself, human differences tend to pale into insignificance.

It seems uncertain if Nietzsche's ideal high peak of cultural development is to be taken as a state of mankind in which there are only Supermen, or as a state in which there are Supermen and others. Both points of view are perhaps compatible, as may be seen from an illustration. The ideal is that *all* men and women should be perfect, should be saints, but the ideal is simply a guiding idea, a motive for constant energy and action, since we recognize that in point of fact there will never be a state of mankind on earth in which all members of the human species are saints. A second ideal is therefore admissible, the appearance of the greatest number of saints concretely possible. In the concrete realization of this ideal 'ordinarily' good men and women will contribute to the function of the more 'godlike' and the saints themselves will have an important influence (not of course always consciously) in the formation of other saints. (In adducing this illustration we have naturally no intention of implying that God Himself is not the Cause of all sanctity; but the history of sanctity, so far as known to the human understanding, shows the part played by e.g. good parents in the formation of this or that saint, as also the influence of one saint on the formation of another. We do not live or die to ourselves alone.) These two ideals are not contradictory; and thus, if Nietzsche sometimes speaks as if the human race as we know it is to be surpassed and give place to a race of Supermen, while at other times he implies that the number of outstanding personalities will be more or less limited, the two viewpoints are not necessarily contradictory, since they may be taken to refer to concrete realization in different ways—the one being merely a guiding ideal, the other referring more directly to a concretely realizable possibility.

The idea of the *Superman*—though the word occurs previously—is characteristic of Nietzsche's later work, i.e. *Also sprach Zarathustra* and the succeeding books. The question then arises, what relation the *Übermensch* of these later works bears to the free and noble aristocracy of culture, the 'good Europeans' of his earlier thought. Is the Superman just another name for the good European, or is he something different—the 'good European' being himself but a preparation for the Superman? The view has been held that the *Übermensch* of *Zarathustra* is of quite a different type to the aristocrat of culture as portrayed in Nietzsche's earlier works. The latter is a type which definitely appears in history from time to time, while the former is a type to be *desired*, a creation of the future, not merely an exceptional man but an *Übermensch*, a Superman, transcending man as man transcends the ape. On this view Nietzsche would have reverted to the earlier type, when he says in *Antichrist* that the higher type of man has definitely appeared, 'but as a stroke of fortune, as an exception, never as *desired*'. It seems to me that the *Übermensch* of *Zarathustra* is Nietzsche's ideal, free from the faults which he recognized even in the exceptional men of history, but not entirely heterogeneous to those higher men that have actually appeared. The complete heterogeneity implied in *Zarathustra* is to be explained as a result of poetic and prophetic emphasis calculated to throw into strong relief the contrast between man, petty and weak, as Nietzsche experienced him, and the ideal man. Precisely because the *Übermensch* of *Zarathustra* is an ideal, which has never yet been realized, he cannot be clearly delineated, but appears dimly in the sunrise of the future, a figure to be desired, in the light of which he must judge of the inadequacy, not only of ordinary men, but also of the more or less faulty approximations to the ideal which have appeared from time to time in the course of history. It is certainly true that Nietzsche uses evolutionary language, which would imply that the *Übermensch* transcends man as we know him—even the exceptional men—as man transcends the ape, and this would imply a radical difference of type between the *Übermensch* and the 'good European', but—as already suggested—this may be no more than a very emphatic way of saying that the ideal, which we must desire and for which we must work, is far greater than anything of which we have had experience. It is difficult to suppose that Nietzsche really envisaged a literally new *species* when he spoke of the *Übermensch*.

The mention of evolution raises the question, what Nietzsche's attitude was towards Darwinism. This is an important question, because it is relevant to the problem whether or not Nietzsche regarded the *Übermensch* as literally a new species. Nietzsche certainly criticizes Darwin. Thus in *Beyond Good and Evil* he classes Darwin, together with John Stuart Mill and Herbert Spencer, among the 'respectable but mediocre Englishmen'. Equally certainly, however, Nietzsche was influenced by Darwin's theory of evolution. But though influenced by Darwin, and though he makes use of evolutionary terms, Nietzsche considered that Darwin's idea of the struggle for existence was essentially inadequate. He spoke of his own view as 'anti-Darwin', and he meant by that that he substituted the struggle for Power in place of the struggle for Existence. Of course, in point of fact the struggle for existence would mean in the concrete a struggle for power, at least if the means of existence are limited (and Nietzsche speaks of Darwinism as reflecting the condition of overcrowded England); but Nietzsche objected that the concept of the struggle for existence is but a poor and pinchbeck conception in comparison with that of the *Wille zur Macht*. Herbert Spencer (whose philosophy is stigmatized by Nietzsche as that of the 'tea-grocer') tried to found a utilitarian ethic on a basis of evolution, and Darwin himself had discovered 'a biological foundation for the moral sentiment' (Höffding) by remarking on the beneficial function of mutual helpfulness in the struggle for existence. Thus the English evolutionists, though accepting the Darwinian hypothesis of the struggle for existence, proceeded to erect a utilitarian ethic, comprising the ideals of altruism, sympathy, etc. Did not T. H. Huxley make man's moral life a realm *sui generis*, a repudiation of the natural principles of the struggle for existence? This is made possible by the gift of intellect, and Nietzsche considered that the use of intellect and the institution of a utilitarian ethic leads to the victory of the weak and the 'decadent'. A herd-morality is excogitated and declared to be the true biological morality, and the values of the herd predominate, preventing the growth of the strong, those in whom the will to power is vigorous. Neitzsche rejected therefore the central principle of *Wille zum Leben*, which, he thought, ended in the victory of the herd and the stunting of the free spirits, the strong aristocrats, and asserted instead the *Wille zur Macht*.

Nietzsche quarrels also with the evolutionists because, while looking on man as the highest type hitherto evolved, they seemed to regard the evolutionary process as stopping there, and did not envisage the evolution of a still higher species, more-than-man, Superman. This would certainly seem to indicate that Nietzsche regarded the future *Übermensch* as a new biological species in a literal sense. Nevertheless I hesitate to accept the view that this was Nietzsche's full meaning at least. If one stresses the eugenic element and the insistence on biological evolution in his thought, then undoubtedly one would have to represent Nietzsche as the pioneer of eugenics and a logical evolutionist on the grand scale; but, while admitting truth in this view, I am inclined to stress much more those passages which would seem to represent Superman as man raised to the nth degree of physical and mental power. For one thing, I cannot imagine Nietzsche sympathizing with the 'stud-farm' view of human nature[1]; and secondly he often supposes that Superman will need 'ordinary' man as a sort of foil, which would not lead one to conclude that the *whole* human species is to give way to Superman or even that between Superman and the 'ordinary' man there will

[1] But cf. *Will to Power*, ii, aph. 734 and 740, where compulsory castration is envisaged in certain cases.

be as *literal* a specific difference as there is between man and the ape. The *Superman* simply represents Nietzsche's ideal man.

The *Will to Power* became a central idea in Nietzsche's philosophy. Life, he declared, is Will to Power, and those who are most alive, those who are the best specimens of the human race, are those in whom the Will to Power is strongest. The outstanding men of history—Napoleon for instance—are the finest embodiments of the Will to Power that have yet appeared; but they will be surpassed by the *Supermen*, in whom the Will to Power will attain its zenith. 'Only where there is life, is there also will: not, however, Will to Life, but—so I teach thee—Will to Power!'[1]

It might appear from this, that Power is the one value in Nietzsche's eyes, and that a man or group of men, who have power, are thereby commendable. But this is very far from being the case. When the 'herd' rules the mediocre majority, and keeps the natural aristocrat, the outstanding man who would fain be free, in subjection to itself, there is power, the power of the herd. The weak and the slaves are living, and in them lives the will to power, and they have so often conspired to retain actual power in their hands and to assert as unchanging values these things which are useful to themselves. 'Wherever I found a living thing, there found I Will to Power; and even in the will of the servant found I the will to be master'.[2] Now if Power were really the one value in Nietzsche's eyes, it should follow that the victorious and reigning herd is justified. It would be useless for the strong individual to complain that the Will to Power was stronger in him and that he was being wrongly enslaved and stunted, bound by the valuation of the herd, since the fact that the herd was actually dominant would be the only justification needed for the herd's supremacy. But Nietzsche constantly and fiercely inveighs against herd-morality, herd-valuation, herd-supremacy: he will not allow that the mediocre majority are entitled to restrain the strong and free-spirited individuals. It follows, then, that for Nietzsche mere power is not the only value: on the contrary, he thinks

---

[1] *Zarathustra*, p. 137.   [2] *Zarathustra*, p. 136.

that those should have power who possess certain characteristics which fit them for power. He certainly upset the old
Tables and asserted new values, but it is a great mistake
to suppose that mere power or domination is the sole
Nietzschean value. Suppose, for instance, that a priesthood
rules in a certain people. It has the will to power and enjoys
actual power, but it is not thereby justified in Nietzsche's
eyes, for the priests may be a decadent type and lack the
characteristics required by Nietzsche in rulers. Nietzsche
does, indeed, state that 'the rank of men is settled and altered
by their degree of power alone, and by nothing else', but
he also states that 'I teach that there exist higher and lower
men'. If the lower type of man is actually dominant, that
is no justification for him. Power is not the only value: there
is a higher type of man, who *should* rule.

What, then, is this higher type of man? As far as the
Übermensch is concerned, the ideal man of the future, the
new 'species', it is extremely difficult to form any very clear
picture of him. This after all is but natural, for a hitherto
unrealized ideal may act as a motive force and guiding star,
a spring of desire, energy, and action, while at the same time
it cannot be clearly conceived and exactly characterized
for the very good reason that it belongs to the *future*. We
can describe men, who exist or have existed, but how can
we describe a man who has not yet existed? And Nietzsche's
poetic modes of expression do not lighten the task of
describing the Superman. Yet, however much we might
like to have a near vision of Nietzsche's ideal, it is not
really just to him if we demand an exact description. For
if he describes the *Übermensch*, he must describe him in
terms of experience, and then we should have a portrait
of the outstanding figures of history. Nietzsche has given
us examples of these noble men, free spirits—and we shall
return to them shortly—but it must be remembered that
they are at the best only approximations to the *Übermensch*,
who is a 'higher man' in a far more exalted sense (even if
he is not literally a new biological species).

There is one point that should be made at once, as it is
important for any understanding of Nietzsche's ideal. The

Übermensch is *not* the same as the barbarian, the blond beast. Nietzsche does indeed affirm that every higher civilization originates in an attack on a weaker, more moral, more peaceful race by 'barbarians in every terrible sense of the word, men of prey, still in possession of unbroken strength of will and desire for power', so that 'at the commencement, the noble caste was always the barbarian caste', that of 'more *complete* men' (which at every point also implies the same as 'more complete beasts')[1]; but his ideal was not simply an exuberant savage but a man of the highest mental, as well as physical, development. Thus Nietzsche says quite explicitly: 'Mankind must surpass itself, as the Greeks did—and no fleshless fantasies must be indulged. The higher mind which is associated with a sickly and nervous character must be suppressed. The goal: the higher culture of the whole body and not only of the brain'.[2] Strength of body is indeed emphasized, but the culture of the mind is included. The higher man is 'a strong, highly-cultured man, skilful in all bodily accomplishments, able to keep himself in check, having a feeling of reverence for himself, and so constituted as to be able to risk the full enjoyment of naturalness in all its rich profusion and be strong enough for this freedom; a man of tolerance, not out of weakness but out of strength, because he knows how to turn to his own profit that which would ruin the mediocre nature, a man unto whom nothing is any longer forbidden, unless it be weakness either as a vice or as a virtue'.[3] This is a picture of man, of Napoleon in fact, as Goethe, according to Nietzsche, conceived him; but it represents very well Nietzsche's own view of the higher man.

Superman then will be the highest example of yea-saying, of positive affirmation of life, in regard to both mind and body. But did not Nietzsche declare Cæsar Borgia (Nietzsche regarded the Renaissance as one of the great ages of the world, second only to the Greek age) to be a 'sort of Superman'? In *Ecce Homo* Nietzsche remarks: 'Once, when I whispered to a man that he would do better to seek for the

---

[1] *Beyond Good and Evil*, aph. 257.   [2] Notes on '*Zarathustra*', 56.
[3] *Twilight of the Idols*, p. 110.

Superman in a Cæsar Borgia than in a Parsifal, he could not believe his ears'.[1] Does he not commend Machiavelli and laud Napoleon, 'in that he called man, the soldier, and the great struggle for power, to life again, and conceived Europe as a political power'?[2] Does it not then appear that Nietzsche admired the 'beasts of prey' precisely as beasts of prey? Does he not speak of 'those marvellously incomprehensible and inexplicable beings, those enigmatical men, predestined for conquering and circumventing others, the finest examples of which are Alcibiades and Cæsar (with whom I should like to associate the *first* of Europeans according to my taste, the Hohenstaufen, Frederick the Second, and amongst artists, perhaps Leonardo da Vinci'?[3] Does Nietzsche not prefer even to the men of the Renaissance the men of antiquity, the Greeks, in whom he saw, as their strongest instinct, the unscrupulous Will to Power?—(as portrayed, e.g. in Thucydides). And must not the conclusion be that Nietzsche's Superman, however developed he may be in body and mind, is a being who could appear to us only as hateful and repulsive, a selfish and unscrupulous egoist on the grand scale?

It must be admitted that there is truth in this criticism. Nietzsche most certainly exalts power, and he most certainly teaches that man must subordinate himself to Superman, i.e. be a means to Superman. 'My desire is to bring forth creatures which stand sublimely above the whole species man: and to sacrifice "one's neighbours" and oneself to this end'.[4] Men must be animated, not by neighbour-love—*die Nächstenliebe*—but by love of the future man— *die Fernstenliebe*—and sacrifice themselves for him, being a means, a bridge, to the coming of Superman. The correlative of this subordination on the part of man is egoism on the part of the Superman. And indeed Nietzsche expressly declares: 'At the wish of displeasing innocent ears, I submit that egoism belongs to the essence of a noble soul, I mean the unalterable belief that to a being such as "we", other beings must naturally be in subjection, and have to

---

[1] p. 58.
[2] *Will to Power*, i, aph. 104.
[3] *Beyond Good and Evil*, aph. 200.
[4] Notes on *Zarathustra*, 46.

sacrifice themselves. The noble soul accepts the fact of his egoism without question, and also without consciousness of harshness, constraint, or arbitrariness therein, but rather as something that may have its basis in the primary law of things:—if he sought a designation for it he would say: "It is justice itself". He acknowledges under certain circumstances, which made him hesitate at first, that there are other equally privileged ones; as soon as he has settled this question of rank, he moves among those equals and equally privileged ones with the same assurance, as regards modesty and delicate respect, which he enjoys in intercourse with himself—in accordance with an innate heavenly mechanism which all the stars understand'.[1] Moreover he demands *hardness*, 'for all creators are hard'. 'This new commandment, oh my brother, I put up over you: become hard'! Not pity, softness, is virtue—it is sickness, a vice: hardness is virtue. 'Only the noblest is quite hard'.

It might very well appear, then, that Nietzsche's Superman is a hard, unfeeling egoist, and that he is heralded by men like Alcibiades, Cæsar Borgia, Napoleon. But we must make certain important reservations, which are not infrequently lost sight of by critics of Nietzsche. The first is that egoism for Nietzsche does not mean petty selfishness, and that hardness does not mean brutal cruelty. The noble man gives—indeed that is a characteristic of the noble man, adorned with *die schenkende Tugend*—but he gives and shines forth, like the sun, out of the abundance of his riches, out of his exuberance of life, not out of a pity which is itself a concealed selfishness, a nauseating and hypocritical delight in the sufferings of others. He does not nose around, prying into the sufferings of others, gloating over them in secret while professing to alleviate their suffering; nor does he indulge in a pity, which is weakness, a sharing in the sickness of others. He gives, not out of weakness, but out of strength. By teaching hardness, *Härte*, Nietzsche has not in mind to inculcate the sadistic cruelty of the Dachau or Buchenwald concentration camps: he rejects pity, not because pity prevents cruelty, but because pity is opposed

[1] *Beyond Good and Evil*, aph. 265.

—in his opinion—to living and vigorous energy. 'Pity is opposed to the tonic passions which enhance the energy of the feeling of life: its action is depressing. A man loses power when he pities'.[1] In pity, therefore, is involved the denial of life.

There is another reason, 'a still more important one', why Nietzsche condemns pity. 'On the whole, pity thwarts the law of development which is the law of selection. It preserves that which is ripe for death, it fights in favour of the dis-inherited and the condemned of life; thanks to the multitude of abortions of all kinds which it maintains in life, it lends life itself a sombre and questionable aspect'.[2] It was one of Nietzsche's constant objections to pity, that it leads to the preservation in life of those who would be better dead— e.g. the incurably cancerous—and the birth of those who should never have been born at all—e.g. mentally defective or syphilitic children. How far Nietzsche would have agreed with euthanasia in practice or in compulsory sterilization at the orders of the state officials it is difficult to say; but it is true that his expressed opinion on these matters are shocking to the Christian conscience. But then Nietzsche never thought that the Christian would agree with him! We reject Nietzsche's opinion in great part at least, but we do so, not out of a mere *feeling* of pity, but out of a con-viction of the value of human life, out of a reverence for suffering, ennobled by the Cross, out of a recognition of the rights of God. If Nietzsche's atheistic position be adopted, what real objection can there be to Nietzsche's con-clusions?

The atheist is, of course, bound by the moral law, and it is to his credit if, in spite of his atheism, he observes the moral law. (The wicked pagans, said St. Paul, were guilty, because they did not observe the Natural Law written in their hearts.) The atheist too is bound by the natural law, the expression of God's Eternal Law, since he, like everyone else is a creature of God, and can recognize the Law even if he does not recognize its Author. But if—*per impossibile*— the atheist's hypothesis were true, and there *were* no God,

---

[1] *Antichrist*, p. 131.   [2] Ibid., pp. 131–2.

if the world and human life had no given τέλος, the individual could have no 'rights' at all, other than those that the strong chose to give him. If religion is actually void of objective validity, then the only rights are the rights of those who have the strength to create their rights, and the other men and women have only such rights as the strong and powerful choose to give them. Take your choice, but do not be so stupid as to imagine that Christian morality can stand without the basis of the Christian religion, or that natural morality is independent of a Transcendental Foundation. If Nietzsche has done nothing else, he has at least—or would have if he were understood—taught us to face the issues honestly.[1]

Yet though Nietzsche condemns pity and teaches 'hardness', he does not suppose that the higher man is an insensitive brute, devoid of all emotion and feeling. Does not Zarathustra declare that 'In indulging and pitying lay ever my greatest danger'?[2] And he asks the soothsayer (Schopenhauer): 'My last sin which hath been reserved for me—knowest thou what it is called'? '*Pity*!' answered the soothsayer from an overflowing heart, and raised both his hands aloft—'O Zarathustra, I have come that I may seduce thee to thy last sin'![3] Zarathustra is not so insensitive that he is unable to recognize the suffering of the world, but he rises above it. 'Woe unto all loving ones who have not an elevation which is above their pity! Thus spake the devil unto me, once on a time: "Even God hath his hell: it is his love for man". And lately did I hear him say these words: "God is dead: of his pity for man hath God died".—So be ye warned against pity: from thence there yet cometh unto men a heavy cloud! Verily, I understand weather-signs! But attend also to this word: All great love is above all its pity: for it seeketh—to create what is loved! "Myself do I offer unto my love, *and my neighbour as myself*"—such is the language of all creators. All creators, however, are

---

[1] Moral obligation is indeed independent of *knowledge* of the Transcendental Foundation; but *if there really were no God*, there could be no moral and rational order in the universe.
[2] *Zarathustra*, p. 226.
[3] Ibid., p. 293.

hard'.[1] For the sake of his creation, for the sake of future man, Zarathustra rises above his pity, and all higher men, the noble type, must rise above their pity, attaining to a state of serenity, characterized not only by *Härte* but also by *Heiterkeit*, joyful serenity.

It is notorious that Nietzsche himself was by no means devoid of pity and feeling—far from it. There is a celebrated incident, in which an Englishwoman of delicate health said to him: 'I know, Herr Nietzsche, why you won't let us see your books. If one were to believe what you say in them, a poor, suffering creature like myself would have no right to live'. Nietzsche was apologetic, but of course the lady's remark was justified. When another lady, alluding to the famous passage in *Zarathustra*, said to him, 'I have been told about your books. You've written in one of them, "If thou goest among women, do not forget thy whip"'. Nietzsche took her hand in his and replied in a pained voice, 'Dear lady, dear friend, do not misunderstand me; it is not thus that I am to be understood'. (Nietzsche did *not* of course mean the whip to be understood literally: it is gross calumny to represent him as advocating such treatment of women.) Nietzsche himself was so sensitive and so understanding of pity that he conceived his ideal man as beyond pity, as having won through to joyful serenity, living as the Epicurean gods. (It is a curious fact that St. John of the Cross speaks of the soul in the highest state of union with God possible here on earth as transcending pity, or rather the sentiments of pity, so that 'even the sensible feeling of compassion exists not now, though the effects of it continue in perfection. . . . As the angels perfectly appreciate all sorrowful things without the sense of pain, and perform acts of mercy without the sentiment of pity, so the soul in this transformation of love'.[2] The saint admits of course, that God can, and does, allow such a soul to feel and suffer on occasion, as in the case of the Blessed Virgin. 'This, however, is not the ordinary condition of this state'. In the merely natural man the absence of the sentiment of pity

[1] *Zarathustra*, p. 105.
[2] *A Spiritual Canticle of the Soul*, trans. David Lewis, p. 163.

would be an imperfection; but in the supernatural *Superman*, the soul elevated to the Spiritual Marriage, 'the weaknesses of its virtues are no longer in the soul, for they are now constant, strong, and perfect'.)

'Hardness' and 'serenity' are therefore characteristics of the higher man and of *Übermensch*. Another is joy, the exuberant joy of life. 'Since humanity came into being, man hath enjoyed himself too little: that alone, my brethren, is our original sin'.[1] Joy, merriment, the spirit of dancing, healthfulness, such are the characteristics of Superman. ('Dance', says Brandes, 'in Nietzsche's language, is always an expression for the lofty-lightness of mind, which is exalted above the gravity of earth and above all stupid seriousness'. *Friedrich Nietzsche*, p. 49.) While beyond the shackles of good and evil, of traditional morality, from which he has set himself free, the noble man will not sink into the abyss of lust and self-indulgence—for he is a free spirit, not a slave. His very winning-through to freedom, joy, and serenity, will necessitate self-discipline, hardness to himself as well as to others. It is freedom that Nietzsche preaches, joyful, powerful, independent freedom: the higher man will not indeed be chaste for 'moral' reasons, but he will certainly not be a slave to the lusts of the body. 'Is it not better to fall into the hands of a murderer, than into the dreams of a lustful woman? And just look at these men: their eye saith it—they know nothing better on earth than to lie with a woman. Filth is at the bottom of their souls; and alas! if their filth hath still spirit in it! Would that ye were perfect—at least as animals! But to animals belongeth innocence. Do I counsel you to slay your instincts? I counsel you to innocence in your instincts. Do I counsel you to chastity? Chastity is a virtue with some, but with many almost a vice. These are continent, to be sure: but doggish lust looketh enviously out of all that they do. . . . And how wisely can doggish lust beg for a piece of spirit, when a piece of flesh is denied it! . . . To whom chastity is difficult, it is to be dissuaded: lest it become the road to hell—to filth and lust of soul. . . . Verily there are chaste

[1] *Zarathustra*, p. 103.

ones from their very nature; they are gentler of heart, and laugh better and oftener than you. They laugh also at chastity, and ask: "What is chastity? Is chastity not folly? But the folly came unto us, and not we unto it. We offered the guest harbour and heart: now it dwelleth with us— let it stay as long as it will" '.[1] Nietzsche demands innocence, complete and joyful wisdom of soul and body, beyond morality, beyond good and evil—an ideal, that is certainly wrong in rejecting 'moral' distinctions and also the Fall, but not the ideal of the libertine. Let us not be unjust to Nietzsche, even when we disagree with him.

The Superman, proud and free, joyful and serene, strong in mind and body, is the supreme yea-sayer to life, the true Dionysos. He says *Amen* even to the Eternal Recurrence, for he says *Amen* to life as it is. 'Not only man but Super-man will recur eternally'—a fearful thought, it is true, but Superman will welcome life with outstretched arms, will affirm it with eyes wide open: he above all will ask himself the question, 'Is this such a deed as I am prepared to perform an incalculable number of times?', and in the joy of his strength will answer 'Yes'. He will bless life—'From people who merely pray we must become people who bless'. This affirmation of life, this yea-saying, will be characteristic of all higher men, the new order of rank, but it will be pre-eminently characteristic of the greatest creation of man, Superman. 'The order of rank develops into a system of earthly dominion: the lords of the earth come last, a new ruling caste. Here and there there arises from them a perfectly Epicurean God, a Superman, a transfigurer of existence. The Superman's notion of the world. Dionysus'.[2]

But if Nietzsche's view of the higher man is of the kind we have depicted, what are we to make of the examples he gives of the lucky strokes of history, the 'almost Superman', e.g. Cæsar Borgia or Napoleon? Nietzsche does indeed say that there is more resemblance between Cæsar Borgia and Superman than between Parsifal and Superman; but his intention is not to advocate poisoning, but to emphasize (besides of course his admiration for Renaissance culture

---

[1] *Zarathustra*, pp. 61–2.   [2] Notes on *Zarathustra*, 81.

and *virtù*) the Superman's position *beyond good and evil*. He does indeed laud Napoleon, but in one place he speaks of him as a synthesis of Monster and Superman; and in this example again his intention is not so much to commend all Napoleon's actions as to emphasize his transcendence of morality: Napoleon is an example of the noble type. This distinction must be understood if Nietzsche is to be understood. He summons mankind *beyond good and evil*, but he does so, not in order to reject *all* valuation, but to substitute a *new* valuation, the distinction *noble—bad* in place of the moral distinction *good—evil*. Of Nietzsche's criticism of Christian morality we propose to treat in another chapter; but something must be said here of the two valuations, the two 'moralities' and corresponding orders of rank, as this is essential to an understanding of his doctrine of Superman.

Nietzsche points out that among the Greeks the antithesis is originally not between good and evil, but between noble and ignoble—or rather that the equation is, good = aristocratic = beautiful = happy = loved by the gods. The man who is κάλος as opposed to δειλός, πονηρός, μοχθηρός is the noble, aristocratic man as opposed to the slavish or vulgar man. The designations of moral value are applied first to *men*, and only derivatively and at a later period to *action*, and 'the noble type of man regards *himself* as a determiner of values; he does not require to be approved of; he passes the judgment: "What is injurious to me, is injurious in itself"; he knows that it is he himself only who confers honour on things; he is a *creator of values*'. In other words the 'good' are originally the noble, the aristocratic class: they *create* values and so make their own morality—which is really a morality of style. 'Bad' denotes the vulgar, slavish man and the actions of such men. Morality is therefore *class* morality, and good = noble = aristocratic. The good is what the noble and strong deem good. In this kind of morality—*master-morality*—'the antithesis "good" and "bad" mean practically the same as "noble" and "despicable" '.

Opposed to this *master-morality* is *slave-morality*, in which the strong and powerful are regarded as evil and the sufferers are looked up to as good. Instead of nobility, strength, beauty, we find those qualities brought into prominence which serve to alleviate the existence of sufferers— 'sympathy, the kind, helping hand, the warm heart, patience, diligence, humility and friendliness'. These are the qualities useful to the 'slaves', to the herd, and these qualities are accounted good in the slave- or herd-morality. (Nietzsche points out—not without perspicacity—that 'a shade of depreciation . . . at last attaches itself even to the "good" man of this morality; because, according to the servile mode of thought, the good man must in any case be the *safe* man: he is good-natured, easily deceived, perhaps a little stupid, *un bonhomme*'.[1])

Judæo-Christian morality is essentially slave- or herd-morality; and Nietzsche demands a return to master-morality. This is the meaning of his summons to man to go forth 'beyond good and evil'. The herd may, and should, retain their own morality; but the strong and virile, the higher men, must cast off the shackles of the slave-morality and adopt their proper valuation, the master-morality, in which good = aristocratic, noble, true, and powerful. The higher men, and above all the Superman, will not allow themselves to be deceived by the herd but will assert their own morality, that of the aristocrat. The herd, fearing and hating the exceptional man, have used various expedients for making out their morality to be the absolute and only morality, to which *all* must conform. Nietzsche demands a return to the twofold morality, one for the higher men, another for the herd.

Let me repeat that although the higher man rejects the herd valuation, which glorifies the qualities useful to the herd, this is not meant by Nietzsche to imply that the noble man never considers anyone but himself in the sense of petty selfishness. In *Beyond Good and Evil* he says expressly of the noble man that, 'In the foreground there is the feeling of plenitude, of power, which seeks to over-flow, the happiness of high tension, the consciousness of a wealth which would fain give and bestow—the noble man

---

[1] *Beyond Good and Evil*, aph. 260.

also helps the unfortunate, but not—or scarcely—out of pity, but rather from an impulse generated by the super-abundance of power'. Thus the noble man, in giving, is discharging the superabundance of his riches: it is part of his nature to bestow. 'A bestowing virtue is the highest virtue. . . . Ye constrain all things to flow towards you and into you, so that they shall flow back again out of your fountain as the gifts of your love'.[1] Nietzsche's Superman may be even more repugnant to us than Aristotle's man of spirit; but there is no justification for distorting Nietzsche's opinion and making him a preacher of a narrow and petty egoism. 'But a horror to us is the degenerating sense, which saith: "All for myself" '.[2]

Leaving aside for later consideration Nietzsche's criticism of morality, what are we to say of his doctrine of the Will to Power and of Superman? We can of course admit the great importance of the will to power as a psychological factor. This has been emphasized particularly by modern psychologists—doubtless largely under the influence, direct or indirect, of Friedrich Nietzsche—and the will-to-power psychology is certainly an improvement on that of Sigmund Freud. The will to power takes an important place in the individual psychology of Prof. Alfred Adler. The instinct of self-preservation is fundamental, and in man this instinct, when confronted with the 'dangers' arising from fellow human-beings, takes the form of a struggle for superiority, the will to power. But this will to power is not necessarily egoistic in a brutal sense: it is 'the very fever-house of human actions, both good and evil'.[3] It may indeed develop into unbridled ὕβρις on the one hand or give rise to the sense of inferiority on the other, but ideally it operates in harmony with the other fundamental tendency in man, the will to community. Over-accentuation of the self belongs, not to the 'normal', but to the 'abnormal'. Individual psychology demands the acceptance of reality as essential to normality: the exaltation of self as the sole value, the unbridled will to power, is a mark of abnormality, of the refusal to accept

[1] *Zarathustra*, p. 86.   [2] Ibid., p. 87.
[3] Rudolf Allers, *The New Psychologies*, Sheed and Ward, 1938, p. 35.

reality, the limitation of the self and the fact of the community.

Individual psychology supplies, therefore, a corrective to Nietzsche's doctrine of the will to power. For the cry *Eritis sicut dii* is the expression of a refusal to accept reality. But a full corrective can be found only in a frank recognition of the truth of theistic philosophy. The egoism of Superman is not only a refusal to accept the reality of man's position *vis-à-vis* the community, but it is also—and especially—a refusal to accept the position of the finite individual in relation to the Infinite Being. It is therefore, as a refusal to accept reality, a monstrosity, an abnormality. An attempt of this sort to free man from his fundamental relation to the Creator will not result in a development and increase of life, but in abnormality and neurosis. While not intending to maintain (indeed we do *not* maintain) that Nietzsche's *Übermensch* has the same characteristics as the Nazi bully and ruffian, it seems clear, to me at least, that the doctrine of Superman would lead *in practice*—though not exclusively—to this abominable type. That Nietzsche *personally* would have been prepared to worship at the shrine of Adolf Hitler, I cannot for a moment imagine; but at the same time I am convinced that the abnormal self-exaltation and unbridled will to power of Adolf Hitler is a *practical* consequence of the Nietzschean doctrine. For if man, denying reality, tries to set himself on an exalted pinnacle, to be as God, the inevitable result is, that he *falls*, and falls very low indeed. The consequence of ὕβρις is disaster. A determined revolt against the limited nature of man is a contradiction of the true will to power, of true ambition, for true ambition must take cognisance of reality, must confine itself within the limits of man's nature. The consequence of such revolt is—from the psychological viewpoint—neurosis. As Rudolf Allers so well remarks: 'Only the saint is free from neurosis and beyond it, because only he has accepted, by an act of "real assent", his position as a finite being, as a mere nothing in face of the Infinite. A really thoroughgoing analysis of neurotic mentality will discover that in all cases of neurosis without exception the real problem is one of metaphysics. The conflict at the root of neurosis is . . . between the original *superbia* of fallen man (which, begotten of sin and leading back to it, makes him strive after infinity) and his recognition of his essential finiteness'.[1]

The root error of Nietzsche's doctrine is thus his atheistic position and his denial of the fundamental value of *humility*. But, if this fundamental error is once clearly conceived, we can then admit a certain value in Nietzsche's doctrine. For one thing the emphasis he lays on the outstanding personality is by no means beside the point. The human race advances, when it does advance, largely through the instrumentality of gifted men and women. Where could Christianity be without Christ? And how much does religion owe to the work of St. Paul, St. Francis, St. Ignatius of Loyola, etc.! The history of art is very largely the history of exceptional artists, and we need not labour the point (despite Tolstoy), how much is owed in the way of political, social, and cultural development to men who had the courage to rise above the past and present, to go before and *lead*. A 'democratic' view of life, which involved a radical mistrust of exceptional talents, would be a wrong view of life—though it does not follow that exceptional men are justified in using the power won by their talents simply for their own ends. Human beings differ, but *every* human being is of value and *no* human being can be made a mere means to another human being.

Nietzsche identifies the Will to Power with Life. We cannot admit this: the will to power is a fundamental tendency of living things, but it is not co-extensive with life. Yet in emphasizing life, vigour, strength, beauty, health, Nietzsche is justified. We are not called upon to value weakness, sentimentality, flabbiness, want of vigour, as such: God is Life, and created life is a gift of God, to be developed, fostered and honoured. And indeed in the highest examples of mankind, the Saints of God, we see—even if in the midst of suffering—an astonishing courage, vigour, and energy of purpose. Supernatural life does not destroy the natural life, but ennobles it, and may even cause

[1] Rudolf Allers, *The New Psychologies*, pp. 76–7.

it to burst forth in unexpected blossom and fruit. Our Lord did not say that He had come to give us less life but that He had come to give us life *more abundantly*. His gift was that of supernatural life, it is true, a gift that does not 'evolve' from natural life but comes from God directly: yet supernatural life and natural life are not opposed —indeed the presence of the former rather enhances the value of the latter. And who is prepared to accuse a woman like St. Teresa of Spain or a man like St. Francis Xavier of weakness, lack of energy, 'degeneracy'? Only those who have never taken the trouble to become acquainted with their lives and understand them.

We may justly honour life and reverence natural vigour, strength, health, and beauty: we honour the supreme examples of natural talents, the great artists, musicians, etc., of mankind; but we will honour, above all, the flowers of the supernatural life, the Saints of God, the true *Über-menschen*—for they are in very truth Supermen, more-than-men, being made, in St. Peter's phrase, 'partakers of the divine nature'. But while we value and reverence the natural vigour of body and mind, we will reverence and honour more the supernatural life of the spirit and we will recognize that this life can develop, and bear marvellous blossom and fruit even in the stunted and suffering body. With Nietzsche we desire life, more life; with Nietzsche we desire the coming of *Übermensch*; but, unlike Nietzsche, we maintain that the highest state open to man, the state of the true *Übermensch*, cannot be attained by man's unaided resources. As against Nietzsche we are *realists*, for we accept all reality, the supernatural as well as the natural; as against Nietzsche we hold that the state of 'more-than-man' is open to *all* who will accept it; and as against Nietzsche we are true optimists, for we believe that the true *Übermenschen* are not mere moments in the Eternal Recurrence, but that they will shine like stars in the firmament of eternity, rejoicing in a perfection of life and vigour, both super-natural and natural. This is not the place to argue logically for our position—for the matter of that Nietzsche does not argue logically for his own position—but we would point out that, for the Christian, man's external end, the Glory of God, coincides with his internal end, his own perfection, and that this end is attainable by all, while for Nietzsche it is but a few who will be Supermen, the end of 'ordinary' men and women being to serve as means to the coming of Supermen. If we compare Nietzsche's Supermen with the mediocre, envious, half-hearted, jealous, and hypocritical Christian, i.e. with the *bad* Christian, then the balance may seem to be weighted in favour of the former; but if we compare Nietzsche's *Übermensch* with the true *Übermensch* of Christianity, there can be no doubt which is the finer flower of humanity. Moreover Nietzsche's Superman hovers in the mists of the future, an unrealized and almost terrifying dream, while the Christian Superman has been realized in the past and will be realized in the future, and he stands clad in the glory of that very *schenkende Tugend* which Nietzsche extols. From the person of the Poor Man of Assisi there streams forth love and light to all that come within the radius of his beams, and behind him and in him we discern the pulsation of that Divine and Infinite Life, which is unceasing Splendour, Power, and Joy.

CHAPTER V

NIETZSCHE'S CRITICISM OF MORALITY

THERE are two classes of people who deny traditional moral values—those who are concerned simply to overthrow, and those who aim rather at clearing the ground for the establishment of new values. From an objective point of view the two courses of action may not infrequently come to the same in the end, but in any case the subjective attitudes of the two classes of destroyers are obviously very different. On the one hand there stands the irresponsible agent, inspired by hatred or by cynicism or by love of sensual pleasure; on the other hand there stands an agent who is inspired by an ideal which transcends himself, a man with a wrong ideal it may be, but with an ideal all the same—an 'idealist' in the practical sense of the word, as contrasted with its philosophical use. In order to understand Nietzsche's attitude in regard to the subject of morality, it is important to realize that he belonged to the second type of destroyer. He hated traditional morality, above all Christian morality, but he hated it, not because he wished to destroy all standards of conduct, still less because he wished to teach 'immorality', but because he regarded the Christian table of values as radically opposed to the true table of values. I have no wish to defend Nietzsche's attack on the absolute Christian morality—far from it, I condemn it most strongly—but a counter-attack on Nietzsche, which involves a misrepresentation of his fundamental inspiration, obviously loses much of its point, besides failing in justice to Nietzsche personally. It is as well therefore, at the very beginning of this chapter, to emphasize the fact that Nietzsche's work on *The Will to Power* has as its sub-title *An attempted Transvaluation of all Values.* He declares himself that he is no mere 'nihilist' or 'anarchist' in the moral sphere, but that he desires to substitute new tables for old, not merely to 'debunk' morality but to assert a new ideal or to reassert an old ideal, which—in his view—has been obscured by the inferior and perverted ideal of Christian morality. His Aristocratic Radicalism—to use a happy phrase of Georg Brandes—is offered to the world as a higher ideal than the morality of 'decadence'.

In *Ecce Homo*, after telling us that he opened his 'campaign against morality' in the *Dawn of Day*, Nietzsche declares, that he was the first to attack and unmask morality. 'No one hitherto has felt Christian morality beneath him; to that end there were needed height, a remoteness of vision, and an abysmal psychological depth, not believed to be possible hitherto'. 'That which defines me, that which makes me stand apart from the whole of the rest of humanity, is the fact that I *unmasked* Christian morality'.[1] *Ecce Homo* is redolent of an exalted state of mind, which may well have been a prelude to the subsequent

---

[1] *Ecce Homo*, pp. 138–9.

mental breakdown: moreover, by the time that Nietzsche wrote his 'autobiography', he had become so isolated and cut off from men that he seems to have been unable to value himself and his thought objectively—at least in what we would term an objective manner. But that very state of exaltation tends to clear, indeed exaggerated, assertion, and Nietzsche leaves us in no doubt as to his meaning. Quoting *Zarathustra* he declares that 'he who would be a creator in good and evil—verily he must be a destroyer, and break values in pieces'. He wills to be a creator of values; but in order to be a creator, he must first destroy. His work of destruction involves a twofold negation, a denial of the type of man that has hitherto been regarded as the highest, the *good*, the *kind*, and the *charitable*, and a denial of Christian morality, the 'morality of decadence'. This second denial is the more decisive, Nietzsche says, since the over-estimation of goodness and kindness is a consequence of decadence and a symptom of weakness: it is 'incompatible with any ascending and yea-saying life'.

Here we have the key to Nietzsche's hatred of morality. It spells decadence or weakness, i.e. a no-saying attitude to life. In *An Attempt at Self-Criticism* (1886), prefixed to *The Birth of Tragedy*, Nietzsche asks, 'Morality itself what? —may not morality be a "will to disown life", a secret instinct for annihilation, a principle of decay, of depreciation, of slander, a beginning of the end'? Christian morality in particular is the crime against life: it teaches—according to Nietzsche—the contempt of all the principal instincts of life. Christian morality is a morality of self-renunciation, and self-renunciation 'betrays the will to nonentity', denying life to its very roots. Christian morality contains as its root-motive and inspiring force an hostility towards life, and is the creation of decadents, of men who hate life and deny it, and who, in their desire to avenge themselves upon life, have set up a table of values and a moral code calculated to shackle the ascending forces of life, to prevent the growth and development of outstanding men, to render impossible the coming of Superman. Hence Nietzsche's definition of morality: 'Morality is the idiosyncracy of decadents, actuated by a desire *to avenge themselves with success upon life'.*[1] 'I attach great value to this definition', says Nietzsche. Moralists and theologians have, it is true, spoken of their intention of improving man, but this was merely a holy pretext, a ruse to conceal their real intention of draining life of its energy and blood. Morality, therefore, so far from being an instrument for the improvement of man, is in reality Vampirism. The man who is in truth weak, ill, and botched, who ought to be wiped out, is declared to be the *good* man, and is offered as a perverted ideal for the true ideal of the 'proud, well-constituted man', who says yeà to life. This latter type of man is declared by the moralists to be *evil*. In passionate loathing of this perversion of values Nietzsche cries out in the words of Voltaire, *Ecrasez l'infâme !*

Nietzsche identified, as we have seen, life with the will to power, and declared that everywhere he discovered the will to power, in the slave as in the master. Morality then is an expression of the will to power—but of whose will to power? That is the crucial question. In Nietzsche's eyes morality expresses the will to power of the *herd*: it is quite distinct from the master-morality, the expression of the will to power of the higher man, the noble type. Nietzsche has unmasked morality and has disclosed three powers lying concealed behind it—'(1) the instinct of the *herd* opposed to the strong and the independent; (2) the instinct of all *sufferers* and all *abortions* opposed to the happy and well-constituted; (3) the instinct of the mediocre opposed to the exceptions'.[2] 'Thus in the *history of morality* a *will to power* finds expression, by means of which either the slaves, the oppressed, the bungled and the botched, those that suffer from themselves, or the mediocre, attempt to make those valuations prevail which favour *their* existence'.[3] Morality, then, has developed at the cost of the ruling classes, at the cost of the well-constituted, strong, and beautiful, and so opposes Nature's efforts to arrive at a higher *type*. It leads to mistrust of life in general, since the tendencies of life are to a great extent thought to be immoral, and to hostility

[1] *Ecce Homo*, p. 141. [2] *Will to Power*, i, aph. 274.
[3] Ibid., i, aph. 400.

to the senses. This conflict between morality and life becomes conscious above all in the higher type of men and the result is their degeneration and self-destruction. Nietzsche's aim was primarily, not to upset the herd, but to make clear to the strong the real nature of morality and so to set them free, to give them courage to be free, and to go forward on the course of ascending life. The herd and the decadents might keep to their 'morality', provided that the freedom of the higher type of man was assured. Hitherto the weak and the decadents have had things their own way, the mediocre have prevailed over the strong by their per-verted morality that equates weakness with goodness and strength with evil.

Morality is the herd's means of self-defence against the strong. Strong instincts, such as 'love of enterprise, foolhardiness, revengefulness, astuteness, rapacity, and love of power',[1] were at first fostered and cultivated, being required for the good of society with a view to warding off common enemies; but, when this outlet is lacking, they are felt by the herd to be dangerous, and so 'are gradually branded as immoral and given over to calumny'. A quality, a disposition, or instinct is judged to be good or evil in so far as it is either advantageous to the society and to common equality—i.e. the gregarious instinct—or disadvantageous to the same. Fear then is the 'mother of morals'. The strongest and loftiest instincts, if followed passionately, carry the individual far beyond the average, and tend to break up the self-reliance of the community; consequently such instincts are condemned and are called immoral. 'Everything that elevates the individual above the herd, and is a source of fear to the neighbour, is henceforth called *evil*; the tolerant, unassuming, self-adapting, self-equalizing disposition, the *mediocrity* of desires, attain to moral dis-tinction and honour'.[2] Nietzsche emphasizes the part played by *resentment* and spite in originating moral valuations. The lambs bear a grudge against the great birds of prey, and so they say that the birds of prey are evil and that the lambs are good. Moreover this resentment is no immediate reaction

[1] *Beyond Good and Evil*, aph. 201.   [2] Ibid.

born of the positive affirmation of self (as is the revenge of the strong), but is a spiteful and venomous resentment, born of the negative attitude of the weak, the dependent, and gregarious, of their no-saying attitude to life. They have not the strength to affirm life themselves or they are resentful and spiteful towards the strong, whom they fear. Impelled by this fear they set up a moral code, which is elevated to the rank of an absolute and universally-binding morality, though it is as a matter of fact nothing but the herd's means of defending itself and expressing its resentment and spite against the strong.

Morality, says Nietzsche, is the enemy of nature. 'All ancient moral-mongers were unanimous on this point, " *il faut tuer les passions*" '.[1] The Church attacks the passions at their roots and so attacks life itself. The same attack on the passions, taught by the Church out of hostility to life, is instinctively adopted by those who are too weak of will, too degenerate, to moderate their passions. 'Only degenerates find radical methods indispensable'; and where we find this radical hostility to the passions, we are justified in suspecting weakness of character on the part of him who goes to such extremes. (This is doubtless sometimes true, but it does *not* follow that a weak man could not be justified in going to extremes. If, for example, a man found by experience that he could not moderate his intemperance, then it is better that he should become a teetotaler.) There can be strength of soul only where there are enemies to overcome: now the Christian desires peace of soul and tries to annihilate his inner enemies. 'The saint in whom God is well pleased, is the ideal eunuch'.

Morality then is hostile to life and an enemy of nature: yet it is a valuation, and a valuation is a valuation of life. Of what kind of life is morality a valuation? 'Of declining, of enfeebled, of exhausted, and of condemned life'. As formulated therefore in the words 'The Denial of the Will to Life' it is the very instinct of degeneration converted into an imperative—'Perish!'—an imperative which hangs like a death sentence over men already doomed. The weak deny

---

[1] *Twilight of the Idols*, p. 26.

life and express this denial in a moral code. By their weakness they are already doomed to perish, and their moral code is really a ratification of this doom. Those, however, in whose veins the tide of life runs strong, must rise above the poisonous and corroding air exhaled by the diseased and dying and affirm, joyfully and courageously, their will to life, their will to power. If man is to be elevated to his highest glory and power, he must place himself above morality: the vital types must not allow themselves to be overcome by the weak and decadent.

The breakdown of morality is assisted by morality itself. Nietzsche expresses this by saying that Christian morality is *nihilistic*. In the Preface to the first volume of *The Will to Power* Nietzsche declares—far-sightedly—that ' The whole of our culture in Europe has long been writhing in an agony of suspense which increases from decade to decade as if in expectation of a catastrophe; restless, violent, helter-skelter, like a torrent that will *reach its bourne*, and refuses to reflect—yea, that even dreads reflection'. He concludes that the triumph of Nihilism—'the absolute repudiation of worth, purpose, desirability'—is at our door, is inevitable. How has this come about? One important explanation is that 'Nihilism harbours in the heart of Christian morals'. Christianity has developed highly the sense of truth, and this truthfulness at length turns against the Christian religion, showing up the falsehood and fictitious character of all Christian interpretation of the world and its history. Thus the Christian view of the universe is ultimately destroyed by Christian morality. What happens then? Some, seeing that interpretation of life, which they thought *the* interpretation, overthrown, conclude that there is no interpretation, that all is senseless, without meaning or purpose, that nothing has value or is desirable. Others attempt to cling to the traditional moral values even without the metaphysical and theological background. Holding on to these values as a means of self-defence, they resist the strong and independent natures and try to tyrannize over them. The result is that the strong turn against the would-be tyrants and their moral values and set out to destroy.

In both cases Nihilism results, though in the first case the Nihilism may be of a passive type, in the second active and dynamic. Morality—false values—leads inevitably therefore to Nihilism.

But though Nietzsche regarded the triumph of Nihilism as inevitable, he was very far from desiring Nihilism as an end. On the contrary he considered it a stage to the assertion of new values: the destruction of the old is preparatory to the creation of the new: the anarchist is condemned by Nietzsche. 'And believe me, friend Hollaballoo! The greatest events are not our noisest, but our stillest hours. Not around the inventors of new noise, but around the inventors of new values, doth the world revolve; *inaudibly* it revolveth'.[1] An important chapter in *Zarathustra* is entitled *Old and New Tables*. Zarathustra cries, 'Break up, break up for me the tables of the never-joyous ones!', and 'Shatter, shatter, O my brethren, those old tables of the pious! Tatter the maxims of the world-maligners!' But the old is broken up to give place to the new: Nietzsche desires to place the *noble* values on the throne. 'The aim should be to prepare a *transvaluation of values* for a particularly strong kind of man, most highly gifted in intellect and will, and, to this end, slowly to liberate in him a whole host of slandered instincts hitherto held in check'.[2] In place therefore of the decadent slave- or herd-morality, Nietzsche will place the aristocratic or master-morality. We have already noted in the chapter on Superman Nietzsche's distinction between these two primary types of morality, the one type originating in a ruling class 'pleasantly conscious of being different from the ruled', the other type originating among the ruled class, 'the slaves and dependents of all sorts'. Nietzsche points out that 'In all higher and mixed civilizations' an attempt is made to reconcile these moralities; 'but one finds still oftener the confusion and mutual misunderstanding of them, indeed, sometimes their close juxtaposition—even in the same man, within one soul'.[3] Hence there is all the more need to set the two moralities in a clear

[1] *Zarathustra*, p. 158. [2] *Will to Power*, ii, aph. 957.
[3] *Beyond Good and Evil*, aph. 260.

light, to bring into relief their distinguishing characteristics and to enable the higher type of man to free himself from the trammels of the slave-morality.

In the master-morality it is the rulers who determine the concept 'good': they denote it by the 'exalted, proud disposition', using the antithesis 'good' and 'bad' in the meaning of 'noble' and 'despicable'. The noble type of man regards *himself* as a determiner of values: knowing that it is he himself only who confers honour on things, he shows himself as a creator of values. In the slave-morality it is the 'slaves', the weak, who determine the values, using the antithesis 'good' and 'evil' in the sense of what is advantageous or disadvantageous to the herd. As strength, beauty, power, nobility, excel the opposite qualities of weakness, vulgarity, meanness, etc., so the master-morality stands higher than the slave-morality and the 'master' higher than the 'slave'. We have therefore an *order of rank*, the higher man representing the ascending line of life, the lower man representing the descending line of life. Nietzsche is constantly insistent on this radical distinction and is opposed to all democratic and socialist views, which stress the equality of men and result in a general level of mediocrity. In *Zarathustra* he says: 'Therefore, O my brethren, a *new nobility* is needed, which shall be the adversary of all populace and potentate rule, and shall inscribe anew the word "noble" as new tables. For many noble ones are needed, and many kinds of noble ones, *for a new nobility!* Or, as I once said in parable: "That is just divinity, that there are Gods, but no God!"' 'My philosophy aims at a new *order of rank*', declares Nietzsche in the *Will to Power*.[1] The herd hates all order of rank: its instinct is in favour of the leveller: it tends to a stationary state of society, merely preserving and unable to create. The type 'man' can only be elevated through a new order of rank. 'I teach that there are higher and lower men, and that a single individual may under certain circumstances justify whole milleniums of existence—that is to say, a wealthier, more gifted, greater, and more complete man, as compared

[1] *Will to Power*, i, aph. 287.

with innumerable imperfect and fragmentary men'. 'Not "mankind", but *Superman* is the goal'![1]

From what has been said it is clear enough that for Nietzsche there is no absolute moral law, but that morals are relative. 'It is *immoral* to say that "what is right for one is proper for another" '. Nietzsche does not preach the destruction of the herd: on the contrary the inferior 'species' is to be regarded as the foundations on which a higher 'species' may live their higher life. This is the justification of the lower race, namely that it exists for the service of a higher and sovereign race 'which stands upon it and can only be elevated upon its shoulders to the task which it is destined to perform'.[2] The existence of the herd is thus even desirable, that it may serve as a foundation for the higher race of men, and that it may be as it were a foil for them. Nietzsche even says that the higher men need the Church, not of course for themselves but as something they can set over against themselves, an enemy to fight. Man needs enemies if he is to keep up to the mark—at any rate a spiritual warfare, the conflict of one valuation with another. But let the herd retain their own valuation and morality—provided the higher men win and retain their freedom. 'The spirit of the herd should rule within the herd—but not beyond it: the leaders of the herd require a fundamentally different valuation for their actions, as do also the independent ones or the beasts of prey, etc.'[3] It was for the independent ones that Nietzsche primarily spoke, to impel them to freedom; he was not concerned to upset the members of the 'herd', and to deprive them of that little they possessed. (It may be as well to point out that when Nietzsche speaks of higher and lower 'races' he is thinking of different types of men, not of races in the sense of the modern Race-theory. Does he not say in *The Genealogy of Morals*, 'Maxim: To associate with no man who takes any part in the mendacious race swindle'? And Nietzsche was a constant opponent of anti-Semitism.)

---

[1] *Will to Power*, ii, aph. 997 and 1,001.
[2] Ibid., ii, aph. 898.
[3] *Will to Power*, i, aph. 287.

Nietzsche's hatred of a morality which did not recognize the order of rank and the relativity of valuation was one of the main reasons why he condemned 'Idealism' so bitterly. He declared that morality was 'the veritable Circe of philosophers'. 'All philosophers, including Kant himself, were building under the seductive influence of morality'—they aimed at certainty and truth only in appearance. The philosophies of e.g. Kant, Hegel, Schopenhauer, all have a *moral* origin: it was a moral interest, the desire to establish an absolute morality, that was their *arrière-pensée*. This being so, Nietzsche depicts the philosophers as enemies of life, inasmuch as absolute morality is itself the enemy of life, hindering the development of the higher men. 'The history of philosophy is the story of a *secret and mad hatred* of the prerequisites of Life, of the feelings which make for the real values Life, and of all partisanship in favour of Life. . . . Up to the present philosophy has been the *grand school of slander* . . . they believed in moral "truths", in these they thought they had found the highest values; what alternative had they left, save that of denying existence ever more emphatically the more they got to know about it? . . . For this life is *immoral*. . . . And it is based upon universal first principles: and morality says *nay* to Life'.[1] Kant comes in for some particularly hard knocks. Kant, a 'moral fanatic', 'entices us into the dialectic by-ways that lead (more correctly mislead) to his "categorical imperative"'.[2] But this Categorical Imperative is hostile to life. 'Nothing is more profoundly, more thoroughly pernicious, than every impersonal feeling of duty, than every sacrifice to the Moloch of abstraction. Fancy no one's having thought Kant's Categorical Imperative *dangerous to life!*—The instinct of the theologist alone took it under its wing'! 'Duty', 'Virtue', these impersonal abstractions are mere fictions, expressing 'the final devitalization of life and Koenigsbergian Chinadom'![3]

In a complete study of Nietzsche's teaching on morality

---

[1] *Will to Power*, i, aph. 461.
[2] *Beyond Good and Evil*, aph. 5.
[3] *Antichrist*, pp. 136–7.

one would have to discuss Nietzsche's attitude to particular moral phenomena, virtues, vices, and institutions. In a brief consideration, such as is undertaken in this book, this cannot be done. It is of interest, however, to consider shortly Nietzsche's general attitude towards marriage. Nietzsche certainly said some hard things about women, but he had no intention of dishonouring women as such: he desired them to fulfil their natural function. 'Have you heard my reply to the question how a woman can be cured, "saved" in fact?—Give her a child'.[1] The people who really try to lower women's rank are those who fight for 'equal rights', emancipation of women, etc.: indeed there are no more certain ways of lowering woman's rank than 'university education, trousers, and the rights of voting cattle'. Ibsen is a 'typical old maid'. The true womanly woman 'fights tooth and nail against rights in general'. Woman's true place therefore is not in the voting-booth or on the judge's bench but in the home.

But though Nietzsche upholds the institution of marriage, he is not of the opinion that 'love-marriages' are the ideal. For lovers, he says, 'the satisfaction of sexual desire is sentimental; it is a mere symbol' (as a matter of fact Nietzsche placed friendship between men above marriage and sexual relations, from the point of view of love and 'soul-intercourse'. Compare the Greeks.). 'Marriage, as understood by the real old nobility, meant the breeding forth of the race . . . that is to say, the maintenance of a fixed, definite type of ruler, for which object husband and wife were sacrificed'.[2] Marriage then must be regulated with this end in view.

'*Concerning the future of marriage.*—A supertax on inherited property, a longer term of military service for bachelors of a certain minimum age within the community.

'Privileges of all sorts for fathers who lavish boys upon the world, and perhaps plural votes as well.

'A medical certificate as a condition of any marriage, endorsed by the parochial authorities, in which a series of

---

[1] *Ecce Homo*, pp. 65–6.
[2] *Will to Power*, ii, aph. 732.

questions addressed to the parties and the medical officer must be answered ("family histories").

'As a counter-agent to prostitution, or as its ennoblement, I would recommend leasehold marriages (to last for a term of years or months), with adequate provision for the children.

'Every marriage to be warranted and sanctioned by a certain number of good men and true of the parish, as a parochial obligation'.[1]

Similar views are found, more poetically expressed, in *Zarathustra*, where Nietzsche urges thirst for the higher man, ultimately for Superman, as the inspiration of marriage. 'Not only onward shalt thou propagate thyself, but upward. For that purpose may the garden of marriage help thee!' 'Marriage: so call I the will of the twain to create the one that is more than those who created it. The reverence for one another, as those exercising such a will, call I marriage'. 'Thirst in the creating one, arrow and longing for the Superman: tell me, my brother, is this thy will to marriage? Holy call I such a will, and such a marriage'.[2] Such is the ideal inspiration of marriage. In actual fact, however, marriages are so often hastily arranged without any such guiding inspiration and often without any inspiration at all save the immediate desire for satisfaction. From this follows marriage-breaking. But marriage-breaking, says Nietzsche, is far better than maintaining a miserable union. 'Thus spake a woman unto me: "Indeed I broke the marriage, but first did the marriage break—me!"'[3] Regarding marriage thus seriously Zarathustra calls for trial marriages: 'Give us a set term and a small marriage, that we may see if we are fit for the great marriage! It is a great matter always to be twain'.[4]

Yes, marriage is a serious thing, and it is indeed a great matter always to be twain; but trial-marriages would be very far from increasing the reverence for marriage. It is perfectly true that people often rush into marriage without due consideration, and it is also true that marriages are not

---

[1] *Will to Power*, ii, aph. 733.
[3] Ibid., p. 258.
[2] *Zarathustra*, pp. 80–1.
[4] Ibid.

infrequently wrecked because one or both of the partners refuse to take those means, whereby the marriage may be made a happy and successful union. One or both are selfish, they refuse to deny themselves, they may even neglect the obligations they have undertaken—and disaster is the result. With due consideration beforehand and with a constant, sincere, and prayerful will to make the marriage a success, there is no reason why any marriage should be a failure. Trial-marriages might conceivably lessen professional prostitution (compare Soviet Russia), but they would certainly degrade marriage. Christian marriage is a sacrament and a holy institution, and spoiled marriages are due—not to the indissolubility of marriage, nor to any Christian doctrine of marriage—but to lack of foresight and consideration or to deliberate sin and selfishness in one or both of the partners. It may be as well, too, to point out, that while the primary biological function of marriage is certainly the procreation of children, and while parents should certainly desire to educate children better than themselves, marriage would be utterly degraded were it to be regarded merely as a breeding-institution. Marriage is a rational act on the part of rational beings, and exists not merely for propagating the race— even upwards—but also for the mutual comfort and help of the partners.   The man and woman who enter upon a contract blessed by the Author of Nature—declared indissoluble by Christ our Lord—have the divine help at their disposal to make their marriage a success.   This may require much self-denial on their part—it may at times be very hard—but it is never impossible, provided that each partner will contribute his or her share. Of course to anyone who disbelieves in an Author of Nature and who rejects Christ and the Christian revelation, such reflection will appear but stale repetition of outworn, even 'immoral', clichés. But it is a hopeless task to attempt to join battle with the atheist on some particular point, such as that of marriage; one must start much further back. One can only point out that his idea of marriage will lead, indeed has led and is leading, to the degradation of marriage. The institution of marriage can only exist on a religious foundation. As a matter of fact Nietzsche, though professedly irreligious, gives it a religious atmosphere, but then Nietzsche's attitude towards life had all the seriousness of a profoundly religious attitude; the levity and utter selfishness of the really irreligious man were far from his character—and it is these deficiencies of character that wreck marriage, even if they be found in those who are professedly religious. Nietzsche's idealism and earnestness deserved a better philosophy than the atheistic philosophy of the Will to Power and the Superman.

After this parenthesis on the subject of marriage, what are we to say of Nietzsche's general teaching on the subject of morality? Did Nietzsche really expose morality? Is morality truly a phenomenon of decadence? No, Nietzsche did not expose Morality: what he did expose, however, was the hollowness of those who are not *truly* moral. Morality itself is not decadence, hostile to life, but the attitude adopted by people, who profess morality, may very well be hostile to life. One might attempt to answer two questions: (i) Has morality biological significance at all or is it hostile to all life? (ii) Is morality hostile to the ascending line of life, i.e. to outstanding men and women? In regard to the first it is quite clear that morality —and I am using morality in the sense of natural ethics, leaving aside for the moment specifically Christian morality —*has* biological significance; and indeed on this fact Nietzsche would be in agreement, since morality for him defends the life of the slaves, the weak, the herd, and expresses their will to power. But the biological significance of morality is not confined to any type of man; it extends to man as such. For example, man, as Aristotle remarked— and as anybody of sense can see for himself—is a social animal, a ζῶον πολιτικόν, and many ethical precepts are concerned with the preservation of society, which certainly has a biological function. The precepts found in the Mosaic Law against stealing and murder, for instance, tend to the preservation of society, society without which man cannot live as a rational animal. Call it 'herd-morality' if you like; but what would any man be without society? He owes his life to society—to the family at least—he owes his education and the possibility of development to society. Without society or without some real relation to society man cannot live, nor can he develop to the full, if at all, those potentialities which belong to him as a living human being. The ethical precepts—they could only be dealt with individually and 'justified' in an ethical treatise, which this book is not—which tend to the preservation and development of society, do not therefore tend to the development of society as *against* its component members, for society is composed of its members. In the history of ethics we find phenomena such as taboo, etc., but these, however strange they appear to those used only to the moral codes of modern Europe, undoubtedly have a biological significance, tending to the preservation of society (even if of a comparatively small group) and so to the preservation and well-being of the members of society. And since society is composed of human beings and man is essentially social in character, it is as true to say that morality has biological significance in reference to the individual, to *every* man, as it is to say that it has biological significance in reference to society.

(In stressing the biological function of morality, I do not mean to suggest that this aspect exhausts the nature of morality. Man, the social animal, and the world in which he finds himself are the effect of a transcendent-immanent Cause, the Creative Principle of Life—God—and morality has thus a transcendental reference, foundation, and justification. But I wish now to bring into relief the biological function of morality, leaving its transcendental basis and reference in the background.)

Morality, then, tends to the preservation and development of the human species, of man, the social animal. But the crucial question then arises, mentioned before—Is morality hostile to the ascending line of life, in the sense of being hostile to the development of outstanding men? It seems to me that the answer largely depends on what you *mean* by an outstanding or higher man. If you mean the barbarian, the blond beast, the bird of prey, the strong man who tramples on the weak, the egoistic adventurer, the unscrupulous seeker for power, then it must be admitted that morality is hostile to such men, since they tend to break up society. But are such men desirable types? If you say yes, and affirm that such men are higher biological productions than the socially conscious and socially bound man, then morality is indeed hostile to life. If you say no, then morality is not hostile to life. If, however, by outstanding man you mean the man of great artistic or scientific or political ability, then morality it not hostile to such men. How is morality hostile to Solon, Augustus, Alfred, Salazar, or to Pheidias, Fra Angelico, Michelangelo, Rubens? It is perfectly true that great men have been persecuted, even done to death, by representatives of society—Socrates, for instance—but it was not morality that was at fault, however much moral principle may have been on the lips of the unjust judges. There is blindness, greater or less, in regard to moral values and there is a possibility of development of insight into moral values, and the progress of the human race is largely conditioned by the development of this insight. Socrates saw more deeply into moral values than his contemporaries and he spoke in the name of morality: he was condemned, ostensibly in the name of morality, but really by men of a less exalted *moral* character than himself. Socrates spoke in the name of morality and desired to elevate man: the human beasts of prey (I do not refer now to Socrates' judges, of course) desire to elevate themselves or their nation or both, but not man. It is moral Socrates who is favourable to life (for life, *pace* Nietzsche, is not originally immoral); it is immoral beasts of prey who are hostile to life, hostile at least to the development of a higher life.

But are not the beasts of prey the full-blooded living men, and the moral men the anæmic, timid and fearful, 'decadent' ones? The question can perhaps best be answered in reference to that Christian morality, the decadent, devitalizing character of which Nietzsche affirms so persistently. We may admit at once that the human beasts of prey are full-blooded, living ones, in that they show energy and activity, and that they seize on the means to attain their ends. When appearing in highly civilized societies they may be highly educated, possessed of intellectual ability and power of judgment of a remarkable order. On the other hand it might be admitted that there are some 'moral' Christians who show little energy or vitality. Do not Christian preachers themselves reprove those whose idea of the practice of brotherly love amounts to little more than refraining from doing others any harm? It may be, as Nietzsche does not hesitate to affirm, that fear has something to do with it, resulting in a perversion of the 'Do as you would be done by' maxim. There are, again, those for whom purity is something predominantly negative in character. Charity, purity, etc., are for these people mainly negative; and there is little perhaps of positive, pulsating life to be found in their lives. Which of us, indeed, would dare to say that we live the Christian life to the full?

All this we admit; but what does the admission amount to? To taking the outstanding examples of the 'immoral' character, contrasting them with the poorest examples of the moral character, and admitting that the latter show a certain lack of vitality in comparison with the former. But take the poorest examples of both. Who is prepared to say that the mean and petty, dishonest and impure little egoist is a more admirable type than the mediocre Christian? Then take the most outstanding examples of both. On the one hand we see the man of power, the unscrupulous, talented 'immoralist', the egoist on a grand scale, who has denied morality: on the other hand we see the Christian saint, filled with the love of God and man, self-sacrificing to the utmost limit and that out of love. Which is the more hostile to life? The man who destroys, overrides, and denies the accepted values, despises the common herd and affirms—himself, turning all to his own advantage, or the man who is the channel of light and love to multitudes, who is steadfast and constant in sacrifice, not out of hatred of life but out of love for Life and for all living men and women? The man who would make his fellow-men stepping-stones to his own ambition or the man who would say with his Divine Master, 'I am come that they may have life, and may have it more abundantly'? Nietzsche may think that Napoleon was a higher type than St. Paul or St. Francis, but it is absurd to say that Napoleon affirmed life more than did St. Paul or St. Francis. The Saints affirmed a wider and a profounder life than any that Nietzsche's higher men—or even his Supermen—did or would affirm. We are at one with Nietzsche in desiring life and vitality, but that desire is not to be fulfilled by the denial of the higher life. Possibly we Christians need Nietzsche's stimulus to affirm the values of natural life—we may indeed tend to be one-sided—but Nietzsche, too, was one-sided, and much more dangerously so, and he denied the values of the supernatural or, if he sought them unknown to himself, he sought them where they can never be found—apart from that God, Who is Life and the Source of life, both natural and supernatural.

CHAPTER VI

ANTICHRIST

IN *Ecce Homo* Nietzsche speaks of his 'incomparable' father, 'delicate, lovable, and morbid, like one who is pre-ordained to pay simply a flying visit—a gracious reminder of life rather than life itself'. Pastor Nietzsche was a devoted Christian clergyman, and Nietzsche's attitude to Christianity was no doubt largely influenced by his pious upbringing. That may sound a strange statement at first hearing; but it is most probably true in its intended meaning. Nietzsche's intense and growing hostility to Christianity, culminating in the defiant cry 'Dionysus *versus* Christ', seems to betray a bond with Christianity that he could not shake off. It is even probable, as has been suggested by other writers, that Nietzsche was troubled by secret doubts as to the value and truth of his own teaching and as to the worthless-ness and falsity of the Christian religion, and that his furious denunciation and defiant attitude had—in part at least—the unconscious function of masking and mastering his unstable conviction as to the reality of his own mission. The tolerant scorn of the cynic and sceptic is conspicuously absent from Nietzsche's writing; he denounces and hates what he knows to be a reality and which he fears—even if he will not admit it even to himself—may be *the* reality. This inner struggle—all the more powerful because it was not brought into the light of day and consciously apprehended —may well have been one of the contributory causes to his mental breakdown.

First of all the Idea of God. In *The Genealogy of Morals* Nietzsche suggests that the idea of God originated in fear. The primitive fear of ancestors and of their power has gradually led to the transfiguration of the ancestor into a god.[1] But however the idea of God may have originated, the Christian notion of God is necessarily unacceptable. 'An omniscient and omnipotent God who does not even take care that His intentions shall be understood by His creatures— could He be a God of goodness? A God who, for thousands of years, has permitted innumerable doubts and scruples to continue unchecked as if they were of no importance in the salvation of mankind, and who, nevertheless, announces the most dreadful consequences for anyone who mistakes his truth? Would he not be a cruel god if, being himself in possession of the truth, he could calmly contemplate mankind, in a state of miserable torment, worrying its mind as to what was truth?'[2] (Apart from the fact that God *has* given mankind means of knowing the truth, it is certainly not the *Catholic* teaching that God announces 'dreadful consequences' for those who unwittingly mistake His truth.)

But Nietzsche's root objection to God is, as we might expect, that He, or the notion of God, is *hostile to life*. Already in *Joyful Wisdom* he speaks of the vistas that are opened up by the report that 'God is dead'. 'In fact, we philosophers and "free spirits" feel ourselves irradiated as by a new dawn by the report that "the old God is dead"; our hearts overflow with gratitude, astonishment, presentiment, and expectation. At last the horizon seems open once more,

[1] *Genealogy of Morals*, pp. 106–8.   [2] *Dawn of Day*, aph. 91.

granting even that it is not bright; our ships can at last put out to sea in face of every danger; every hazard is again permitted to the discerner; the sea, *our* sea, again lies open before us; perhaps never before did such an "open sea" exist'.[1] (The report that 'the old God is dead' means, of course, that life is without given meaning. But when man, the adventurous sailor, sets out on the 'open sea' without the Divine Pilot he encounters such storms as we are witnessing to-day, from which he cannot save himself by his own unaided efforts.) The God-believers are despisers of life, decaying ones, blasphemers of the earth: 'I conjure you, my brethren, *remain true to the earth*, and believe not those who speak unto you of superearthly hopes. Poisoners are they, whether they know it or not'.[2] 'The concept "God" was invented as the opposite of the concept life—everything detrimental, poisonous and slanderous, and all deadly hostility to life, was bound together in one horrible unit in Him'.[3] So speaks Nietzsche in *Ecce Homo*, when all moderation of tone has been flung aside. The same spirit and tone find expression in *Antichrist*, when Nietzsche speaks of 'the miserable God of Christian monotono-theism', a 'hybrid creature of decay, nonentity, concept, and contradiction, in which all the instincts of decadence, all the cowardices and languors of the soul find their sanction'.[4] This 'miserable God' of Christianity is a step down from the *national* God. The transition from the God of Israel, the God of a people, to the Christian God, marks, not a step forward, but a decline—'the decline and fall of a god', in the words of Nietzsche. (We are reminded of the words of Shatov in Dostoievsky's *The Possessed*: 'It is a sign of the decay of nations when they begin to have gods in common . . . the stronger a people the more individual their God'.[5])

Nietzsche was never given to bringing forward logical arguments: indeed he tended to despise rational argument. He never really attempted a scientific proof of the Eternal

---

[1] *Joyful Wisdom*, aph. 343.
[2] *Zarathustra*, p. 7.
[3] *Ecce Homo*, p. 142.
[4] *Antichrist*, p. 147.
[5] C. Garnett, Heinemann, 1913, p. 233.

Recurrence (the 'proofs' he offers cannot be termed seriously scientific), nor did he ever really attempt a 'proof' of atheism: he attempted the 'exposure' of the concept of God, stating that it is a degenerate idea, hostile to life. What he has to say of the origin of the idea is not much more than a dogmatic assertion, backed up by notions taken from current history of religion, of which he had made no profound study; and when, in *The Twilight of the Idols*, he declares: 'the concept "God" has been the greatest objection to existence hitherto. . . . We deny God, we deny responsibility in God', it is mainly of the *effect* of this denial that he is thinking—'the great deliverance', 'thus alone do we save the world':—he offers no serious arguments for his position. Of course this does not of itself demonstrate that Nietzsche is wrong in what he says; but it is a point worth drawing attention to.

According to Nietzsche, then, the Christian concept of God is a concept of a God Who is the contradiction of life. 'With God war is declared on life, nature, and the will to life! God is the formula for every calumny of this world and for every lie concerning a beyond! In God, nonentity is deified; and the will to nonentity is declared holy'![1] Of course, as a matter of fact the Christian conception of God does not involve the denial of life, even of this life, though it does involve the belief that this life is not the only life nor even the richest life—a belief that in no way detracts from the value of this life, but rather ennobles and enhances it. However, thinking as he did, Nietzsche naturally adopted an anti-God attitude. He looks forward to the man of the future, the 'Antichrist' and Antinihilist, this conqueror of God and of Nothingness,[2] and suggests, whether seriously or not, a sort of anti-God league. 'Scattered among the different nations of Europe there are now from ten to twenty millions of men who no longer "believe in God"— is it too much to ask that they should give each other some indication or password? As soon as they recognize each other in this way, they will also make themselves known to each other; and they will immediately become a power in

[1] *Antichrist*, p. 146.   [2] *Genealogy of Morals*, p. 117.

Europe, and, happily, a power *among* the nations! among the classes! between rich and poor! between those who command, and those who obey! between the most restless and the most tranquil, tranquillizing people'.[1]

To turn more specifically to Christianity. In an early essay Nietzsche has a good word for Christianity. 'In fact here and there sometimes an exuberant degree of compassion has for a short time opened all the flood gates of Culture-life; a rainbow of compassionate love and of peace appeared with the first radiant rise of Christianity and under it was born Christianity's most beautiful fruit, the gospel according to St. John.' (*The Greek State*, 1871.) Nor is this the only passage in which Nietzsche ascribes a positive and beneficial function to religion. For instance in *Beyond Good and Evil* he says, that 'Asceticism and Puritanism are almost indispensable means of educating and ennobling a race which seeks to rise above its hereditary baseness and work itself upward to future supremacy. And finally, to ordinary men, to the majority of the people, who exist for service and general utility and are only so far entitled to exist, religion gives invaluable contentedness with their lot and condition, peace of heart, ennoblement of obedience, additional social happiness and sympathy, with something of transfiguration and embellishment, something of justification of all the commonplaceness, all the meanness, all the semi-animal poverty of their souls. . . . There is perhaps nothing so admirable in Christianity and Buddhism as their art of teaching even the lowest to elevate themselves by piety to a seemingly higher order of things, and thereby to retain their satisfaction with the actual world in which they find it difficult enough to live—this very difficulty being necessary'. (*Beyond Good and Evil*, p. 81.) This is a long quotation, but we make bold to add yet another, in which Nietzsche writes appreciatively of the continuance of the religious cult in the feelings. 'The Roman Catholic Church, and before that all antique cults, dominated the entire range of means by which man was put into unaccustomed moods and rendered incapable of the cold calculation of judgment or the clear

---

[1] *Dawn of Day*, aph. 96.

thinking of reason. A church quivering with deep tones; the dull, regular, arresting appeals of a priestly throng, unconsciously communicates its tension to the congregation and makes it listen almost fearfully, as if a miracle were in preparation; the influence of the architecture, which, as the dwelling of a Godhead, extends into the uncertain and makes its apparition to be feared in all its sombre spaces—who would wish to bring such things back to mankind if the necessary suppositions are no longer believed? But the *results* of all this are not lost, nevertheless; the inner world of noble, emotional, deeply contrite dispositions, full of presentiments, blessed with hope, is inborn in mankind mainly through this cult; what exists of it now in the soul was then cultivated on a large scale as it germinated, grew up, and blossomed'.[1]

But though Nietzsche thus recognizes some beneficial effects of religion, and though he grants its usefulness for the herd, he rejects Christianity altogether so far as the higher men are concerned, and his attack is of course based on his belief that Christianity is hostile to life—which, *if 'life' be interpreted as the will to power and lust for dominion of the strong man*, we may well admit. '*Paganism* is that which says yea to all that is natural, it is innocence in being natural, "naturalness". *Christianity* is that which says no to all that is natural, it is a certain lack of dignity in being natural; hostility to Nature. "Innocent":—Petronius is innocent, for instance. Beside this happy man a Christian is absolutely devoid of innocence'.[2] (This is absurd—Petronius *versus* Agnes, Thomas More, the Curé d'Ars—is *Petronius* the more innocent?) Christianity, according to Nietzsche, has waged a deadly war upon the higher type of man, declaring him to be a villain, and has sided with everything weak, low and botched, corrupting even the strongest intellects 'by teaching that the highest values of intellectuality are sinful, misleading and full of temptations'.[3] Christianity is the religion of the herd, expressing the will to power of the oppressed of all kinds, the mediocre of all

---

[1] *Human, All-too-Human*, i, aph. 130.
[2] *Will to Power*, i, aph. 147.   [3] *Antichrist*, p. 130.

kind, and the dissatisfied and diseased of all kinds'. 'The *first* struggle against the politically noble and their ideal; the second contend with the exceptions and those who are in any way privileged (mentally or physically); the third oppose the *natural instinct* of the happy and the sound'.[1]

Nietzsche declared that he had scented out the guiding inspiration and emotion of the oppressed and mediocre people, 'the decaying and excremental elements', whom we call Christian. Christianity, he says, 'consists of a founda- ton of resentment against all that is successful and dominant: it is in need of a symbol which represents the damnation of everything successful and dominant. It is opposed to every form of *intellectual* movement, to all philosophy: it takes up the cudgels for idiots, and utters a curse upon all intellect. Resentment against those who are gifted, learned, intellectually independent: in all these it suspects the element of success and domination'.[2] Now there may be resentment, fear, and even envy in the souls of some Christians in their attitude towards Nietzsche's strong and outstanding men; but in so far as such emotions pre- dominate, they are not acting precisely as Christians. A Christian who was envious of a successful and unscrupulous egotist would not be acting as a Christian, and his envy cannot be laid at the door of Christianity. The Christian as Christian will not envy the successful tyrant for instance, but he will condemn the unscrupulous lust for power. He has *another* ideal. 'Precisely', Nietzsche might say, 'the Christian has another ideal, and it is a perverted, a degenerate ideal. It is with this ideal that I quarrel. Have I not written in the first volume of the *Will to Power*, that it is not with the theology and cobweb-spinning of Christians that we need concern ourselves, but that one thing must be utterly destroyed, the ideal of mankind which Christianity advances?' It is worth quoting the relevant passage, even though somewhat lengthy, as it brings out clearly Nietzsche's main quarrel with Christianity. Recognizing the meaning of Nietzsche's attack on Christianity, we can see easily enough

---

[1] *Will to Power*, i, aph. 215.
[2] Ibid., i, aph. 154.

how it follows from his philosophy of the Will to Power and Superman.

'Christianity should never be forgiven for having ruined such men as Pascal. This is precisely what should be combated in Christianity, namely that it has the will to break the spirit of the strongest and noblest natures. One should take no rest until this thing is utterly destroyed: the ideal of mankind which Christianity advances, the demands it makes upon men, and its "Nay" and "Yea" relative to humanity. The whole of the remaining absurdities, that is to say Christian fable, Christian cobweb-spinning in ideas and principles, and Christian theology, do not concern us; they might be a thousand times more absurd and we should not raise a finger to destroy them. But what we do stand up against is that ideal which, thanks to its morbid beauty and feminine seductiveness, thanks to its insidious and slanderous eloquence, appeals to all the cowardices and vanities of wearied souls—and the strongest have their moments of fatigue—as though all that which seems most useful and desirable at such moments—that is to say confidence, artlessness, modesty, patience, love of one's like, resignation, submission to God, and a sort of self-surrender —were useful and desirable *per se*; as though the puny, modest abortion which in these creatures takes the place of a soul, this virtuous, mediocre animal and sheep of the flock—which designs to call itself man, were not only to take precedence of the stronger, more evil, more passionate, more defiant, and more prodigal type of man, who by virtue of these very qualities is exposed to a hundred more dangers than the former, but were actually to stand as an ideal for man in general, as a goal, a measure—the highest desideratum. The creation of *this* ideal was the most appalling temptation that had ever been put in the way of mankind; for with it the stronger and more successful exceptions, the lucky cases among men, in which the will to power and to growth leads the whole species "man" one step farther forward, this type was threatened with disaster. By means of the values of this ideal, the growth of such higher men would be checked at the root. . . . What is it we combat in Christianity? That it aims at destroying the strong, at breaking their spirit, at exploiting their moments of weariness and debility, at converting their proud assurance into anxiety and conscience-trouble; that it knows how to poison the noblest instincts and to infect them with disease, until their strength, their will to power, turns inwards, against themselves—until the strong perish through their excessive self-contempt and self-immolation: that gruesome way of perishing, of which *Pascal* is the most famous example'.[1]

Admiring the Greeks as he did, Nietzsche could not but look on the triumph of Christianity in the ancient world as a cultural disaster of the first magnitude. His views on the relation of Christianity to Antiquity are of considerable interest. Nietzsche naturally stresses the opposition between Christianity and pagan Antiquity—'a sincere leaning towards antiquity renders one unchristian'[2]—and declares that the Christian religion corresponds to a pre-Greek condition of mankind—'belief in witchcraft in connection with all and everything, bloody sacrifices, superstitious fear of demoniacal punishments, despair in one's self, ecstatic brooding and hallucination; man's self become the arena of good and evil spirits and their struggles'.[3] And as Christianity corresponds to pre-Greek conditions, so it corresponds to the 'subterranean cults' of the Roman Empire, which it absorbed. The same thought occurs also in the first volume of *The Will to Power*, when Nietzsche says that Christianity met the needs and level of intelligence of the religious masses in Empire, who believed in Isis, Mithras, Dionysos, and the 'great mother', and who demanded of a religion that it should supply hopes of a future life, sacrifice and mystery, holy legend and redemption, asceticism and 'purifications', hierarchy.[4]

There is nothing extraordinary in these ideas or peculiar to Nietzsche. Moreover there is a certain truth in them; for Christianity certainly did meet the needs of religiously-minded sections of the population who were groping after a

---

[1] *Will to Power*, i, aph. 252.   [2] *We Philologists*, aph. 42.
[3] Ibid., aph. 151.   [4] Aph. 196.

more spiritual and personal religion than was supplied by the official pagan cult, and the Church certainly did make use of certain external features of paganism—without compromising her own message to mankind. But is it not astonishing that Nietzsche can *also* declare, not only that Christianity is itself a piece of antiquity and has preserved antiquity, but also that 'it has never been in combat with the pure ages of antiquity?' Is this a gross inconsistency or is there a way of reconciling the two points of view, first that Christianity corresponds to a pre-Greek condition and to the 'subterranean cults', second that Christianity has never been in combat even with the *pure* ages of antiquity? Although Nietzsche does not professedly note and solve the apparent contradiction, he says enough to show what he meant. The Christian *life* in his view is the essence of Christianity and is anarchical in character (v. *Will to Power*), but the Christian Church, in order to remain, had to let itself be overcome by the spirit of antiquity—'for example, the idea of empire, the community, and so forth'. It would appear then, that Nietzsche distinguishes several elements of Christianity,— the original Christian *life*, which is essentially hostile to the finest, noble and aristocratic tradition of Greece, Christian *belief*, which corresponds to certain phenomena of antiquity, and Christian Church organization and pretensions, which are inherited from pagan political and imperial ideas. The 'contradiction' in Nietzsche's thoughts may not be fully resoluble, but these thoughts may suggest what he apparently meant, and how he could say that 'in the end, all the forces of which antiquity consisted have reappeared in Christianity in the crudest possible form: it is nothing new, only quantitatively extraordinary'[1] and 'a criticism of the Greeks is at the same time a criticism of Christianity'. For to Nietzsche the bases of the spirit of belief are the same in Greek antiquity as in Christianity, together with the religious cult and witchcraft. Therefore he asserts, that 'With the dissolution of Christianity a great part of antiquity has become incomprehensible to us, for instance, the entire religious basis of life'.

[1] *We Philologists*, aph. 159.

We will return later to the relation of Christian life to Christian belief and to the Church; but with the question of the Church's adaptation of certain externalities of paganism we cannot deal here. Nor is it a really important question in connection with Nietzsche: what *is* important is the alleged hostility of Christianity to the aristocratic ideal, and that topic we will consider briefly now. We have seen that Christianity, according to Nietzsche, fitted the needs of the religious masses and absorbed the mystery cults. Now, although the cults were within paganism, they represent an *anti-pagan* tendency, in that they were 'the religions proper to the lower herd, women, slaves, and ignoble classes'.[1] Christianity then is the religion proper to the herd, and it grew 'among the outcasts, the condemned, and the leprous of all kinds, as also among "publicans", "sinners", prostitutes, and the most foolish of men (the "fisher folk"); it despises the rich, the scholarly, the noble, the virtuous, . . .'[2] By flattering people's vanity—making them think that they had immortal souls and that the salvation of each individual had eternal importance—it 'lured all the bungled and the botched, all revolting and revolted people, all abortions, the whole of the refuse and offal of humanity, over to its side'.[3] In this way the aristocratic attitude of mind was undermined: in fact 'Christianity is the revolt of all things that crawl on their bellies against everything that is lofty: the gospel of the "lowly" *lowers*'[4]—Christians, actuated by a hatred of all that is great and lofty, a 'cowardly, effeminate and sugary gang', were the vampires of the Roman Empire and destroyed the aristocratic principle of Greece and Rome.

How was this rendered possible? In the Empire the ruler and the ruling classes became degenerate, and so it was that men were led to discover that there are virtues among the inferior and suppressed classes and that all are equal before God—'which is the *non plus ultra* of all confounded nonsense that has ever appeared on earth'! 'When Nero and Caracalla stood at the helm, it was then that the paradox arose: "the lowest man is of more value than that one on the throne"!

---

[1] *Will to Power*, i, aph. 196. [2] Ibid., aph. 207.
[3] *Antichrist*, p. 186. [4] Ibid., p. 187.

Without the Roman Cæsars and Roman society, Christianity would never have prevailed'.[1]

Now, that Christianity grew up for the most part among the lower classes of the Empire, is true. It is probably also true that these early Christians were by no means all ideal characters. We certainly know of scandals; and it is quite unhistorical to speak of early Christianity as a sort of earthly Paradise, after the fashion of Protestants at various times. But Ancient Society, as Nietzsche himself admits—he could hardly do otherwise—had become extremely corrupt in its higher strata, and when St. Paul condemns the pagan, he is condemning the pagan's vices, he is not saying, that natural virtue and nobility of character are valueless. Christian writers have at times exaggerated, and, believing that *merely* natural virtue and nobility has no direct reference to man's supernatural end, have spoken as if the higher attainments of paganism—boasted of by pagan apologists—were possessed of no value at all. But it is not fair to judge the Christian attitude to natural nobility simply by the exaggerated or very emphatic statements of Christian apologists. And in any case, as we have remarked before, it is hopelessly unjust to contrast the best examples of paganism with the worst examples of Christianity. Nietzsche may dislike men like St. Augustine, but he cannot sincerely accuse them of being unintellectual, anti-cultured or effeminate and degenerate. It was these very men, who helped to lay the foundations for the culture that later succeeded the culture of pagan antiquity. They owed much to pagan culture—we willingly admit it—but that they were not swamped in the foul morass and debâcle of pagan culture, but rose above it and left a monument *aere perennius* they owed to Christianity. The seeming hostility that Christianity at first displayed towards pagan culture, was conditioned by historical circumstances, but it is not in itself hostile to culture. Nor is it hostile to great men. The question is, what do you mean by great men? and, which is the higher type? Nietzsche admits the historical existence of fine Christians, but he tries to make out that what is fine in them is in no

---

[1] *Will to Power*, ii, aph. 874.

way due to Christianity. Well, no one would maintain that Pascal's mathematical genius was due precisely to Christianity, but it is due to the same God Who revealed Himself in Christ; and what evidence is there for affirming that Pascal was ruined and spoilt by Christianity? Would he have been any more admirable had he been a Caesar Borgia? It is not that Christianity has *no* aristocratic ideal, but that it has a *different* aristocratic ideal from that of pagan antiquity, from that of the purely humanistic Renaissance and from that of Nietzsche himself. And the aristocratic ideal of Christianity can be called hostile to life, only if the whole Christian religion is a tissue of lies, legends, and fiction—which Nietzsche asserted freely enough, but never attempted to prove. This we can understand, since a false statement *cannot* be proved.

I declared my intention of saying something concerning Nietzsche's views on the relation of Christian life to Christian belief and to Christian ecclesiastical organization. Perhaps this can best be done by discussing briefly Nietzsche's attitude towards Christ and to St. Paul. His opinions on this subject have nothing particularly novel or peculiarly 'Nietzschean' about them—save in his notions as to the hostility towards 'Life' displayed by the Apostle and in the uncompromising vigour with which he attacks him. The attempt to separate the Founder of Christianity from the great Apostle of the Gentiles and to derive Christianity as an organized religion from St. Paul and not from Christ, was common enough in past years, as was also the tendency to treat as later interpolations passages in the Gospels, which ill befitted the picture of Christ *assumed* by the critic. Nietzsche's suggestions in this respect could be paralleled in the works of the more extravagant 'Higher Critics', and he makes no attempt to argue for his assertions. At Pforta, and no doubt at the University and later, he had picked up a certain amount of 'Higher Criticism', which he simply adopted and used for his own purposes. It is not my intention to attempt to deal with the assertions of 'Higher Criticism': this has been done by others, and in any case the more extravagant views of the older 'Higher Critics' have been discarded by modern critics. But in treating of Nietzsche's attitude towards the Christian religion it is obviously imperative to say something of his attitude towards Christ Himself.

In the first place Nietzsche draws a sharp distinction between Christianity as an historical reality and Christ Himself. 'What did Christ deny?—Everything which to-day is called Christian'.[1] In the first place the Christian *creed* is mere 'idle falsehood and deception' and was not taught by Christ: in the second place the *ecclesiastical organization* of Christianity is radically anti-Christian. 'To be really Christian would mean to be absolutely indifferent to dogmas, cults, priests, church, and theology'.[2] Christ preached simply a *life*—offering 'a real life, a life in truth, to ordinary life'. He did not tell men what they should believe, but how they should behave. He bids 'not to resist, either by deeds, or in our heart, him who ill-treats us; He bids us admit of no grounds for separating ourselves from our wives. . .'[3]. Therefore the man who refuses to be a soldier, who 'lays no claims to the services of the police', etc. would be a Christian: the doctrines of a personal God, of sin and redemption, faith and immortality are irrelevant dogmas, foreign to essential Christianity.

Now it is quite true that Christ preached a way of life and that He laid immense stress on conduct, but it is not true that He gave man nothing to believe. For example, He certainly taught the existence of a personal God, the Father in Whom we must trust: He speaks of Himself as the Eternal Son of God and declares the mission of the Holy Spirit. According to Nietzsche the doctrines of judgment and of rewards and punishments, are 'subsequent additions', interpolations in the Gospels foreign to the mind of Christ. But this is a ridiculous assertion, worthy of a German 'Higher Critic' of the old School. We have no less reason, and every bit as much reason, for accepting the doctrine of the Last Judgment as *Christ's* doctrine as for accepting the doctrine of forgiveness, of love, of the indissolubility of

---

[1] *Will to Power*, i, aph. 158.   [2] Ibid., aph. 159.
[3] Ibid., aph. 163.

marriage, as Christ's doctrine. Our only source of knowledge as to the actual words of Christ is the Gospels, and the
only reason for picking and choosing among words of Christ
as there recorded, is an *a priori assumption* as to what Christ
must have taught. If the Gospels are authoritative and trust-
worthy records (we cannot attempt here to prove that they
are such), they must be taken as they stand and not mutilated
according to caprice. When Nietzsche declares that nothing
could have been more foreign to His mind than the somewhat heavy nonsense of an 'eternal Peter', he is being
arbitrary in the extreme—and needless to say he attempts
no exegesis of the 16th chapter of St. Matthew's Gospel.

Nietzsche's notions on 'subsequent additions' and interpolations are unworthy of serious consideration. But for his
insistence that Christ taught a way of life, and that the
'Counsels' were seriously meant, we have profound sympathy
—was not Christianity once known as ἡ ὁδός? Nietzsche's
words are a challenge to Christians, a prick for the Christian
conscience. Too often does one find believing Christians, who
pay lip-service to the higher ethical demands of Christ, and
then proceed to water them down, in order to suit their own
low ideals. If we do not intend to fulfil His demands, if we
have not the courage to attempt it, let us admit it like honest
men, instead of behaving like paltry hypocrites. Nietzsche
said that there never was a Christian—that from the very
beginning Christians began to adopt all those practices
which were rejected by Christ—'the Christian becomes a
citizen, a soldier, a judge, a workman, a merchant, a scholar,
... a priest, ... a farmer, an artist, a patriot, etc.', 'he defends
himself, he establishes tribunals, he punishes, he swears, etc.'
We might of course ask *when* and *where* Christ forbad people
to be workmen, merchants, scholars, priests, farmers, artists,
patriots or even soldiers, but I cannot enter into details here.[1]
I wish simply to point out that there *have* been Christians,
who took Christ's words seriously—e.g. St. Francis of Assisi,
St. Vincent de Paul, St. Peter Claver—and that the historical
fact of these great *livers* of the Christian life are a standing

---

[1] For the question of 'Pacifism' see my article in the *Church Quarterly
Review* for Oct. 1937.

rebuke to those who would make Christianity—practically, if not theoretically—either a mere 'do-no-harm-to-anyone' ethic or a mere set of beliefs. Nietzsche was often extremely exaggerated, one-sided, inaccurate, and perverse in his assertions, but his words are none the less a challenge. He did not like the Christian ideal of life, but he admitted that there *is* a Christian ideal of life (even if he depicted it in a very one-sided manner, making no distinction between precepts obligatory on all and counsels of perfection), and woe to us Christians if, in our eagerness to make ourselves acceptable to the 'world', we whittle down, pare away and explain away the demands of Christ and the call of Christ.

Nietzsche's Christian upbringing is no doubt largely responsible for his attitude towards Jesus Himself. He admits that Jesus is 'attractive in the highest degree',[1] that He had 'the warmest heart'[2] (Nietzsche contended that the warmest heart and the highest intelligence cannot coexist in one man, and that Christ 'retarded the production of the greatest intellect'), the He represents 'the rare, sudden flashing of a single sunbeam' in the gloomy Jewish landscape, that He was filled with a 'marvellous, fantastic pity' (an error, however, in Nietzsche's eyes), that He put 'the highest significance and value' into the life of the common people of Palestine, that He suffered 'the martyrdom of the most innocent and most craving heart, that never had enough of any human love', that He was 'the incarnate gospel of love', that He 'died as he lived and as he taught' (*Ant.*, p. 174)— 'there never was more than one Christian, and he *died* on the Cross'. But Nietzsche does not like the teaching of Jesus, and in *Zarathustra* he has the hardihood to make the blasphemous assertion, that Jesus 'would have disavowed his doctrine had he attained to my age! Noble enough was he to disavow! But he was still immature. Immaturely loveth the youth, and immaturely also hateth he man and earth. Confined and awkward are still his soul and the wings of his spirit'. 'Verily, too early died that Hebrew whom the preachers of slow death honour: and to many hath it proved a calamity that he died too early.'

---

[1] *Human, All-too-Human*, i, aph. 144.　　　　[2] Ibid., aph. 235.

'As yet had he known only tears, and the melancholy of the Hebrews, together with the hatred of the good and just—the Hebrew Jesus: then was he seized with the longing for death.

'Had he but remained in the wilderness, and far from the good and just! Then, perhaps, would he have learned to live, and love the earth—and laughter also!' (*Zarathustra*, p. 84).

But if Christ Himself taught only a way of life and neither a creed nor an ecclesiastical organization, who was responsible for Creed and Church? Chiefly St. Paul, that 'decadent' and 'blockhead' Paul. Paul, 'one of the most ambitious and importunate souls that ever existed, of a mind full of superstition and cunning', had been filled with zeal for the Jewish Law, but had become aware, that a man of his nature— 'violent, sensual, melancholy, and malicious in his hatred'— *could* not fulfil the Law. However, at what we know as the vision on the way to Damascus, he was seized with the thought that it was unreasonable to persecute Jesus Christ: rather had he in Jesus an opportunity to become the destroyer of the Law. Thus he became 'the apostle of the *annihilation of the Law*',[1] and through his doctrine of incorporation with Christ and a glorious resurrection and eternity, sharing in the glory of Christ, he satisfied 'his ungovernable ambition'. It was Paul too, who founded the Church, who transformed Christianity into 'a mysterious pagan cult, which was ultimately able to accord with the whole of *state organization*—and which carries on war, condemns, tortures, conjures and hates'.[2] It was Paul who introduced the sacrificial cult, salvation through faith, who distorted the life and character of Jesus, who paved the way for the full growth of priesthood and Church, concocting 'an appalling stew of Greek philosophy and Judaism', etc. All this was contrary to the true spirit of Jesus. 'The Church', says Nietzsche, 'is precisely that against which Jesus inveighed—and against which He taught His disciples to fight'.[3] 'Paul is the incarnation of a type which is the

---

[1] *Dawn of Day*, aph. 68.
[2] *Will to Power*, i, aph. 167.
[3] Ibid., i, aph. 168.

reverse of that of the Saviour; he is the genius in hatred, in the standpoint of hatred, and in the relentless logic of hatred'.[1] He desired *power*, and so he invented concepts, doctrines, and symbols by which the masses might be tyrannized over and herds might be formed—e.g. the doctrine of the Last Judgment. He saw that he needed the belief in immortality in order to 'depreciate' the world, that the notion of 'hell' would become master of Rome, that with a 'Beyond' *this life* can be killed.[2]

What are we to say of all this? In the first place, St. Paul did *not* invent the conception of redemptive suffering (cf. Mt. 20/28), nor the doctrine of the Last Judgment (cf. Mt. 25), nor the Church (Mt. 16/17 ff.), nor the doctrine of the sacrificial cult (cf. Luke, 22/19 ff., I Cor. 11/23 ff.). In the second place he was filled with a sincere love of Christ, whom he had not seen before the Ascension, but whom he saw for the first time—as far as we know—on the road to Damascus. The charity of Christ urged him on (II Cor. 5/14), he longed to be with Christ (Philipp. 1/23), to suffer for Christ (Philipp. 3/10). He burnt with the love of his disciples (II Cor. 12/15) and with love for all men (Rom. 1/14, I Cor. 9/22). His Master was the loving Saviour and Redeemer, he himself was the Apostle of Love. The other apostles never accused him of *distorting* Christ's teaching: he himself insisted that his gospel was not his own personal message (Galat. 1/11–12). In the third place, so far was Paul from being driven by an ungovernable ambition, that he was ready to become anathema for his brethren (Rom. 9/3), and declared that he was not worthy to be called an Apostle because he had persecuted the Church of Christ. In the fourth place, he did not preach the annihilation of the Law, but the fulfilment of the Law. In the fifth place, Nietzsche has no justification—save his own imagination—for attributing all manner of sins to St. Paul before his conversion. No, if Christianity is to be condemned, then Christ must be condemned also, for it is not Paul but Christ, who is responsible for Christianity. We can hardly exaggerate the importance of St. Paul in the work of evangelizing the Roman

[1] *Antichrist*, p. 184.   [2] Ibid., p. 224.

world, it is true,—is he not the 'vessel of election', chosen to carry the Name of Jesus to the Gentile world?—but he was not the founder of Christianity. He preached what he had received, not what he had invented.

We have dwelt somewhat on Nietzsche's opinion as to the opposition between essential Christianity and the super-structure erected by St. Paul and others; and to a student of Nietzsche these opinions are naturally of interest, though they are without value in themselves. Church, sacrifice, sacraments, judgment, and sanctions, find their place in the Gospels along with the call to universal love, forgiveness to the utmost limit, etc., and one cannot be justified in sub-tracting the so-called 'institutional' element from the rest in virtue of an *a priori* assumption as to the nature of essential Christianity. Moreover there is no reason for asserting a radical opposition between Christian Church, Belief and Sacraments on the one hand and Christian Life on the other. The doctrine of Christianity supplies the setting and the justification for that life, the Church is the visible union of all those living that life and the Sacraments are the divinely appointed means of initiating, fostering, and increasing that Life. There have undoubtedly been abuses— for example, political, egoistic, and worldly motives have predominated at times in the minds of the highest eccle-siastics—but abuses are irrelevant, when it is a question of essential characteristics, oppositions, etc. And history and experience show that a religion of *mere behaviour* does not bear the fruits that it pretends to. Nietzsche bears tacit witness to this fact, when he says that Christianity is simply a way of believing, but that there has been only *one* Christian, Christ Himself. To this we would reply that Christ is indeed the one absolutely perfect Example of the Christian Life, but that the Christian Life has been lived by historical men and women, and that the life has not been without essential reference to Belief and Institution.

Nietzsche was gifted with a certain power of psychological penetration, and it is probably this fact that accounts very largely for the feeling some people experience, that 'there is something in what Nietzsche says'. For example, in *The*

Dawn of Day, after remarking that among the ancients there were many who *acted* virtue ('Of what use was a virtue which one could not display, and which did not know how to display itself!'), Nietzsche says: 'Christianity put an end to the career of these actors of virtue; instead it devised the disgusting ostentation and parading of sins: it brought into the world a state of *mendacious sinfulness* (even at the present day this is considered as *bon ton* among orthodox Christians)'.[1] Now it is true that there have been certain phenomena among Christians, which might be characterized as disgusting exhibitions of sin-parading—staged 'conversions', public and rhetorical 'confession', etc. It may also be true that some Christians—human nature being what it is—have pretended to 'sinfulness' without real conviction, to make themselves 'interesting', to exhibit their 'humility', etc. To some indeed the protestations of saints, that they were great sinners, might appear examples of 'mendacious sinfulness', but when we are tempted to think this, we are really judging the saints by ourselves. We have not the saint's living realization of the utter holiness of God, in Whose sight the very heavens are not pure, nor have we the saint's realization of ourselves. On our lips the saint's protestations of sinfulness would ring hollow—not because they would be untrue, but because they would not proceed from a realization of the truth—and so we tend to imagine that the saint is acting. But the conclusion does not follow.

To take another example. Nietzsche asserts that the doctrine of eternal rewards and punishments was an expression of the will to power. Now it is obvious enough that the doctrine of hell for example *might* be used by priests or preachers with a view to dominating the Christian 'herd', and so we may experience the uneasy suspicion, that Nietzsche is exposing the doctrine. But a few minutes' quiet reflection should be sufficient to show us that though the doctrine *might* be so used, even if it *has* on occasion been so used, it does not follow that it was invented for that purpose, that it is in itself an expression of the will to power, a human invention devoid of objective reference. If a doctrine has

[1] *Dawn of Day*, aph. 29.

been *used* for a personal end, that does *not* prove that the doctrine is false.

In the concluding paragraphs of this chapter I propose to say something more of Nietzsche's fundamental objection to Christianity, that it is hostile to culture. I have already spoken of his accusation that Christianity is hostile to the development of 'higher men', and I have shown that so much depends on what you mean by higher men. For Christianity is undoubtedly hostile to the development of Nietzsche's *Übermensch*—it cannot regard the development of the free, immoral, and atheistic individual, however strong and beautiful and virile, however talented and intellectual and artistic as desirable—but it is not hostile to the development of higher men in the sense of men living to the fullest degree the supernatural life and the natural life in due harmony. Yet we should perhaps admit this much, that human finitude and the fact that intensity is so often proportionate to canalization (cf. Ritschl's advice to Nietzsche), render it difficult at least to attain in one individual a full and harmonious development of both the supernatural and the natural, to the highest degree. Such a development is the *ideal*, but whether it is practically possible, is doubtful —at least as regards *full* development. There have indeed been great saints who were also great intellectuals—St. Thomas Aquinas and St. Robert Bellarmine for instance— great artists who were saintly men—Fra Angelico for instance—but generally speaking a certain specialization seems the natural course. Michelangelo was a great artist, he lived and died a convinced Catholic; but it would perhaps cause us a certain surprise, if we found that he was a great mystic as well, just as we would be surprised if St. Bernard had written *Othello* or St. John of the Cross had composed *Faust*. Nietzsche would say that there is *opposition* between the supernatural and the natural. This I would deny: a man of Michelangelo's artistic genius might, without contradiction, have been a great mystic; and a man of St. Bernard's holiness might, without opposition, have written *Othello*. But all the same I do not see how it can be denied that there is a natural tendency to specialization when outstanding eminence is in question. The *ideal* is an all-round eminence, in the supernatural and in the natural spheres, but *practically* there is a tendency to specialization. This fact may lead unreflecting people to suspect an essential opposition, when there is no essential opposition. If there were an essential opposition, then St. Thomas Aquinas, Fra Angelico, St. Robert Bellamine, St. John of the Cross—a Castilian poet—Pasteur, General de Castelnau, Marshal Foch, etc. would have been impossibilities—we should have St. Simon Stylites on the one hand, Napoleon on the other, and no intermingling. And it is not that Christianity is hostile to the development of great natural talents—Christians believe that these outstanding talents were given by God to be used and developed—but Christianity is a supernatural religion, primarily interested in man's eternal salvation. The words used by Christian writers in regard to the body (showing, thought Nietzsche, a contempt for the body) should be taken as emphatically expressing the relative importance of the supernatural as compared with the natural, of the things of the spirit in comparison with natural talents. A literal *contempt* for the body and natural talents would be, not Christian, but definitely unorthodox.

Christianity therefore has nothing in its nature which is essentially hostile to culture, for, although it teaches the doctrine of original sin, it does not hold that the natural man is totally corrupted or worthless. On the contrary, it teaches that the *whole* man comes from God, and that God, the Author of all being, is glorified, not only by supernatural virtue but also by outstanding natural talents. God is glorified, not only by the prayer of St. Teresa or the heroic charity of St. Vincent de Paul, but also by the art of Michelangelo and Velasquez, of Rembrandt and Rubens, by the music of Beethoven, by the literature of Dante, Shakespeare, and Goethe. Whether all these talented people *intended* to glorify God, is irrelevant to the point at issue: objectively speaking their great achievements glorify the God who gave them their talents and the possibility of developing them. Christianity is not Manichaeanism—the latter is heretical—

and physical beauty, strength, and vigour are not in themselves evil but *good*. It is much less important that a man should be possessed of bodily strength and vigour than that he should possess strength and vigour of soul; but bodily gifts are by no means valueless. Of course, if the supernatural is a fiction, then the doctrine of the greater importance of the supernatural as compared with the natural, would reasonably be construed as involving an opposition to the natural—and this is Nietzsche's position—but it has first to be demonstrated that the supernatural is only a fiction, and this can never be done—for it is not a fiction. Once the premises of Christianity are granted, it is unreasonable and unjust to declare that Christianity is anti-natural. The charge would be true in reference to certain heresies; but no level-headed and sincere critic will judge Christianity by the heresies, for, in so far as they are heretical, they are non-Christian, anti-Christian.

Is the contention that there is no quarrel between Christianity and culture empirically justified, i.e. in history? Nietzsche, as we have seen, contended that Christianity has in history proved itself the foe of culture, destroying pagan culture, the culture of Moorish Spain, the culture of the Renaissance. Now if culture = secularist culture, then Christianity is certainly hostile thereto—that point need not be laboured—but has it been hostile to culture in general? Was Christianity hostile to pagan culture as culture?—for it is obvious that Christianity was hostile to paganism as a religion. We must admit at once that some Christian writers spoke in a very hostile tone about the pagan world; but this was but natural, for the myths and morals of the ancient world are reflected, not only in legend and cult, but in literature, sculpture, and so on. But to conclude from the attacks of Christian writers and apologists that Christianity adopted a radically hostile attitude to the culture of the ancient world without further distinction, would be premature. If we look at the historical facts, we find the Church—when external circumstances permitted—utilizing the literary and artistic forms of antiquity, adapting its philosophy, stressing the beneficent aspect of the Empire.

St. Augustine was greatly influenced by the pagan philosopher Plotinus and transposed his philosophy into a Christian setting. It is true that, in the course of his controversy with the Pelagians, the African Doctor came to speak more severely of the pagans than he had formerly, but who would count St. Augustine among the forces of anticulture, Augustine who continued his literary work even when the barbarians were knocking at the gates and the Empire was crumbling in ruins before his eyes ? And who was it but Christian monks, that preserved something of the culture of Antiquity and transmitted it to the early Middle Ages ?

That the natural culture of Moslem Spain was far in advance of the contemporary culture of Christian Europe is an undeniable fact ; but it would scarcely be correct to conclude from the somewhat slow growth of culture in Medieval Europe to an anti-cultural attitude on the part of the Church. When we think of the work of men like Alcuin and Rhabanus Maurus at the beginning of the Middle Ages, of the humanism of the School of Chartres in the twelfth century, of the Universities of Paris, Oxford, Bologna, etc. in the thirteenth century, of the growing interest in empirical science in the fourteenth century, when we think of the Gothic Cathedrals and Abbeys, of the works of art and literature of Filippo Lippi, Fra Angelico and Dante, it can scarcely be denied that the peak period of medieval culture was one of the great periods of culture in the world's history. People may speak of medieval crudity and barbarity, of oppression, poverty and misery, but these phenomena are not peculiar to medieval Europe. Was not Athenian culture founded on a slave-basis, and was not imperial Rome stained by far fouler blots than ever darkened medieval Europe ?

Nietzsche asserted that the Church, in the period of the Counter-Reformation, was hostile to Renaissance culture. But he himself admits that Renaissance Humanism, in the period before the Reformation and the Counter-Reformation, threatened Christianity in its very foundations. It was therefore not so much that the Church was hostile to

Renaissance humanism, as that the latter—in certain aspects —was hostile to the Church, and that the Church defended herself. And it must be remembered that these features of the Renaissance, which were frowned upon by the Church at the time of the Counter-Reformation, tended to undermine that very culture of Europe, which had been so laboriously built up. The Church never showed herself hostile to culture as such, but extended her patronage to painting, literature and sculpture. Instances can certainly be adduced, in which ecclesiastics have shown themselves narrow, suspicious, and over-timorous in admitting new cultural influences, but 'culture' includes the development of *all* the powers and potentialities of man and the spiritual potentialities of man are the most important; and if the influence of the Church has seemed at times to be somewhat hostile to fresh forms of the natural side of culture, her attitude was determined by her zeal to preserve those spiritual values, which alone render a true and profound culture possible.

This assertion might have appeared somewhat bold, had it not been for the present condition of Europe. But if anyone reflects on the condition of the world to-day, it should become obvious that no real culture is possible that is not based on the firm recognition of spiritual values, and that the Church, through her constant assertion of these values, has proved herself to be a truly cultured force and a true custodian of culture. We have been led by recent cataclysmic events to recognize, not only the evils of Totalitarianism but the *lacunae* and flaws in liberal Democracy. Now Totalitarianism tends to the practical denial of the supernatural (though not always explicitly perhaps) and so to the denial of the eternal worth of the individual: the result is a crushing tyranny, a stifling of freedom, and a hopeless mediocrity in the achievements of even natural culture. Democracy does indeed hold to the value of the individual but it offers no sure foundation for this tenet and so often tends to a despicable materialization of human life. Christianity, however, supplies a dogmatic foundation for the eternal value of the individual. It was this Christian doctrine that triumphed over Roman slavery, and it is the influence of this Christian doctrine that has passed over into Democracy, as Nietzsche himself recognized and clearly asserted. But in Democracy the tenet of the individual's value and importance is set adrift from its moorings, and it cannot survive alone: it can survive only if securely rooted in the Christian Faith. And let no one quote the splendour of the Greek or Roman slavery-culture as a proof that culture is independent of the doctrine of the individual's value, for to do so is tantamount to denying the possibility of a profounder development of culture in the future. We who believe that a development of culture is possible in the future, which will be profounder than the culture of Antiquity, which will embrace not only the *whole* man but *every* man—as far as is possible,—take our stand on the Christian Faith, and recognize that without Faith secularization and materialization inevitably result, which mean the degradation of man and are the very antithesis of culture. Those secularist writers among us who oppose totalitarianism and profess to uphold a free culture, unhampered by the shackles of Christianity, are anti-historical dreamers, who do not see that they are busy sawing off the very branch on which they hope to sit. These men, who think themselves friends of culture and foes of 'superstition' and 'bigotry', are in truth enemies of culture and of man, all the more dangerous because their poison-fangs are concealed from the unsuspecting and easily hood-winked.

There are some who recognize that spiritual values are essential to culture, but who at the same time assert that the Christian religion has outlived its usefulness, that it is unacceptable to the modern man and that a new religion is needed. And what do they offer in its place? A watery soup of their own concoction, which is scarcely superior to sheer atheism. And do they hope to build a strong culture on this miserable foundation? Not a bit of it: their substitute-religion is thrown out as a sop to the religious-minded, that is all. They have not recognized, first that Europe is heading straight to Nihilism (as Nietzsche, a far clearer thinker, prophesied years ago), and secondly that the remedy can only be found in building culture on the firm foundation of the dogmatic Christian Faith. Nietzsche denied this second assertion; but it is not absurd to suppose that if he had lived to see what we have seen, he might—had he the necessary humility—have returned to the Christian fold, not out of cowardice or despair, but from a recognition of the truth. Nietzsche said that if Christ had lived longer, He would have changed His doctrine; we suggest that if Nietzsche were alive to-day, he might by God's grace have returned to Christ.

CHAPTER VII

SCHOPENHAUER AND NIETZSCHE

'I BELONG to those readers of Schopenhauer who know perfectly well, after they have turned the first page, that they will read all the others, and listen to every word that he has spoken. My trust in him sprang to life at once, and has been the same for nine years'.[1] So wrote Nietzsche in *Schopenhauer as Educator*, an essay completed in August, 1874, and forming part of *Unzeitgemässe Betrachtungen*. In 1888, however, in *Ecce Homo*, Nietzsche is speaking of 'the bitter odour of corpses which is peculiar to Schopenhauer' (p. 69), and tells us how the man who understands the concept 'Dionysian', 'does not require any refutation of Plato, or of Christianity, or of Schopenhauer—for his nose *scents decomposition'*. (p. 71.) A remarkable change of attitude, reminding us somewhat of Nietzsche's change of attitude in regard to Richard Wagner who, from being an ideal, a man in whose defence Nietzsche was willing to risk his reputation as a serious scholar, is depicted in *Nietzsche contra Wagner* as 'a cranky and desperate *décadent'* (p. 73). There is of course one important difference between the one case and the other, namely that the greatest friendship of Nietzsche's life had been his friendship with Wagner

[1] *Thoughts out of Season*, ii, p. 114.

(whom indeed he never eradicated from his heart), while he had never known Schopenhauer personally. If Nietzsche had ever known the great Pessimist personally, it is not fanciful to think that his rejection of the doctrine of Schopenhauer would have been complicated by a severe disappointment in regard to the man himself. The philosopher was hardly the type of character that would have attracted Friedrich Nietzsche. But though Nietzsche's relationship with Schopenhauer shows this marked difference from his relationship with Wagner, yet Nietzsche's own explanation of his change of front is similar in both cases. He had read himself, his own ideal, into both Schopenhauer and Wagner, and in both cases he had been disappointed. Thus Nietzsche tells us that 'it is not "Schopenhauer as Educator" but "Nietzsche as Educator", who speaks his sentiments in it' (i.e. in the essay *Schopenhauer as Educator*), and that 'The essay *Wagner in Bayreuth* is a vision of my own future; on the other hand, my most secret history, my development, is written down in *Schopenhauer as Educator*'.[1] Similarly in *Nietzsche contra Wagner* Nietzsche observes: 'You see how I misinterpreted, you see also what I *bestowed* upon Wagner and Schopenhauer—myself'.[2]

Yet even if we grant that Nietzsche seizes upon Schopenhauer as a type, as a convenient means of expressing his own ideas, the fact remains that at first Nietzsche undoubtedly was attracted towards Schopenhauer. What was the point of attraction? Is it not difficult to understand how the great Renouncer, the philosopher who preached renunciation of the will to live, who afforded a metaphysical basis for the sentiment of pity, who advocated—in word at least—an ascetic ideal, could have attracted the upholder of the Will to Power, who preached, not the ascetic saint, but the Superman, who advocated, not pity, but hardness? Nietzsche tells us himself: 'It was atheism that had drawn me to Schopenhauer'.[3] Nietzsche made his first acquaintance with the works of Schopenhauer when he was a student at

[1] *Ecce Homo*, p. 81.
[2] *Nietzsche contra Wagner*, p. 65.
[3] *Ecce Homo*, p. 78.

the University of Leipzig, i.e.—after he had separated himself from Christianity, for it was at Easter in 1865 (he went to Leipzig in the autumn of that year) that he had refused to go with his mother and sister to partake of the Protestant Communion. Nietzsche was of course brought up in an atmosphere of piety—his father was Pastor of Röcken and his mother was always an earnest Christian—and in early years he had wished to follow the calling of his excellent father. But it was not the influence of Schopenhauer that first turned him from the Christianity of his boyhood. Apart from the independent tendencies of his own character, the 'free spirit', he had come under influence at the School or College of Pforta which helped to alienate him from religion. For example, one or two of the masters at Pforta expounded ideas of the higher criticism in class. Thus one cannot be surprised that, although Nietzsche had studied both philology and theology when he first went to the University of Bonn in 1864, he soon abandoned theology and devoted himself entirely to philology. This period of doubt is symbolized by the act of abstention from Communion at Easter, 1865, and so he was already well prepared for the reception of the doctrine of Schopenhauer when he came upon his works at Leipzig. 'I happened to be near the shop of Rohn, the second-hand bookseller, and I took up *The World as Will and Idea*, glancing at it carelessly, I do not know what demon suggested that I should take the book home with me. Contrary to my usual practice—for I did not as a rule buy second-hand books without looking through them—I paid for the volume and went back home. Throwing myself on the sofa I gave myself up to the thoughts of that gloomy genius. From every line I heard the cry of renouncement, denial, and resignation; I saw in the book a mirror in which the world, life itself, and my own soul were all reflected with horrifying fidelity. The dull, uninteresting eye of art looked at me; I saw sickness and recovery, banishment and restoration, hell and heaven'.[1]

To imagine that Friedrich Nietzsche was attracted to atheism and to Schopenhauer in the spirit of a superficial

[1] *Das Leben Friedrich Nietzsches*, i, 232.

'free-thinker', would be to make a capital mistake which would involve a radical misunderstanding of Nietzsche's character. Nietzsche displays none of the levity of the ordinary free-thinker, he was no Strauss (on whose spirit he pours the vials of his scorn in *Thoughts out of Season*); still less did he adopt atheism as a pretext for moral licence. No, Nietzsche was impressed by the picture of human life as given by Schopenhauer, that sombre picture which embodies an earnest outlook on life, the vision of a man who sees the universe as the phenomenon of a blind Will, without purpose, without ultimate meaning—a changing scene, dominated by fruitlessness, frustration, suffering, inevitable death, in which happiness is but negative and beatitude a dream.

'The life of every individual, if we survey it as a whole and in general, and only lay stress upon its most .significant features, is really always a tragedy, but gone through in detail it has the character of a comedy. For the deeds and vexations of the day, the restless irritation of the moment, the desires and fears of the weak, the mishaps of every hour, are all through chance, which is ever bent upon some jest, scenes of a comedy. But the never-satisfied wishes, the frustrated efforts, the hopes unmercifully crushed by fate, the unfortunate errors of the whole life, with increasing suffering and death at the end, are always a tragedy. Thus, as if fate would add derision to the misery of our existence, our life must contain all the woes of. tragedy, and yet we cannot even assert the dignity of tragic characters, but in the broad detail of life must inevitably be the foolish characters of a comedy'.[1]

The conclusion is, in the words of Calderón,

> 'Pues el delito mayor
> Del hombre es haber nacido'.
> ('For the greatest crime of man
> Is that he ever was born'.)

But if it is not difficult to understand how Nietzsche was attracted by the sombre picture of Schopenhauer, one would expect, even *a priori*, that he would be unable to find abiding

---

[1] *The World as Will and Idea*, Trans. Haldane and Kemp, pp. 415–16.

satisfaction in Schopenhauer's Pessimism and his doctrines of renunciation and asceticism. In the first place Nietzsche's own joyous spirit would certainly revolt from Schopenhauer's pessimism. The latter's pessimism was due, not merely to his study of the Upanishads and their doctrine of Mâya, but, as Professor De Witt Parker points out, 'had its primary source in his own temperament and character'. It seems probable that his father committed suicide and we may well suppose that Schopenhauer inherited from him a tendency to form a sombre view of life, which was accentuated by his estrangement from his mother who was of a very different type of character. Nietzsche, however, contrary to what is sometimes supposed, was not naturally of a sad and sombre disposition, even if he was always possessed of a serious outlook on life. True, ill-health, overwork, lack of recognition, and increasing loneliness affected him deeply as time went on, yet we read how even at a late period of his life, before his mental breakdown, other guests at the 'pension', where he was staying in the south of France, vied with one another to be next him at table, as he was always the centre of a lively, cheerful and interesting conversation. When staying once at a hotel he and his sister laughed together so much that an old general, who had a neighbouring room, sent to ask why they laughed so constantly—it was infectious, he said; and, when travelling by train in Italy, Nietzsche and his sister exchanged nonsense rhymes with one another, accompanied by so much merriment that an Englishman got up and left the carriage in disgust, under the mistaken impression that they were laughing at him. A man of this description, joyous and active, could hardly rest in the Schopenhauerian pessimism.

It may not be fanciful to suggest another reason why we should expect, even *a priori*, that Nietzsche would pass beyond Schopenhauer. Schopenhauer's philosophy was certainly atheistic, but his ethical teaching borrows elements from religious thought and practice, not only from Indian but also from Christian sources. Indeed his outlook on life, apart from the metaphysical framework, bears an obvious resemblance to the picture of this world as a vale of tears given by Christian moralists—and it is not without significance that Schopenhauer quotes from the *Vida es sueño* of Calderón, who was a great Christian dramatist. Indeed certain German pastors went so far as to make use of Schopenhauer's thoughts in their sermons, exchanging of course the atheistic for a theistic background, and offsetting the pessimistic outlook on this life by the doctrine of immortality and future happiness. And did not Schopenhauer himself attach value to the writings of the Spanish Jesuit Balthasar Gracian (1584–1638), some of whose work he translated into German? Indeed in 1832 Schopenhauer wrote that his favourite Spanish author was Gracian, all of whose works he had read. Gracian naturally presented his ideas in a Christian framework; but Schopenhauer recognized in him a kindred spirit from the point of view of a common outlook on the world and man's life in it. Gracian has even been placed by some writers, together with Schopenhauer and Leopardi, among the great pessimists. Now we might well expect that Nietzsche would come to recognize the religious element in Schopenhauer—despite all the latter's atheism—and to see that Schopenhauer's ethical teaching owed much to that very Christianity which Nietzsche himself had already abandoned before he met Schopenhauer. While we cannot subscribe to the judgment of a contributor to the *Times Literary Supplement* that Schopenhauer was 'philosophus christissimus', we willingly admit that there is not a little common to Christianity and to the philosophy of Schopenhauer. (This point has been well elaborated by Professor Umberto Padovani of Milan.)[1] When Nietzsche came to recognize this we would expect him to abandon Schopenhauer as he had abandoned Christianity. And in actual fact, in proportion as his opposition to Christianity deepened and the idea of the 'Transvaluation of all Values' took hold of him, his opposition to Schopenhauer was also deepened.

In *Schopenhauer as Educator* Nietzsche analyses the influence of Schopenhauer on him—i.e. at a time when he was still under the influence of the philosopher or, if

[1] *Arturo Schopenhauer*, by Umberto A. Padovani. Milano, 1934.

preferred, at the period when he was unconsciously using Schopenhauer as a peg on which to hang his own ideas. Nietzsche tells us that he was seeking for a true philosopher and educator, 'and with such needs and desires within me did I come to know Schopenhauer'. He found in him an absence of pose, a fundamental honesty, a speaking for himself alone, a bracing air of candour. 'I only know a single author that I can rank with Schopenhauer, or even above him, in the matter of honesty; and that is Montaigne'. Besides honesty Nietzsche found in Schopenhauer—strange to say—'a joy that really makes others joyful'. This is not the joy of mediocre writers like David Strauss, who 'do not see the sufferings and the monsters that they pretend, as philosophers, to see and fight', but the joy of facing the suffering and the monsters and of gaining the victory as consequence. The third element in Schopenhauer's influence on Nietzsche was his consistency. 'Analysing it, I find that this influence of Schopenhauer has three elements, his honesty, his joy, and his consistency. He is honest, as speaking and writing for himself alone; joyful, because his thought has conquered the greatest difficulties; consistent, because he cannot help being so'. And thus Nietzsche found in Schopenhauer 'the educator and philosopher I had so long desired'.

Now that Schopenhauer was honest in the sense of saying what he thought, can scarcely be denied. He certainly believed that in giving to man *The World as Will and Idea* he was giving to the world the truth. It cannot be said that he followed his own ethical prescriptions; but then, as he remarked, it is no more necessary that the philosopher should be a saint than that the saint should be a philosopher. That Schopenhauer did not make his statements without conviction, merely in order to appear brilliant or unusual, we may allow; but that joy was a characteristic of his spirit and thought will not so easily escape criticism. There is indeed in the thought of Schopenhauer a certain negative 'joy', which is rather the restrained calm of the dispassionate beholder. It is not the vigorous joy of the man who looks his enemy in the face and conquers him, but the pitying gaze of the onlooker who, on the island of his philosophic calm, stands apart from the fruitless struggle. The Schopenhauerian saint is not the man in whose soul pulsates the energy of a divine life, a God-given love, but the man who has renounced—and that is all. He is not the man who sees the suffering and follies of this mortal life set against the white light of eternity, but the man who sees the suffering and follies of this life against a background of darkness. In the thought of Schopenhauer there is room for the 'joy' of the artist, room for the 'joy' of the Indian ascetic, but there is certainly no room for the joy of St. Francis of Assisi, and— here is the point—there is no room for the joy of Friedrich Nietzsche, no room for the joy of the fighter, the creator, the devotee of *Dionysus*. When Nietzsche found in Schopenhauer the joy 'that really makes others joyful', he was—as he came to realize later—not finding but *bestowing*. He read into Schopenhauer a joy which is not there to find: he clothed Schopenhauer in his own ideals. And consistency? Well, it might be supposed that suicide would be the logical conclusion to the Schopenhauerian philosophy, the evidence of consistency. Suicide was indeed condemned as surrender, as giving-in; but the conquest of the monster, as taught by Schopenhauer, was but a phantom conquest, an acquiescence, an escape. The Schopenhauer of *Schopenhauer as Educator* is not the real Schopenhauer. Just as Nietzsche wove a peculiar ideal of his own about the form of Wagner and suffered bitter disappointment when he was at length forced to realize that Richard Wagner was Richard Wagner and no one else, so he wove a peculiar ideal of his own pattern about the form of Schopenhauer and later came to realize that Schopenhauer after all was but Schopenhauer.

An indication of Nietzsche's misunderstanding of Schopenhauer the man is afforded by this passage. 'Schopenhauer makes small account of the learned tribe, keeps himself exclusive, and cultivates an independence from state and society as his ideal, to escape the chains of circumstance: that is his value to us'. That Schopenhauer passed some very bitter criticism on 'the learned tribe', on professors of philosophy, is true enough; but it is notorious that this proceeded mainly from exasperation at non-recognition and from jealousy. Schopenhauer did not start as a University professor as Nietzsche did (who occupied the Chair of Philology at Bâle, until ill-health forced him to relinquish it); but so far from its being his 'ideal' to cultivate this state of independence, he made abortive attempts to obtain a chair for himself. On one occasion he even advertised lectures at Berlin at the same hour as that at which Hegel was lecturing to crowded audiences; and then had to leave in humiliation and disgust when he discovered that the students could not be enticed from their allegiance to their Master, despite Hegel's obscurity and laboured style. On this point Schopenhauer was not so much a free spirit as a disgruntled spirit. Does not Nietzsche himself say: 'Schopenhauer has at all events an advantage over him' (i.e. Kant); 'for he at least was distinguished by a certain fierce ugliness of disposition, which showed itself in hatred, desire, vanity, and suspicion: he was of a rather more ferocious disposition, and had both time and leisure to indulge this ferocity'.[1]

Nietzsche was attracted to Schopenhauer by the latter's atheism, by his denial of supernaturalism and transcendentalism, by his doctrine of the fundamentally irrational character of the universe—in strong contrast to Hegel, who was wormwood and gall to both Schopenhauer and Nietzsche —and by his subordination of intellect to will. These elements remained common to both but, as Nietzsche's peculiar ideas developed and took concrete shape, he came to realize in ever clearer light the antithesis between Schopenhauer and himself. In the philosophy of Schopenhauer the ideal of man is the denial of life, in the philosopby of Nietzsche it is the affirmation of life. In *Thus Spake Zarathustra* Nietzsche speaks of his period of Schopenhauerian pessimism: 'All life had I renounced, so I dreamed'. But the way of the 'Soothsayer', the way of the world-weary, was rejected by Nietzsche as an evil dream; he came to preach the affirmation of Life, the great Yea to life. Man is not to renounce life, to stand aside from life, to pursue an

---

[1] *Dawn of Day*, aph. 481.

ideal of asceticism, but to welcome and embrace life. Even in the fatalistic doctrine of the 'Eternal Recurrence', the notion that the process of the Universe is one of eternally recurrent cycles (a fatalistic doctrine which, as has often been remarked, is scarcely favourable to the Nietzschean doctrine of the Superman), the same theme appears. Men are 'not to shun life like pessimists', but 'just as revellers at a banquet desire their cups refilled, will say to life: Once again'! Thus Nietzsche developed away from Schopenhauer, and if we have on the one side the pessimism of Schopenhauer, combined with a predominantly negative ideal of conduct, we have on the other hand the optimism of Nietzsche, combined with a predominantly positive and activist ideal of conduct.

But what is life for Nietzsche? Life is Will to Power. It is not a mere struggle for existence, but is above all a struggle for power, the Will to Power. This is observable both in the animal and human kingdoms, but in the main it must be consciously affirmed and realized. Here at once we see another important difference between Nietzsche and Schopenhauer. The latter held up the ideal of pity and taught that all individuals are metaphysically united and identical in the one Will: Nietzsche, on the other hand, rejected the ideal of pity and passionately affirmed, not the unity of all men, but the *difference* of men, the order of rank, the existence of natural aristocracy. It is true no doubt that the system of Schopenhauer also culminates in an aristocracy, the aristocracy of geniuses and ascetics, but then they attain this position, not by the affirmation of the Will to Power, but by renunciation, self-denial, stepping aside as it were from the struggle. Nietzsche, believing firmly that men are *not* equal, and that the doctrine of equality is the truly *immoral* doctrine, denounced Socialistic egalitarianism and the Christian doctrine of the equality of all men before God (both of which doctrines Nietzsche considered decadent and degenerate), and he came to consider that the philosophy of Schopenhauer was tarred with the same brush. The aristocrats of Schopenhauer are precisely those who have *seen through* the principle of individuation, who have realized that individuality and particularity are Mâya and that all are metaphysically one, identical in one Will. Realizing this they pity all; for is not the suffering of all ultimately their own suffering, in virtue of the metaphysical unity of all being? Nietzsche's aristocrats, on the other hand, are precisely those who realize their *difference* from the many, who separate themselves from the herd outlook and herd values, who go their own way, leaving the herd to its own pettiness. The aristocrats of Schopenhauer gaze downwards with eyes of pity: the aristocrats of Nietzsche gaze upwards and forwards, triumph, joy, and dominion—not pity—in their eyes. (Not, of course, that Nietzsche advocated cruelty or barbarity. The Supermen are not the swashbucklers of the S.S., but the 'European men'—not the 'blond beasts', but men who have conquered littleness in themselves, cramping of intellect and slavery of the passions, men who are completely 'free'.)

The Schopenhauerian 'saint' reaches his position of superiority by asceticism and renunciation, by saying 'no' to life: the Nietzschean Superman realizes himself by affirmation, by saying 'yes' to Life. Nietzsche, of course, preached a certain asceticism, in that man must conquer himself: it is not the message of libertinism and self-indulgence that he proclaims, but power in restraint and self-mastery. Libertinism is weakness, not strength. But the negative ideal of Schopenhauer became abhorrent to him: the ideal is affirmation, is positive and not negative.

At the beginning of this chapter we mentioned the parallel between Nietzsche's change of attitude in regard to Schopenhauer and his change of attitude in regard to Richard Wagner. But there is a closer connection than merely that of a similar *volte-face* in Nietzsche's personal relations with the two men (if one can speak of personal relations in regard to Schopenhauer, whom he never knew personally). Wagner expressed in music the metaphysics of Schopenhauer; it has even been suggested that Wagner stands to Schopenhauer as Dante to St. Thomas. Wagner was strongly inclined to pessimism, and in 1853 he wrote to Liszt that his life was but a dream, and that when he awoke it was only to suffer. He writes again, that 'as for hope, there remains for me but one: that of sleeping with a sleep so profound that every sense of human misery be blotted out in me'. It was in this state of mind that Wagner discovered Schopenhauer. 'I am at present', he writes to Liszt, 'exclusively occupied with one man, who appeared to me in my solitude as a messenger from heaven: it is Arthur Schopenhauer, our greatest philosopher since Kant. . . . His central thought, the final negation of the will to live, is of a terrible seriousness; but it is the only way of salvation. Naturally this thought was not new to me but it is this philosopher who has for the first time revealed it to me with perfect clarity . . '. The *Ring* was conceived before Wagner had come to know Schopenhauer's philosophy, but *Tristan* was conceived (1854) under the direct influence of Schopenhauer. It is true that in *Parsifal* Wagner tends towards a concept of positive redemption but it is still by way of negation and not through the affirmation of life.[1]

Now Nietzsche, it is true, shows disgust principally at Wagner's later development, as manifested in *Parsifal*. In *Ecce Homo* he speaks of his reception of 'a splendid copy of the *Parsifal* text', with the following inscription from Wagner's pen: 'To his dear friend Friedrich Nietzsche, from Richard Wagner, Ecclesiastical Councillor. . . . At about this time the first Bayreuth Pamphlets appeared: and I then understood the move on my part for which it was high time. Incredible! Wagner had become pious' (pp. 89–90). Similarly in *The Case of Wagner* Nietzsche comments: ' "Lohengrin" contains a solemn ban upon all investigation and questioning. In this way Wagner stood for the Christian concept, "Thou must and shalt *believe*" ' (p. 7). But it must be remembered that in Nietzsche's eyes Christianity and Schopenhauerianism were akin in that both are manifestations of decadence, of weakness, of negation. In rejecting *Parsifal* Nietzsche was rejecting also the Wagner of the interpretation of the *Ring* and the Wagner of *Tristan*,

---

[1] Kuno Fischer mentions that Wagner, in his contribution for the jubilee celebration of Beethoven, recognized and accepted Schopenhauer's theory of music as revealing the essence of the world.

not only the 'Christian' Wagner but also the Schopenhauerian Wagner.

Nietzsche indeed explicitly recognizes and rejects the Schopenhauerianism of Wagner. In his Preface to *The Case of Wagner* he is speaking of his preoccupation with 'the problem of *decadence*' and his combat with morality, which denies life and has as its concealed foundation '*impoverished* life, the will to nonentity, great exhaustion'. He comments: 'I had to side against all that was morbid in myself including Wagner, including Schopenhauer, including the whole of modern *humanity*' (p. xxx). Speaking of the *Ring* and Wagner's subsequent interpretation of it, Nietzsche writes: 'What happened? A misfortune. The ship dashed on to a reef; Wagner had run aground. The reef was Schopenhauer's philosophy; Wagner had stuck fast on a *contrary* view of the world. What had he set to music? Optimism? Wagner was ashamed. It was moreover an optimism for which Schopenhauer had devised an evil expression—*unscrupulous* optimism. He was more than ever ashamed. He reflected for some time; his position seemed desperate. . . . At last a path of escape seemed gradually to open before him: what if the reef on which he had been wrecked could be interpreted as a goal, as the ulterior motive, as the actual purpose of his journey? To be wrecked here, this was also a goal. *Bene navigavi cum naufragium feci* . . . and he translated the *Ring* into Schopenhauerian language. Everything goes wrong, everything goes to rack and ruin, the new world is just as bad as the old one: Nonentity, the Indian Circe beckons. . . . Brunnhilda, who according to the old plan had to retire with a song in honour of free love, consoling the world with the hope of a socialistic Utopia in which 'all will be well'; now gets something else to do. She must first study Schopenhauer. She must first versify the fourth book of 'The World as Will and Idea'. *Wagner was saved* . . . Joking apart, this *was* a salvation. The service which Wagner owes to Schopenhauer is incalculable. It was the *philosopher of decadence* who allowed the *artist of decadence* to find himself' (pp. 10–11).

This theme of the connection of Wagner, Schopenhauer,

and Christianity with 'decadence' is most clearly stated by
Nietzsche. 'Wagner had the virtue of *décadents*—pity . . .'
(p. 22). Again, '. . . Wagner is a seducer on a grand scale.
There is nothing exhausted, nothing effete, nothing
dangerous to life, nothing that slanders the world in the
realm of spirit which has not secretly found shelter in his
art; he conceals the blackest obscurantism in the luminous
orbs of the ideal. He flatters every nihilistic (Buddhistic)
instinct and togs it out in music; he flatters every form of
Christianity, every religious expression of decadence. . . .
Music is the form of Circe . . . in this respect his last work in
his greatest masterpiece. In the art of seduction *Parsifal*
will for ever maintain its rank as a stroke of genius . . .'
(pp. 39–40). What was it that Nietzsche missed in Wagner?
He answers the question in *The Case of Wagner*. It was
'*la gaya scienza*; light feet, wit, fire, grave, grand logic,
stellar dancing, wanton intellectuality, the vibrating light
of the South, the calm sea—perfection'—in fact all that
Nietzsche thought he had found in Bizet and in his friend
Peter Gast—life, in short, as opposed to decadence, corruption, death. This may seem strange in view of what
Nietzsche had affirmed of Wagner at an earlier period; but,
just as he had formerly read himself into Schopenhauer, so
he had formerly read himself into Wagner. 'I began by
interpreting Wagner's mind as the expression of a Dionysian
powerfulness of soul. In it I thought I heard the earthquake
by means of which a primeval life-force, which had been
constrained for ages, was seeking at last to burst its bonds,
quite indifferent to how much of that which nowadays calls
itself culture, would thereby be shaken to ruins. You see
how I misinterpreted, you see also, what I *bestowed* upon
Wagner and Schopenhauer—myself. . . '. In reality Wagner
and Schopenhauer 'both deny life, they both slander it but
precisely on this account they are my antipodes'.[1] '*Parsifal*
is a work of rancour, of revenge, of the most secret concoction of poisons with which to make an end of the first
conditions of life; *it is a bad work*'.[2]

---

[1] *Nietzsche contra Wagner*, pp. 65–6.
[2] Ibid., pp. 72–3.

As a matter of fact, although Nietzsche accuses Wagner of being 'a crawly and desperate *décadent*', who 'suddenly fell helpless and broken on his knees before the Christian cross', he was under no illusion concerning Wagner's credentials as a spokesman for Christianity. 'To cast side-long glances at master-morality, at *noble* morality . . . and at the same time to have the opposite teaching, the 'gospel of the lowly', the doctrine of the *need* of salvation, on one's lips! . . . Incidentally, I admire the modesty of Christians who go to Bayreuth. As for myself, I could *not* endure to hear the sound of certain words on Wagner's lips. There are some concepts which are too good for Bayreuth . . . What? Christianity adjusted for female Wagnerites, perhaps *by* female Wagnerites—for, in his latter days Wagner was thoroughly *feminini generis*? Again I say, the Christians of to-day are too modest for me. . . . If Wagner were a Christian, then Liszt was perhaps a Father of the Church! The need of *salvation*, the quintessence of all Christian needs, has nothing in common with such clowns. . .'[1]. In spite of his hostility to Christianity, Nietzsche always respected genuine Christians.

Thus Nietzsche came to reject his 'great teacher Schopen-hauer' because of the latter's negative attitude towards life, because of his assertion of 'the value of the "unegoistic" instincts, the instincts of pity, self-denial, and self-sacrifice which Schopenhauer had so persistently painted in golden colours, deified and etherealized, that eventually they appeared to him, as it were, high and dry, as "intrinsic values in themselves", on the strength of which he uttered both to Life and to himself his own negation'. It was in these instincts that Nietzsche came to see 'the *great* danger of mankind, its most sublime temptation and seduction— seduction to what? to nothingness?—in these very instincts I saw the beginning of the end, stability, the exhaustion that gazes backwards, the will turning *against* Life. . .: I realized that the morality of pity which spread wider and wider, and whose grip infected even philosophers with its disease, was the most sinister symptom of our modern European

[1] *Case of Wagner*, pp. 49–50.

civilization . . .' (Preface to *Genealogy of Morals*, pp. 7–8). But in spite of this rejection Nietzsche maintained the value of Schopenhauer as an educator, as representing a stage on the road to spiritual freedom. Thus although he did not want his friend Heinrich von Stein, 'who died at such an unpardonably early age', to remain in the swamp of Schopenhauerianism, he recognized the value of such a phase in his intellectual development.[1] For the philosophy of Schopenhauer continued to have for Nietzsche this merit, that it exposed the falsity of transcendental and super-natural views and acted as a corrective to optimism of the Hegelian type. In other words, Nietzsche considered that Schopenhauer might well perform for others the office he had performed for Nietzsche himself, of convincing him of atheism. But though Schopenhauer has his value, it is necessary to pass beyond him, to use him against himself 'I counsel everybody not to fight shy of such paths (Wagner and Schopenhauer). The wholly *unphilosophic* feeling of remorse has become quite strange to me'. 'I leave my loftiest duty to the end, and that is to thank Wagner and Schopenhauer publicly, and to make them as it were take sides against themselves'.[2]

If Nietzsche passed beyond Schopenhauer, what did he profess to substitute for Schopenhauerian pity and Schopen-hauerian pessimism, for Schopenhauer's 'no' to Life? He professed to substitute strength, joy, affirmation of Life, the creative work of preparing for the Superman. But this substitution rests on the same foundation as that of Schopenhauer, on atheism and the doctrine of the irrationality and meaninglessness of Life. Nietzsche maintained the Eternal Recurrence, the cyclic return of all phenomena, and though he may possibly stress the doctrine to a less degree in his later period, when his hopes and aspirations are centred on the coming of the Superman, it certainly does not appear that he ever abandoned the doctrine. But the doctrine of the Eternal Recurrence logically involves pessimism, for it

---

[1] Nietzsche's friend, Professor Paul Deussen of Kiel, remained an adherent of Schopenhauer.
[2] *Selected Aphorisms*, 74 and 73.

excludes the notion that there is any given end for life—all teleology is banished. Nietzsche, of course, realized this, and so he declared that an end must be given to life, that man himself must give that end and must construct a meaning for Life through his own creative work. 'The Superman is the meaning of the earth. Let your will say: the Superman *shall be* the meaning of the earth!' [1] But is this more than the petulant cry of the man who realizes the meaninglessness of things and who rebels against that frightful vision, who refuses to resign himself and sets his will against the blind Will that lies at the heart of all phenomena? That there is a gulf between Schopenhauer and Nietzsche is undeniable, for the one preaches resignation, the other defiance, the one conformity, denial, asceticism, the other rebellion, affirmation, strength, and action; but the same vision is common to both, the vision of the irrationality of things. Is there, then, any place for real joy, for a real optimism in the philosophy of Nietzsche: is not his 'optimism' an optimism of despair, that refuses to recognize itself as such? Does it not seem that the difference between Schopenhauer and Nietzsche is not so much a difference of philosophy as a fundamental difference of tone and of temperament? The Indian resignation of the one is profoundly different from the European activism of the other, but the metaphysical basis is the same. Nietzsche may affirm Life, Life as the Will to Power, but nothing can alter the fact that that Will is a blind Will. Schopenhauer and Nietzsche are as two brothers who are unlike in temperament yet spring from a common parentage.

To pass beyond Schopenhauer it is necessary to pass beyond Nietzsche, too. If to pass beyond Schopenhauer means to pass beyond pessimism, then it is necessary also to pass beyond a philosophy, which, however much it may affirm joy, is founded on a pessimistic basis. Possibly one may be accused of misusing the term 'pessimism'. Schopenhauer's philosophy can justly be termed pessimistic in that he emphasizes the suffering and misery of existence and represents life as evil and undesirable. Nietzsche, on the contrary, represents life as good and desirable: he calls, not

[1] *Prologue to Zarathustra*, p. 7.

for less life, for not-being, for Nirvana, but for more life, more vigorous life, more joyful life. How, then, can his philosophy be termed pessimistic and coupled with that of Schopenhauer? As a matter of fact, Nietzsche, as mentioned before, ascribes joy as one of the chief characteristics of Schopenhauer: the latter is joyful, 'because his thought has conquered the greatest difficulties'. No doubt he later considered that in *Schopenhauer as Educator* he had been attributing his own joy to Schopenhauer; but Nietzsche's concept of joy remained the same, that 'there is only joy where there is victory'. Victory over what? Victory over the clear vision of suffering, of the irrationality of life. The Schopenhauerian ascetic achieves victory over this vision in one way, the Nietzschean in another way; but the vision is the same. Both thinkers view life as without ultimate meaning, and so both may justifiably be termed pessimistic. The pessimism of the ordinary man who is temperamentally inclined to look on the black side of things—though he may believe that life has some ultimate meaning and value— is but superficially a pessimist: his pessimism is but a surface-pessimism in comparison with the pessimism of him whose gaze has penetrated to the roots of things and has seen there the abyss of irrationality. And on this fundamental pessimism both Schopenhauer and Nietzsche are agreed. They may have reacted very differently to this vision and their respective 'ethics' may widely diverge, but beneath them both is the yawning abyss.

At the present time we are concerned with the struggle for the preservation of cultural values, and Nietzsche's ideal was certainly the man of the deepest and widest culture, as opposed to the 'blond beast' on the one hand or the *merely* learned on the other. But who will be so bold as to assert that Nietzsche provides us with a philosophy which can be of real service to the contemporary war-racked world? Some of his ideas are of permanent value (how could it be otherwise with a man of Nietzsche's calibre?)—the idea of European unity for instance—but these are incidental elements in his thought. His failure to construct a philosophy which can have a real message for us to-day, is precisely that

notion which attracted him in the philosophy of Schopenhauer—the notion of atheism. 'God is dead', proclaimed
Zarathustra—and thereby the Nietzschean man became
only-man, a man condemned to death, the abyss of meaninglessness. The end given to the world may be the Superman,
but what is the end of the Superman? Life? But this life
is a life to death, a mere moment in the Eternal Recurrence,
a bubble on the sea of irrationality. The world has no
meaning, life has no meaning, man has no meaning—
because 'God is dead'. The Nietzschean man is like the man
of Martin Heidegger, whose very existence is a *Gegenwart
aus Vergangenheit in Zukunft*, who is always in the grip of
death. 'Death', says Heidegger, 'is a kind of being which
seizes upon man from his birth'. Death, that is only death,
is the seal of meaninglessness, and man, who is only man, is
a figure of unrelieved tragedy. It is only if God is not dead,
only if man is not simply a being-to-death but a being-to-
God, that life can have meaning and that talk of the conservation of values and of culture can be more than a
pastime.

Schopenhauer's   metaphysic   excludes   Christianity;
Nietzsche despised Christianity as decadent, weak, anti-Life.
In point of fact the Christian philosophy includes all that
is of value in the thought of both Schopenhauer and
Nietzsche.   Christian philosophers have certainly not
failed to recognize that there is a problem of suffering and
evil; they have certainly not attempted to justify everything that is or to characterize everything as rational
precisely as it stands, even if it is used to subserve a rational
end. Though few would go so far as to declare with
Dostoievsky in *Letters from the Underworld*, 'You can say anything about the history of the world; anything that the
wildest brain can conceive, but you cannot pretend one
thing: that it is reasonable. Your tongue would refuse to
utter the words', yet Augustine, Thomas Aquinas, Pascal,
etc., would show some sympathy with Schopenhauer's
reaction against Hegel (though Hegel, of course, never denied
the *existence* of suffering: he was no Christian Scientist).
Even if the 'theodicies' of Augustine, Aquinas, Leibniz, etc.,

have not completely solved the mystery of suffering (how should they?), they have not failed to realize that there is a problem. But they did not allow their vision of the fact of suffering and evil to absorb them: they saw also the reality of values, and they saw them against the Transcendent Background. (The validity of their metaphysical arguments on this question is obviously not a subject that can be here discussed.)

Nietzsche accused Christians of saying 'no' to Life, of encouraging weakness and decadence, of reducing everybody to the equality of the herd. But he forgets the words of the Founder of Christianity: 'I am come that they may have Life and may have it more abundantly'. True, supernatural life is for Nietzsche an empty concept, a thin, ghostly illusion; but so it must be for all for whom 'God is dead'. Yet, whatever may be the case with less perfect Christians, the 'Supermen' of Christianity have been conspicuous for their Yea-saying to Life in its fullest and deepest sense. That great thinker, Henri Bergson, speaking of the Christian mystics, points out how 'from their increased vitality there radiated an extraordinary energy, daring, power of conception and realization. Just think of what was accomplished in the field of action by a St. Paul, a St. Teresa, a St. Catherine of Sienna, a St. Francis, a Joan of Arc, and how many others besides!' [1] Of the soul united to God Bergson says again, 'Let us say that henceforth for the soul there is a superabundance of life. There is a boundless impetus. There is an irresistible impulse which hurls it into vast enterprises. A calm exaltation of all its faculties makes it see things on a vast scale only, and, in spite of its own weakness, produce only what can be mightily wrought. . . .' [2] The yes to Life of the Christian 'Superman' is far truer than the yes of the Nietzschean *Übermensch*, for it is a yes to Life in its totality, not merely to the natural life but to the supernatural life, and ultimately a yes to the superabundant Source of all Life, the God Who is not dead but Life itself.

And what of the equalizing reduction to the herd?

---

[1] *The Two Sources of Morality and Religion*, Macmillan, p. 194.
[2] Ibid., p. 198.

Christian philosophers obviously do not consider that men are all equally strong or equally beautiful or equally clever. Nor do they even consider that all men are equal before God—since they are no more equally good and holy than they are equally intelligent. But what Christian philosophers do hold is that each human person is of value, and that no human person can legitimately be made a mere means to any other human person—agreeing in this with that 'old Kant', who was one of Nietzsche's *bêtes-noires*. That human beings should be made mere means to the fulfilment of the Will to Power of 'Superman', some megalomaniac Führer, is to them irrational and absurd. We have argued elsewhere that the Nazi leaders are but a caricature of Nietzsche's ideal Superman, and that he would have held the National-Socialism of modern Germany in abhorrence. But Nietzsche certainly admired Napoleon (a hero of the younger Hegel too); and in any case it is difficult to see how in Nietzsche's philosophy the man-in-the-street could have any real value other than contributing in some way to the coming of the *Übermensch* and furthering his development. The Christian philosopher agrees with Schopenhauer in inculcating the virtues of compassion and sympathy, while denying the metaphysical identity of all men in the one blind Will, for he affirms their unity-in-diversity as children of the one Father. He agrees with Nietzsche that man must be free, a bearer of life, but he affirms that man must be free with the freedom of the sons of God, and that his highest privilege is to be a bearer of the life which springs from an undying Fountain in the invisible depths of Eternity.

CHAPTER VIII

THE COLD MONSTER

THOUGH I cannot believe that Nietzsche would have looked with favour on the National-Socialist Movement of modern Germany (he would have considered it a caricature of his doctrine), Nietzsche's doctrine of the new Table of Values, of egoism, of the denial of pity, etc., would appear to lead *in the concrete* to such phenomena as that of the unscrupulous and ruthless dictator. But that Nietzsche is to be esteemed a 'Totalitarian', an Absolutist in regard to the State, is entirely incorrect. Nietzsche was essentially individualist and neither the State nor the nation nor the race were to him the highest productions of human culture. The Superman is the meaning of the world (as far as there can be any talk of 'meaning of the world' on Nietzsche's theories), and certainly not an impersonal, or even 'superpersonal', institution. There is certainly a sense in which it is true to say that Nietzsche stands in the line of German philosophical thinkers, but his attitude towards the Hegelian doctrine of the State is one, not of acceptance, but of reaction and rejection. Nietzsche states his point of view in unequivocal terms: for instance in *Schopenhauer as Educator* he remarks, that 'We are feeling the consequence of the doctrine preached lately from all the housetops, that the State is the highest end of man, and there is no higher duty than to serve it: I regard this not a relapse into paganism, but into stupidity'.[1]

Nietzsche will not allow that the State originated in a contract or compact—he calls this a 'fantastic theory'[2]: on the contrary the State has a 'horrible origin', being the creation of violence and conquest. 'A herd of black beasts of prey, a race of conquerors and masters, which with all its warlike organizations and all its organizing power pounces with its terrible claws on a population, in numbers possibly tremendously superior, but as yet formless, as yet nomad. Such is the origin of the "State".'[3] The State is thus born of the Will to Power, and at the root of its foundation lies the maxim, that 'Power gives the first *right*, and there is no right, which at bottom is not presumption, usurpation, violence'.[4] The State is thus 'of ignominiously low birth, for the majority of men a continually flowing source of hardship', and one can see on all sides 'the monuments of its origin—devastated lands, destroyed cities, brutalized men,

---

[1] *Thoughts out of Season*, ii, p. 135.　　[2] *Genealogy of Morals*, p. 103.
[3] Ibid.　　[4] *Greek State*, p. 10.

devouring hatred of nations'. Yet in spite of all this it comes about that the State 'is even contemplated with fervour as the goal and ultimate aim of the sacrifices and duties of the individual'; it becomes 'a battle cry, which has filled men with enthusiasm for innumerable really heroic deeds, perhaps the highest and most venerable object for the blind and egoistic multitude which only in the tremendous moments of State life has the strange expression of greatness on its face!' This transformation of the creation of violence and rapine into the object of fervent devotion and self-sacrifice is brought about by Nature herself. Nature has a purpose to be realized in and through the State, and she spreads as it were a veil over the terrible origin of the State, so that 'hearts involuntarily go out towards the magic of the growing State with the presentiment of an invisible deep purpose, where the calculating intellect is enabled to see an addition of forces only'.[1] What is this purpose of Nature? It is the foundation of Society. The 'final end' is the 'birth' of these privileged Culture-men, 'in whose service everything else must be devoured', and Society is necessary as a basis for the higher men. Nature, then, 'in order to arrive at Society, forges for herself the cruel tool of State', by which the 'raw material of a semi-animal populace was not only thoroughly kneaded and elastic, but also moulded'.[2] The majority of men are in the dark as to what Nature intends in her 'State-instinct' and follow it blindly; but there are some who stand outside the instinct and who know what *they* want from the State. The latter will gain influence in the State and use it as a *means*, whereas the majority, being under the sway of the unconscious purposes of the State, 'are themselves only means for the fulfilment of the State purpose'.

The State has thus a function to play in the promotion of culture, since it is the means of moulding society, which is the necessary presupposition for the aristocracy of the higher men. Nietzsche, for instance, fully recognizes the repellent aspect of Greek city-life—the 'bloody jealousy of city against city, of party against party, this murderous greed

---

[1] *Greek State*, p. 10. [2] *Genealogy of Morals*, p. 103.

of those little wars, the tiger-like triumph over the corpse of the slain enemy'—and asks, 'What is its excuse before the tribunal of eternal justice ?' He answers: 'Proud and calm, the State steps before this tribunal and by the hand it leads the flower of blossoming womanhood: Greek society. For this Helena the State waged those wars—and what grey-bearded judge could here condemn ?'[1] In Nietzsche's opinion the ancient State did not recognize as culture only what was directly useful to the State itself, and so was far more favourable to culture than the modern-Prussian-State, which 'assumes the attitude of a mystagogue of culture', and while professing to promote education and culture is really only serving its own interests and spreading a pseudo-culture that has little in common with the real German spirit.[2] The self-interest of the State requires the greatest possible breadth and universality of culture, and to that extent it certainly promotes culture; (there is an important qualification to be introduced, which we will mention presently); but Nietzsche remarks rather caustically, that 'in large States public education will always be extremely mediocre, for the same reason that in large kitchens the cooking is at best only mediocre'.[3] A further service of the State to culture is that in the State or organized society there is—historically at least—a division of classes, and a higher culture can only originate where there exists such a division, 'that of the working class, and that of the leisured class who are capable of true leisure'.[4]

But though the State has a function to play in the promotion of culture, in that it is a tool for the moulding of that Society without which a true culture is impossible, the State is but a *means* to culture and not the end. 'He who cannot reflect upon the position of affairs in Society without melancholy, who has learnt to conceive of it as the continual painful birth of those privileged Culture-men, in whose service everything else must be devoured—he will no longer be deceived by that false glamour, which the moderns

---

[1] *Greek State*, p. 12.
[2] *Future of our Educ. Instit.*, lect. 3.
[3] *Human, All-too-Human*, i, aph. 467.
[4] Ibid., 439.

have spread over the origin and meaning of the State. For what can the State mean to us, if not the means by which that social-process described just now is to be fused and to be guaranteed in its unimpeded continuance?' The fruit of true culture is the Superman, and the Superman is beyond the State. 'There, where the State ceaseth—there only commenceth the man who is not superfluous: there commenceth the song of the necessary ones, the single and irreplaceable melody.

'There, where the State *ceaseth*—pray look thither, my brethren! Do ye not see it, the rainbow and the bridges of the Superman?'[1]

The State, however, is only too inclined to look on itself as the be-all and end-all of the historic process and to plume itself as the 'mystagogue of culture': its concrete tendency is thus to render culture mediocre and static, subservient to the practical interests of the State, and to hinder the growth of true culture. A highly civilized state 'generally implies at the present time the task of setting free the spiritual forces of a generation just so far as they may be of use to the existing institutions', and this 'setting-free' comes to mean rather 'chaining-up'. Nietzsche takes as a comparison 'what the self-interest of the state has done for Christianity', thinking primarily no doubt of the Protestant religion. 'Christianity is one of the purest manifestations of the impulse towards culture and the production of the saint, but being used in countless ways to turn the mills of the State authorities it gradually became sick at heart, hypocritical, and degenerate, and in antagonism with its original aim'.[2] The root of the matter is that 'the State has never any concern with truth, but only with the truth useful to it, or rather with anything that is useful to it, be it truth, half-truth, or error'.[3] That the state for example should attempt a coalition with philosophy and demand of candidates for degrees in universities an examination in philosophy (Nietzsche is thinking of course of the system of State universities) is absurd. 'It would certainly be a noble thing

[1] *Zarathustra*, p. 57.   [2] *Thoughts out of Season*, ii, p. 161.
[3] Ibid., p. 196.

for the state to have truth as a paid servant; but it knows well enough that it is the essence of truth to be paid nothing and serve nothing'.[1]

The State therefore, which is concerned with the formation of obedient citizens, tends to hinder the growth of free culture: it statifies and stereotypes. In *Human, All-too-Human* Nietzsche passes a severer judgment on the Greek city than he had done in his essay on *The Greek State*. In the latter composition he had compared the Greek city's attitude to culture with that of the German State greatly to the advantage of the former, but in *Human, All-too-Human* he declares that 'The Greek *polis* was like every organizing political power, exclusive and distrustful of the growth of culture; its powerful fundamental impulse seemed almost solely to have a paralysing and obstructive effect thereon . . . the education laid down in the State laws was meant to be obligatory on all generations to keep them at *one* stage of development'.[2] Yet Nietzsche always maintained that the State tends to exercise a retarding influence on the growth of culture, as he understood it; and we can therefore have no difficulty in understanding that for him 'Totalitarianism'—whether Nazi, Fascist, or Socialist—is condemned in advance. I have already quoted his comment in *Schopenhauer as Educator*, to the effect that the doctrine of man's highest end being the service of the state represents a relapse into stupidity; and I will now refer to the chapter in *Zarathustra*, entitled *The New Idol*. It is a famous chapter, which has often been quoted and is essential to an understanding of Nietzsche's attitude towards the State. 'A state? What is that? Well! open now your ears unto me, for now will I say unto you my word concerning the death of peoples.

'A state is called the coldest of all cold monsters. Coldly lieth it also; and this lie creepeth from its mouth: "I, the state, am the people".

'It is a lie! Creators were they who created peoples, and hung a faith and a love over them: thus they served life.

'Destroyers are they who lay snares for many, and call it the state: they hang a sword and a hundred cravings over

---

[1] *Thoughts out of Season*, i, p. 196.   [2] *Human, All-too-Human*, i, aph. 474.

them'. The State is false and rotten, it 'lieth in all languages of good and evil: and whatever it saith it lieth; and whatever it hath it hath stolen.

'False is everything in it; with stolen teeth it biteth the biting one. False are even its bowels'. Nietzsche shows his complete disagreement with the Totalitarian doctrine, with the 'Hegelian' doctrine of the State, in the following passage. 'On earth there is nothing greater than I: it is I who am the regulating finger of God—thus roareth the monster. And not only the long-eared and short-sighted fall upon their knees'! The State is 'the new idol' which tries to attract around it in an attitude of wondering worship the heroes and honourable ones. 'Gladly it basketh in the sunshine of good consciences—the cold monster'! The State exists for the 'many too many', it swallows up indiscriminately 'good' and 'bad'. In the State men seek for wealth as the lever of power, clambering over one another and thus scuffling into the mud and the abyss. It is only where the State ceaseth that Superman, the product of true culture, can begin.

When Nietzsche condemns idolatry of the State, the 'cold monster', we can only applaud: Man does not exist for the State but the State for man. And it is only too true that when the State sets itself up as the great idol, a mortal deathblow is inevitably dealt at culture. How for example can philosophy flourish in a society like that of Soviet Russia, where it is made into an instrument of the Proletariat Revolution and thinkers are bound hand and foot? How can the study of history advance if historians are bound to expound the Nazi myth of the Race Theory? Moreover it can scarcely be denied that when universal education is imparted by the State, according to the exclusive standards of the State, practical efficiency in citizenship is the one end aimed at and a mediocre level of culture is like to result. The passion for uniformity, for moulding all minds to a pattern, has a disastrous result, since those who are not naturally contented to think as the State prescribes, will either surrender in the end to mediocrity or they will become revolutionary in mentality, even if not in practice. (It is significant that F. H. Bradley, who certainly tended to the

Hegelian doctrine of the State, recognized a *non-social* sphere of culture.) But while recognizing the dangers inherent in all worship of the State, whether Fascist, Socialist, or Democratic, it is a mistake to go to the opposite extreme and to regard the State as essentially anti-cultural. On the contrary man is a social animal by nature, and it is only in organized society that he can develop his powers to the full: to society we owe our education, the social milieu, which is essential to the development of character and talent, and to society we owe the means of extending and deepening culture, whether in the masses or in outstanding individuals. Nietzsche recognizes, as we have seen, the part played by the State in the promotion of culture, but he certainly also speaks as though the State were of its very nature a drag on culture. This is true, if by State be meant the self-idolatrous State, the 'cold monster', but it is not true if applied to the State simply as such. We have no wish to uphold the 'liberal' idea of the State as a police force for the protection of property (in my opinion Hegel rightly refuses to recognize in such a society the real notion of the State), but there is a half-way house between the 'liberal' idea of the State and the 'totalitarian' idea of the State. The State is a 'perfect society', as canonists say, on the temporal plane, and it is to a great extent in and through organized society or the State that culture arises and develops: it is only when the State regards itself as an absolute end and subordinates all the phenomena of culture to its own immediate practical interests, that it becomes inimical to culture.

The State is not the absolute end of man—but neither is the production of Superman the absolute end of man. In condemning State-idolatry Nietzsche was right, but in regarding Superman (in his sense) as the end of culture he was equally certainly wrong. The end of culture is the development of the powers of man, including those of outstanding men, to the *glory of God*. If we wish to borrow Hegelian language we can say that the end of the historical process is the manifestation of God or the Absolute, and that the Absolute is manifested—or God glorified—in the fullest harmonious unfolding of man's powers. Such a doctrine would of course be abhorrent to Nietzsche who denies all 'Transcendentalism'; but it must never be forgotten that Nietzsche merely stated his philosophy, he never proved it. Indeed on his premises it could never be proved, for—once atheism is granted—the world has no meaning: it can be *given* a meaning, it is true, but then what right has one man to claim that the meaning *he* wishes to give to life shall be accepted by others? To speak of the purposes of Nature is but metaphor. The 'world-historical' men have been often treated in a sorry way by 'Nature', and there is no reason to suppose that Nietzsche's Supermen would fare any better. In any case they themselves would be swallowed up in the Eternal Recurrence. To the questions: 'Why should the majority of men serve as a foundation for the Superman?' or 'What right has the Superman over against State and society?' Nietzsche could offer no satisfactory answer. It is useless to speak of Nature's purposes, for 'Nature'—in an atheistic philosophy—can have no 'purpose'. We can only speak of 'purpose' if ultimate Reality is God or Mind, and it would scarcely be an easy task to show that God had made man a social animal, while at the same time the end of society is simply the production of a Superman who stands beyond society, a law to himself, the free and atheistic aristocrat of culture.

In treating of Nietzsche's doctrine of the State it seems only right to say something of his opinions concerning War, which have sometimes been misrepresented. That Nietzsche in places extols war and the benefits conferred by war, that he lauds the warrior and the warlike spirit, is quite true, but these passages should not be stressed to the exclusion of those other passages in which he clearly recognizes the evils due to war. Moreover war *has* its good aspects: if it were an unmixed evil, then under *no* circumstances would it be justified. It would be far preferable if man were so disposed inwardly that wars never took place, but, given the concrete historical situation and given the actual behaviour of man, war must be admitted as a legitimate means of securing right, even if it should be adopted only in the last resort. This is not the place to canvass the question, whether a just war is or is not a possibility in modern society. The author of this book believes that it is a possibility, and he believes in the justice of the Allies' recourse to arms in the present war, but in any case it follows from the natural right of self-defence that war cannot be condemned as always and intrinsically evil. Every Catholic must admit this. And if war is not always and intrinsically evil, it follows that it has its good aspects and that true benefits may accrue from war. But to see the good side of war is not at all the same thing as loving war for its own sake. If a human body has become so diseased that the surgeon's knife is necessary, we may recognize the beneficial function of the knife, while deploring the facts that the body has been permitted to get into such a state, supposing that the progress of the disease could have been arrested earlier by less drastic means.

In his essay on *The Greek State* Nietzsche states that 'Against the deviation of the State-tendency into a money-tendency . . . the only remedy is war and once again war, in the emotions of which this at least becomes obvious, that the State is not founded upon the fear of the war-demon as a protective institution for egoistic individuals, but in love to fatherland and prince it produces an ethical impulse, indicative of a much higher destiny'. One cannot help feeling a bit sceptical as to war's power of upsetting the 'money-aristocracy', at least if its remedial power be cate-gorically asserted. Nietzsche considers war the only remedy —and presumably a sure remedy—for a condition of affairs, in which the 'international homeless money-hermits' 'abuse politics as a means of the Exchange, and State and Society as an apparatus for their own enrichment'. He accordingly says that we will have to pardon his 'occasionally chanting a Paean on war'. 'Horribly clangs its silvery bow, and although it comes along like the night, War is nevertheless Apollo, the true divinity for consecrating and purifying the State'. A similar conception of war as a purifying force is to be found in *Human, All-too-Human*. 'War as a remedy.— For nations that are growing weak and contemptible war may be prescribed as a remedy, if indeed they really want to go on living. National consumption as well as individual admits of a brutal cure. The eternal will to live and inability to die is, however, in itself already a sign of senility of emotion. The more fully and thoroughly we live, the more ready we are to sacrifice life for a single pleasurable emotion. A people that lives and feels in this wise has no need of war'.[1]

Nietzsche thus extols war as a remedy for national enervation and decrepitude. Now war may afford a rallying-ground for the more vigorous and patriotic members of a nation, who, if victorious, may help to revivify their country; but it is never legitimate to embark on war as a remedy for national enervation. War in self-defence is legitimate, but not as a sort of gymnastic exercise. Moreover war is by no means always a remedy. If a nation embarks on an aggressive and unjust war from lust of power and greed of conquest, the effect of the war, if victorious, is to confirm the worst elements in that State and prolong the very evil— evil in our eyes at least—which caused the war. The wound enters deeper into the nation's soul. True, it may be healed, but it is through defeat that it will be healed. And did not Nietzsche explicitly deplore the evil effects of Germany's victory in 1870 on her own culture?

In *Thus Spake Zarathustra* Nietzsche devotes a chapter of the first part to *War and Warriors*, in which he addresses the warriors in these words: 'Ye shall love peace as a means to new wars—and the short peace more than the long'. 'War and courage', he says, 'have done more great things than charity. Not your sympathy, but your bravery hath hitherto saved the victims'. And in the same book Nietzsche says: 'Man shall be trained for war, and woman for the recreation of the warrior—all else is folly'.[2] Similar thoughts may be found in *The Twilight of the Idols*, when Nietzsche inveighs against the Christian desire for 'peace of soul', and maintains that 'the man who has renounced war has renounced a grand life'.[3] But it seems to the present writer that these passages should not be unduly pressed, for it is not necessary to suppose that Nietzsche is thinking primarily

[1] *Human, All-too-Human*, II, ii, aph. 187.   [2] *Zarathustra*, p. 75.
[3] *Twilight of the Idols*, p. 29.

of wars between States—or at any rate not exclusively—
he is thinking most of all of the warlike spirit. After all,
Christians exhort one another to be 'warriors', not to aim at
slothful ease and indifference. 'Warfare', 'victory', etc.—
such terms play an important part in the Christian
vocabulary. They refer to 'spiritual warfare', warfare against
self and against the 'powers of darkness', it is true, whereas
what Nietzsche says of warfare in *Zarathustra* certainly
includes warfare in the ordinary sense; but it would appear
that he includes a good deal more than warfare with swords,
guns, and shells—he is primarily thinking of an *attitude of
soul*, of the active, dynamic personality. It is absurd to
make a great deal of such a statement as the one quoted, that
'Man shall be trained for war'—i.e. as interpreted in the
exclusively militaristic sense—since Nietzsche's ideal man,
though a 'conqueror' and 'warrior' was by no means simply
a soldier. In the chapter on *War and Warriors* Nietzsche
exhorts his warriors: 'Let your love to life be love to your
highest hope, and let your highest hope be the highest
thought of life! Your highest thought, however, ye shall have
it commanded unto you by me—and it is this: man is
something that is to be surpassed'. He is thinking primarily
of the struggle for the advent of Superman and the fight
against all which hinders his coming.

In any case war is not an end in itself in Nietzsche's eyes:
he sees it in its relation to culture. He may no doubt
exaggerate or even mis-state the intimate relation of war
to culture, but the fact that culture, as he understands it,
is the end, should be sufficient to dispel the illusion that
Nietzsche was a bloodthirsty militarist, whose highest
ideal was that men should be slaughtering one another. In
the essay on David Strauss he remarks that 'it must be
confessed that a great victory is a great danger. Human
nature bears a triumph less easily than a defeat; indeed,
it might even be urged that it is simpler to gain a victory
of this sort than to turn it to such account that it may not
ultimately prove a serious rout'. In *Human, All-too-Human*,
he acknowledges that 'Against war it may be said that
it makes the victor stupid and the vanquished revengeful',

though he goes on to assert, 'In favour of war it may be said that it barbarizes in both its above-named results, and thereby makes more natural; it is the sleep or the winter period of culture; man emerges from it with greater strength for good and for evil'.[1] The same thought of the relation of war to culture is strikingly stated in aphorism 477 of the same book, *War Indispensable*. In this aphorism Nietzsche repeats his notion that war is necessary for the recovery of enervated nations. 'For the present we know of no other means whereby the rough energy of the camp, the deep impersonal hatred, the cold-bloodedness of murder with a good conscience, the general ardour of the system in the destruction of the enemy, the proud indifference to great losses, to one's own existence and that of one's friends, the hollow, earthquake-like convulsion of the soul can be as forcibly and certainly communicated to enervated nations as is done by every great war'. 'Culture', he says, 'can by no means dispense with passions, vices, and malignities'. He admits that the Engish, 'who appear on the whole to have . . . renounced war', adopt other means in order to generate anew vanishing forces of the soul—means such as 'dangerous exploring expeditions, sea-voyages, and mountaineerings', which 'bring home surplus strength from adventures and dangers of all kinds'. He thinks, however, that 'such a highly cultivated and therefore necessarily enfeebled humanity as that of modern Europe not only needs wars, but the greatest and most terrible wars—consequently occasional relapses into barbarism—lest, by the means of culture, it should lose its culture and its very existence'. It may be true that war serves to unsettle the condition of bourgeois contentment and shake the conviction of inevitable progress and of the all-sufficing character of materialistic civilization, but war is certainly not the only means of effecting this result. Christianity effected a renewal of soul, but it did so by a spiritual and not by a 'militaristic' warfare.

That war occasions acts of heroism and self-sacrifice, that it reveals depths of goodness and of evil hitherto unsuspected, is obvious to all; but one of the great objections to

---

[1] *Human, All-too-Human*, i, aph. 444.

war is that it is precisely the heroic and self-sacrificing elements that are destroyed. The young and ardent go forth to battle, and so may never return. Now Nietzsche recognized of course this waste of war, and stated it in clear terms. A relevant passage from the first volume of *Human, All-too-Human*, merits quotation. It is headed *The National Army*.

'The greatest disadvantage of the national army, now so much glorified, lies in the squandering of men of the highest civilization; it is only by the favourableness of all circumstances that there are such men at all; how carefully and anxiously should we deal with them, since long periods are requred to create the chance conditions for the production of such delicately organized brains! But as the Greeks wallowed in the blood of Greeks, so do now Europeans in the blood of Europeans: and indeed, taken relatively, it is mostly the highly cultivated who are sacrificed, those who promise an abundant and excellent posterity; for such stand in the front of the battle as commanders, and also expose themselves to most danger by reason of their higher ambition. At present, when quite other and higher tasks are assigned than *patria* and *honor*, the rough Roman patriotism is either something dishonourable or a sign of being behind the times'.[1]

The mention of Europeans wallowing in the blood of Europeans naturally leads to Nietzsche's conception of a United Europe. Greek civilization had been marred by the constant wars between the various City States, in which Greek shed the blood of Greek: they never really succeeded in uniting, though they were subsequently subjected to the common domination of a foreign ruler. Similarly, European State fights European State, and it is not the worst men who lose their lives. This absurd state of affairs indicates the need for unity, which has been prefigured by the great culture-men of the past who were more than mere citizens of their own European culture and belong over and above their national allegiance to Europe as a whole. According to Nietzsche, it was 'only in their weaker moments, or when

[1] *Human, All-too-Human*, i, aph. 442.

they grew old', that they fell back into the national narrow-ness of the 'Fatherlanders'. He mentions Napoleon, Hein-rich Heine, Goethe, Beethoven, Stendhal, Schopenhauer. 'Perhaps Richard Wagner likewise belongs to their number, concerning whom, as a successful type of German obscurity, nothing can be said without some such "perhaps" '.[1]

These higher men already, if tentatively, anticipate the European synthesis of the future, but owing to the 'nationality-craze' and owing to the 'short-sighted and hasty-handed politicians' whom this craze helps to power, 'the most unmistakable signs that *Europe wishes to be one*, are now overlooked, or arbitrarily and falsely misinterpreted'.[2] This United Europe is, Nietzsche thinks, slowly preparing itself. 'I see over and beyond all these national wars, new "empires", and whatever else lies in the foreground. What I am concerned with—for I see it preparing itself slowly and hesitatingly—is the United Europe'.[3] Nietzsche does not enter into any detailed description of the new Europe; but how should he? What does not yet exist for itself, but is only in germ, can hardly be described. But he backs up his assertion by reference to the economic situation of contem-porary Europe. 'Money is even now compelling European nations to amalgamate into one Power'. 'The small States of Europe—I refer to all our present kingdoms and "empires" —will in a short time become economically untenable owing to the mad, uncontrolled struggle for the possession of local and international trade'.[4] The ease of travel is also a con-tributing factor. 'With the freedom of travel now existing, groups of men of the same kindred can join together and establish communal habits and customs. The overcoming of "nations" '.[5] Narrow nationalism is attacked by Nietzsche. 'A little more fresh air, for Heaven's sake! This ridiculous condition of Europe *must* not last any longer. Is there a single idea behind this bovine nationalism? What possible value can there be in encouraging this arrogant self-conceit when everything to-day points to greater and

---

[1] *Genealogy of Morals*, pp. 224–5.   [2] *Beyond Good and Evil*, aph. 256.
[3] *Genealogy of Morals*, p. 224.   [4] Ibid., p. 225.
[5] Ibid., p. 227.

more common interests?—at a moment when the spiritual dependence and denationalization, which are obvious to all, are paving the way for the reciprocal *rapprochements* and fertilizations which make up the real value and sense of present-day culture!'[1]

But let no one suppose that Nietzsche is envisaging a union of socialistic democracies as his ideal. On the contrary, he clings to his central notion of the 'order of rank', and democracy and socialism have seldom met with a more trenchant critic. Much of Nietzsche's criticism is very much to the point, especially when levelled against political theories that make no reference to a spiritual and religious foundation. To speak of 'freedom', of 'equality', of the 'rights of man' and so on, is all very well if man is the creature of God, if man has an immortal soul possessed of an eternal value: but what if man is just a moment in the development of a godless universe? How can there be any talk of 'rights' in such a universe? There may be conventional rights, true, but apart from this unstable factor it is difficult to see how there can be any 'right' save the right of the successful. This will sound shocking to the secularist democrat but if he would only deliver himself of his sentimentality—perhaps of his better *feelings*—and look on the world, i.e. *his* world, with a cold and rational mind, he would see the absurdity of his position. As a matter of fact the non-Christian democrat is enjoying a Christian inheritance, only he imagines that he can maintain conclusions of Christianity while dispensing with Christianity itself. Nietzsche was right when he remarked in *Beyond Good and Evil* that 'the *democratic* movement is the inheritance of the Christian movement'.[2] I do not mean to assert that Christianity necessarily implies a democratic form of government, but that the fundamental notions of the democrats—'rights of man', etc.—are *historically* derived from Christian thought.

Nietzsche allows that the democratic movement, with its accompanying 'levelling and mediocrizing of man', prepares a field for the rise of exceptional men—for the herd require a commander, a master—and 'that the democratizing of

---

[1] *Will to Power*, ii, aph. 748.   [2] Aph. 202.

Europe is at the same time an involuntary arrangement for the rearing of *tyrants*—taking the word in all its meanings, even in its most spiritual sense'.[1] But the democratic movement in itself, being a herd-movement, hates the élite— ' "The Will to Power" is so loathed in democratic ages that the whole of the psychology of these ages seems directed towards its belittlement and slander'.[2] However, inasmuch as it prepares the way for the new aristocracy, it may be said to be 'redeemed' in the coming aristocracy, the lords of the earth. 'And would not the democratic movement itself find for the first time a sort of goal, salvation, and justification, if some one appeared who availed himself of it—so that at last, besides its new and sublime product, slavery (for this must be the end of European democracy), that higher species of ruling and Cæsarian spirits might also be produced, which would stand upon it, hold to it, and would elevate themselves through it? This new race would climb aloft to new and hitherto impossible things, to a broader vision, and to its task on earth'.[3]

The motive power of socialism Nietzsche finds in 'envy and laziness'[4]—laziness, for the crowd desire to do as little work as possible, envy, because they hate 'the better social caste'. But he clearly recognizes that Socialism is provoked by the luxurious living of the wealthy and by the same lust for possession that animates the *bourgeoisie*. 'The only remedy against Socialism that still lies in your power is to avoid provoking Socialism—in other words, to live in moderation and contentment, to prevent as far as possible all lavish display, and to aid the State as far as possible in its taxing of all superfluities and luxuries. You do not like this remedy? Then you rich bourgeois who call yourselves "Liberals", confess that it is your own inclination that you find so terrible and menacing in Socialists, but allow to prevail in yourselves as unavoidable, as if with you it were something different. As you are constituted, if you had not your fortune and the cares of maintaining it, this bent of

---

[1] *Beyond Good and Evil*, aph. 242.
[2] *Will to Power*, ii, aph. 751.
[3] Ibid., 954.
[4] *Human, All-too-Human*, i, aph. 480.

yours would make Socialists of you. Possession alone differentiates you from them. If you wish to conquer the assailants of your prosperity, you must first conquer your-selves'.[1] Surely Nietzsche is right. When one hears the 'haves' deploring the greed of the 'have-nots', one cannot but suspect that if they themselves were in the position of the 'have-nots' they would manifest identical symptoms. Nietzsche's words sound like those of a preacher, when he addresses the bourgeoisie in reference to their selfish hedonism—'your houses, dresses, carriages, shops, the demands of your palates and your tables, your noisy operatic and musical enthusiasm; lastly your women, formed and fashioned but of base metal, gilded but without the ring of gold, chosen by you for show and considering themselves meant for show—these are the things that spread the poison of that national disease, which seizes the masses ever more and more as a Socialistic heart-itch, but has its origin and breeding-place in you. Who shall now arrest this epidemic ?'[2]

There is an interesting passage in the second volume of *Human, All-too-Human* in which Nietzsche distinguishes Democracy and Socialism, and declares that 'The masses are as far as possible removed from Socialism as a doctrine of altering the acquisition of property. If once they get the steering-wheel into their hands, through great majorities in their Parliaments, they will attack with progressive taxa-tion the whole dominant system of capitalists, merchants, and financiers, and will in fact slowly create a middle class which may forget Socialism like a disease that has been over-come'.[3] The practical result of this victory of democracy will, says Nietzsche, 'be a European league of nations, in which each individual nation, delimited by the proper geo-graphical frontiers, has the position of a canton with its separate rights. Small account will be taken of the historic memories of previously existing nations, because the pious affection for these memories will be gradually uprooted under the democratic régime, with all its craze for novelty and

[1] *Human, All-too-Human*, ii, aph. 304.   [2] Ibid.
[3] *Wanderer and his Shadow*, aph. 292.

experiment. The corrections of frontiers that will prove
necessary will be so carried out as to serve the interests of the
federation, but not that of any venerable memories'.[1] Not
that Nietzsche desires a democratized League of Nations as
an end in itself—far from it—though it may be desirable, in
so far as it may form a substructure for the coming
aristocracy.

From the somewhat disjointed remarks contained in this
chapter it should be clear that the political thought of
Nietzsche is conditioned by his ruling idea, the higher man,
the aristocratic culture. The State is beneficial in so far as
it effects the close formation of Society, which is necessary
to the rise of true culture, but harmful in so far as it turns
itself into an idol, subordinates all elements to its own
practical interests, and hinders the rise of free and creative
spirits. War is beneficial in so far as it revivifies the flagging
spirit of a nation, affords an outlet for military ardour and
heroic devotion, and breaks down materialistic contentment
and conventionality, but harmful and disastrous inasmuch
as it involves the sacrifice of the best elements of the nation
as a hecatomb on the altar of the Fatherland. Democracy
may be considered a blessing in that it fashions that mediocre
and slavish herd that *requires* a master, but a curse in that
it involves catchwords and fictions derived from Christianity
and carries with it a mistrust and hatred of the true élite.
In other words Nietzsche's judgments on political and social
phenomena are conditioned by their reference to the coming
of 'Superman'. Man is a being to be surpassed—what hinders
that surpassing is condemned, what favours it is commended.
There may be inconsistencies and contradiction in
Nietzsche's pronouncements, but there is a deep underlying
unity, and it is in function of this unity that they should
be regarded if we are to begin to understand Nietzsche as
politician and sociologist.

Many of Nietzsche's observations are clear-sighted, free
from cant and humbug, some are 'prophetic' (e.g. concerning a European catastrophe), but here as elsewhere
his philosophy is vitiated by its denial of the supernatural

[1] *Wanderer and his Shadow*, aph. 292.

and its assertion of a false goal. Man is indeed something to be 'surpassed', but he is to be surpassed not by his own efforts but by the grace of God; and the ideal is not an aristocracy of Supermen on the basis of a slavish and mediocre herd, but the union of redeemed and super-naturalized mankind in the Body of Christ. There is one true Superman, and to all who will receive Him He gives power to become the sons of God. Christianity is based on historic fact, the philosophy of Nietzsche on the cry for an unrealizable ideal.

CHAPTER IX

THE JEWS

IN *Ecce Homo* Nietzsche declares that he sought in vain among the Germans for a sign of tact and delicacy towards himself. 'Among the Jews I did indeed find it, but not among Germans'.[1] Nietzsche's distaste for his own country-men had, of course, become highly exaggerated by the time he wrote *Ecce Homo*, and it is not with his anti-Germanism that I am now concerned, but with his sentiments towards the Jews. The friends to whom Nietzsche was the most deeply attached were, first of all, Richard Wagner and then, in the second place, Erwin Rohde, and neither of these was a Jew; but he was on terms of friendship with the Jew, Dr. Paul Rée, from whom he received considerable help and attention, though the friendship was broken off as a sequel to the Lou Salomé incident. But though Nietzsche con-sidered—whether rightly or wrongly—that Rée had not behaved as a sincere friend in that matter, he was, and remained, a consistent opponent of racial anti-Semitism, and those contemporary anti-Semites who look with a favourable eye on Nietzsche's *Übermensch* philosophy cannot appeal to him for support in their anti-Semitic policy.

Nietzsche was opposed to his sister's marriage with Förster, largely on the ground of the latter's well-known

[1] p. 129.

anti-Semitism. His sister protested that she was marrying
Förster the man and the colonist, and not the anti-Semite;
but Nietzsche found it difficult to reconcile himself to the
match as he could not stomach 'Racialism'. Of course
Nietzsche's resentment against the marriage may have been
partly due to a feeling that his sister would thereby be with-
drawn from him—she announced her intention of following
Förster to Paraguay—but his hostility to anti-Semitism was
no passing phase, occasioned merely by a desire not to lose
his sister. He numbered 'the anti-Semitic folly' among other
follies, which he ascribed to contemporary Germans, for
example 'the Teutonic folly' and 'the Prussian folly'.[1]
Nietzsche recognized that Germany 'has amply *sufficient*
Jews', and that there was sense in the cry 'Let no more
Jews come in!'; but at the same time he pointed out that this
was the cry of a people 'where nature is still feeble and
uncertain, so that it could be easily wiped out, easily
extinguished, by a stronger race'. In Nietzsche's opinion the
Jews 'are beyond all doubt the strongest, toughest, and
purest race at present living in Europe'. If the Jews desired
—'or if they were driven to it, as the anti-Semites seem to
wish'—they *could* have the ascendency over Europe; but
Nietzsche goes on to declare that 'they are not working
and planning for that end'. On the contrary 'they rather
wish and desire, even somewhat importunately, to be insorbed
and absorbed by Europe; they long to be finally settled,
authorized, and respected somewhere, and wish to put an
end to the nomadic life, to the "wandering Jew";—and one
should certainly take account of this impulse and tendency,
and *make advances* to it'. 'One should make advances with
all prudence and with selection; pretty much as the English
nobility do'. Hence Nietzsche suggests that 'it would
perhaps be useful and fair to banish the anti-Semitic brawlers
out of the country'.

The anti-Semites make great play with moral principles,
but Nietzsche retorts that 'an anti-Semite does not become
the least bit more respectable because he lies on principle',[2]
and he deplored Wagner's hatred of the Jews. That bad

---

[1] *Beyond Good and Evil*, aph. 251.   [2] *Antichrist*, p. 213.

Jews exist, Nietzsche admits: he even says that 'perhaps the young Stock Exchange Jew is, in general, the most repulsive invention of the human species'.[1] But it is absurd to make the bad Jews the sole representatives of the Jewish people. 'Every nation, every individual, has unpleasant and even dangerous qualities—and it is cruel to require that the Jew should be an exception'. Nietzsche's criticism of anti-Semitism would seem here to be perfectly justified, and he rightly deplores the habit 'of sacrificing the Jews as the scape-goats of all possible public and private abuses'. That the Jews have exercised an immoral influence through press, plays, cinema, etc., is not infrequently pleaded as an excuse for their persecution. But if a given State sincerely desires to suppress immoral productions in literature, drama, and so on, it is always possible for it to pass laws which will render the authors and producers of immoral works, dramas, etc., liable tǫ prosecution. If a given Jew is really a pernicious influence in the community, let a restriction be put on his activities; but let any such measure be directed against him, not as a member of the Jewish race, but as a bad citizen, a deleterious influence in the State. If a nation has not the moral strength of character to set its own house in order, it is mere cowardly hypocrisy to throw all the blame on the Jews, casting stones at the Semites as though the anti-Semites were without sin. The upholders of the Racial Theory are bad enough, but it is at least an open question if they deserve so much contempt as those who deny the Racial Theory in principle, and then proceed to buttress their practical anti-Semitism with moral reflections and high-sounding phrases. It may be that open and crude brutality is preferable to Pharisaic hypocrisy.

Nietzsche emphasizes the debt which Europe owes to the Jews. To the Jews, he says, 'we owe the most loving of men (Christ), the most upright of sages (Spinoza), the mightiest book, and the most effective moral law in the world'.[2] Nietzsche maintained that a high culture requires a broad basis of mediocrity to stand on. Now the power of the middle

---

[1] *Human, All-too-Human*, i, aph. 475.
[2] Ibid.

classes who represent the mediocre, is upheld by means of commerce, and the Jews are the great financiers. They have an interest then in preserving the *status quo* of the middle classes, and in opposing anarchic and revolutionary elements. He concludes that 'on this account the Jews are, for the present, the most *conservative* power in the threatening and insecure conditions of modern Europe. They can have no use either for revolutions, for socialism, or for militarism'.[1] (Nietzsche hated anarchic and revolutionary political tendencies.) There is, no doubt, a certain truth in this, but it may well be doubted whether it is altogether borne out by the subsequent history of Europe. There seems to be a type of Jew, who, cut off from the religious tradition of his people, is yet not content to sink into practical materialism, but, fired by a non-religious 'Messianism', betrays a markedly revolutionary tendency. After all Jews have played a prominent part in Bolshevism, and was not Marx himself a Jew? The *deraciné* Jew may be a very dangerous man— for he may lend the genius and religious fervour of his race to the service of a perverted 'ideal'. All the same, it would be ridiculous to attempt to fasten all nihilistic tendencies and activities on the Jews: the phenomenon of Nazism should be a sufficient check to any attempt of this kind.

Nietzsche also emphasizes the direct services of the Jews to culture. 'The Jews, with Heinrich Heine and Offenbach, approached genius in the sphere of art'.[2] Heine was a favourite of Nietzsche's. 'It was Heinrich Heine who gave me the most perfect idea of what a lyrical poet could be. In vain do I search through all the kingdoms of antiquity or of modern times for anything to resemble his sweet and passionate music. He possessed that divine wickedness without which perfection itself becomes unthinkable to me, —I estimate the value of men, of races, according to the extent to which they are unable to conceive of a god who has not a dash of the satyr in him. And with what mastery he wields his native tongue! One day it will be said of Heine and me that we were by far the greatest artists of the German language that have ever existed, and that we

---

[1] *Will to Power*, ii, aph. 864.   [1] Ibid., ii, aph. 832.

left all the efforts that mere Germans made in this language
an incalculable distance behind us'.[1] It may be objected that
Heine was by no means an ornament to culture, certainly not
in regard to spiritual values. That may be admitted; but
are we to conclude that Heine was no poet? Lord Byron,
an Aryan, had grave defects in his moral character, but
did he make no contribution to English literature? In the
present century we can surely admit a debt to Einstein, while
agreeing that the views he has expressed on theism are worthless. And we certainly owe a debt to the Jew, Henri Bergson,
who dealt a mortal wound to Positivism and to mechanistic
science in France.

I have quoted a passage from Nietzsche in which he
declares that the Jews only wish to settle down. There is an
earlier passage in which he speaks of a future ascendency
of the Jews in Europe. It is a long passage; but since it is
important for Nietzsche's attitude towards the Jews, I
venture to quote it in full. It comes from *The Dawn of Day*,
and is headed *The People of Israel*:

'One of the spectacles which the next century will invite
us to witness is the decision regarding the fate of the
European Jews. It is quite obvious now that they have cast
their die and crossed their Rubicon: the only thing that
remains for them is either to become masters of Europe or
to lose Europe, as they once centuries ago lost Egypt, where
they were confronted with similar alternatives. In Europe,
however, they have gone through a schooling of eighteen
centuries such as no other nation has ever undergone, and the
experiences of this dreadful time of probation have benefited,
not only the Jewish community, but, even to a greater
extent, the individual. As a consequence of this, the
resourcefulness of the modern Jews, both in mind and soul,
is extraordinary. Amongst all the inhabitants of Europe
it is the Jews least of all who try to escape from any deep
distress by recourse to drink or to suicide, as other less gifted
people are so prone to do. Every Jew can find in the history
of his own family and of his ancestors a long record of
instances of the greatest coolness and perseverance amid

[1] *Ecce Homo*, pp. 39–40.

difficulties, amid dreadful situations, an artful cunning in fighting with misfortune and hazard. And above all it is their bravery under the cloak of wretched submission, their heroic *spernere se sperni* that surpasses the virtues of all the saints.

'People wished to make them contemptible by treating them contemptibly for nearly twenty centuries and refusing them access to all honourable positions and dignities, and by pushing them further down into the meaner trades—and under this process indeed they have not become any cleaner. But contemptible? They have never ceased for a moment from believing themselves qualified for the very highest functions, nor have the virtues of the suffering ever ceased to adorn them. Their manner of honouring their parents and children distinguishes them among all Europeans. Besides this they have been able to create for themselves a sense of power and eternal vengeance from the very trades that were left to them (or to which they were abandoned). Even in palliation of their usury we cannot help saying that without this occasional pleasant and useful torture inflicted on their scorners they would have experienced difficulty in preserving their self-respect for so long. For our self-respect depends upon our ability to make reprisals in both good and evil things. Nevertheless, their revenge never urges them on too far, for they have all that liberty of mind, and even of soul, produced in many by frequent changes of place, climate, and customs of neighbours and oppressors, they possess by far the greatest experience in all human intercourse, and even in their passions they exercise the caution which this experience has developed in them. They are so certain of their intellectual versatility and shrewdness that they never, even when reduced to the direct straits, have to earn their bread by manual labour as common workmen, porters, or farm hands. In their manners we can still see that they have never been inspired by chivalric and noble feelings, or that their bodies have ever been girt with fine weapons: a certain obtrusiveness alternates with a sub-missiveness which is often tender and almost always painful.

'Now, however, that they unavoidably intermarry more and more year after year with the noblest blood of Europe, they will soon have a considerable heritage of good intellectual and physical manners, so that in another hundred years they will have a sufficiently noble aspect not to render themselves, as masters, ridiculous to those whom they will have subdued. And this is important! and therefore a settlement of the question is still premature. They themselves know very well that the conquest of Europe or any act of violence is not to be thought of; but they also know that some day or other Europe may, like a ripe fruit, fall into their hands, if they do not clutch at it too eagerly. In the meantime, it is necessary for them to distinguish themselves in all departments of European distinction, and to stand in the front rank: until they shall have advanced so far as to determine themselves what distinction shall mean. Then they will be called the pioneers and guides of the Europeans whose modesty they will no longer offend.

'And then where shall an outlet be found for this abundant wealth of great impressions accumulated during such an extended period and representing Jewish history for every Jewish family, this wealth of passions, virtues, resolutions, resignations, struggles, and conquests of all kinds—where can it find an outlet but in great intellectual men and works! On the day when the Jews will be able to exhibit to us, as their own work, such jewels and golden vessels as no European nation, with its shorter and less profound experience, can or could produce, when Israel shall have changed its eternal vengeance into an eternal benediction for Europe: then that seventh day will once more appear when old Jehovah may rejoice in Himself, in His creation, in His chosen people—and all, all of us, will rejoice with Him'.[1]

The foregoing passage is appreciative in regard to the Jews; but when treating of Nietzsche's attitude towards the Jews, it is necessary to show the other side of the picture to make it clear what he thought of their ideology. The Jews, according to Nietzsche, have shown a remarkable love of

[1] *Dawn of Day*, aph. 205.

life—even more than the Greeks. They did not wish to get rid of their bodies, but hoped to preserve them for ever. (Nietzsche quotes the Jewish martyr of Macabees ii, 7, who 'would not think of giving up his intestines, which had been torn out: he wanted to have them at the resurrection': quite a Jewish characteristic![1]) But though the Jews loved life, they are guilty of an inversion of values, 'by means of which life on earth obtains a new and dangerous charm for a couple of millenniums'.[2] Nietzsche means that the Jews, finding themselves dubbed a people born for slavery (cf. Tacitus), turned values upside down by exalting the slave-values. Thus by canonizing, as it were, the position in which they found themselves, they gave fresh meaning to life, *their* life, and so fed their love of life. They began the revolt of the 'slaves' in the sphere of morals and changed the aristocratic equation (good = aristocratic = beautiful = happy = loved by the gods) into the contrary equation (good = wretched, poor, weak, lowly, suffering, needy, etc. = pious = blessed) with its complement of aristocratic or men of power = evil, horrible, covetous, godless = cursed and damned.[3] (The Jews themselves, of course, were very much preoccupied with temporal prosperity, wealth, and good repute, and it is notorious that the Jewish tendency was to harp on temporal prosperity as a mark of God's favour. Did not Job's 'comforters' think that he *must* have committed sin since he suffered so much? There was very little of Nietzsche's Jewish equation in their minds. However, it is true that the Prophets introduced much more spiritual ideas, and Nietzsche often regards Judæo-Christian ideology as a whole.)

The root of the Jewish valuation is a profound feeling of resentment and hate, 'Jewish hate—that most profound and sublime hate, which creates ideals and changes old values to new creations, the like of which has never been on earth'.[4] Nietzsche, as mentioned before, makes great play with the concept of resentment and finds it to be strong,

---

[1] *Dawn of Day*, aph. 72.
[2] *Beyond Good and Evil*, aph. 195.
[3] Cf. *Genealogy of Morals*, pp. 30–1.
[4] *Genealogy of Morals*, p. 31.

not only among the Jews—'the priestly notion of resentment *par excellence*', but also in the Church, that '*œcumenical* synagogue'. And when the revival of the classical ideal or aristocratic valuation at the time of the Renaissance was overcome, Nietzsche depicts the situation as a fresh triumph of Judea, 'thanks to that fundamentally popular (German and English) monument of revenge, which is called the Reformation'.[1] Similarly 'Judæa proved yet once more victorious over the classical ideal in the French Revolution', when the last political aristocracy of Europe was 'broken in pieces beneath the instincts of a resentful populace'.

In this matter, as so often with Nietzsche, we have to be careful not to allow the truth contained in what he says to blind us to his exaggeration and one-sidedness. That resentment and desire for revenge were powerfully operative in the ordinary Jewish attitude towards other nations and other ideals is most probably true; but in the Old Testament we see men like the prophets rising superior to the more popular viewpoint, and in the Books of *Jonas* and *Wisdom*, for instance, we find God's *universal* love clearly stated. As to the French Revolution, resentment certainly played a considerable part in the revolutionary attitude and ideology, but it is at least very doubtful whether the nobler motives, which were also operative, can be simply resolved into hatred and resentment—unless one is prepared to agree with Nietzsche, that all values are relative and that the values asserted in the Revolution were merely the values of the herd, impelled by hatred of the noble valuation of the aristocracy. And Nietzsche's view of the Reformation is certainly false. The Reformation in England, for instance, cannot possibly be called a fundamentally popular movement: on the contrary, it was forced upon the people from above. For my part I consider Nietzsche's analysis of resentment a valuable contribution to psychology—it may even be that resentment has been operative, to a certain extent, in the souls of modern Jewish revolutionaries—but it is necessary to point out that the presence of resentment or hatred or desire of revenge in a person or people does not, of

[1] *Genealogy of Morals*, p. 55.

itself, show that the values asserted by the resentful person or people are devoid of objective validity. A man might assert a true value, possessed of objective and universal validity, out of resentment; and though the man's psychological state would scarcely be admirable, the value itself would not be vitiated. Accordingly, one must beware of saying: 'Nietzsche's analysis of popular Jewish psychology is right' (supposing for the moment that it *is* right without further qualification being necessary), '*therefore* the Jewish valuation is merely relative to the resentful soul and has no objective validity'. For the resentful Jews might quite well assert an objective valuation from undesirable psychological motives.

The history of Israel is, in Nietzsche's eyes, 'the typical history of every *denaturalization* of natural values'.[1] In the early period of Jewish history, particularly in the period of the kings, Israel's attitude was the *right* or natural one. Jehovah was the expression of the people's consciousness of power, and victory was expected from Him. 'Jehovah is the God of Israel, and *consequently* the God of justice: this is the reasoning of every people which is in the position of power and which has a good conscience in that position'. But as time went on it was found that 'The old God was no longer able to do what he had done formerly'. What happened then? Instead of simply dropping the old God, the priests changed the idea of Him, and began to interpret all happiness as a reward, all unhappiness as a punishment for disobedience, for 'sin'. Thus they arrived at the conception of a moral order of the Universe, and morality, from being the expression of the conditions of life and growth, becomes abstract and the very opposite of life. But the Jewish priesthood went further than this: they interpreted Jewish history in a religious manner, and began to measure peoples, ages, and individuals according to whether they favour or oppose the ascendancy of the priesthood: they inverted the concept of revelation or the 'holy scripture' and so ensured their own domination. What *they* wanted was the Will of God. Disobedience to the God =

[1] *Antichrist*, pp. 156 sq.

THE JEWS 191

disobedience to the Law = disobedience to the priest = sin. Their supreme axiom becomes 'God forgiveth him that repenteth—in plain English—*him that submitteth himself to the priest*'. The priest had become the dominant power, but the priest exists only by depreciating and desecrating nature.

It would certainly be difficult to deny that the Jewish priesthood desired domination: one of the motives prompting the delivery of Christ to the Roman authority for execution was *envy*. The priests feared that their position might be assailed. Nor can it be denied that the attitude ultimately adopted by the ruling classes of Israel, the priests, Scribes, and Pharisees, was hostile to 'life': in their intemperate zeal for the Law, and for their own additions thereto, they chained and enslaved the spirit of man: the letter was exalted over the spirit. In this sense we might speak of a 'denaturalization of values': what had been meant to bind together, invigorate, and strengthen the Jewish people became an instrument of slavery and tyrannical oppression: sanctity was external, forced, priestly. But there is another side to the picture. The development of moral ideas in the Jewish people, the broadening-out for instance of the concept of the God of Israel to the God of the whole world, of all men, was a 'denaturalization' of values only in the sense that it was a 'spiritualization' of values—a gradual process which was, on the human side, a growing insight into values, on the Divine side, a progressive revelation.

It may seem somewhat strange that Nietzsche should speak of the Jews as a life-loving, a power-loving people, a strong and tough people, and that he should then represent the history of Israel as a growing 'denaturalization of values', a growing hostility to life, i.e. a growing decadence. But the seeming contradiction tends to disappear if we look at what he says in *Antichrist* concerning the Jewish people and decadence.[1] 'From the psychological standpoint', says Nietzsche, 'the Jewish people are possessed of the toughest vitality', and again, 'The Jews are the opposite of all *decadents*'. Why is it then that they have taken the side of the instincts of decadents and invented their 'no-saying

[1] pp. 155–6.

morality'? Not because they were dominated by decadent instincts, but because they saw that by their means they could attain to power. The Jews 'have known how to set themselves at the head of all decadent movements (St. Paul and Christianity for instance), in order to create something from them which is stronger than every party *saying Yea to Life'*. In Judaism and in Christianity we find a class of men—the sacerdotal class—who have used decadence as a *means*. 'This category of men has a vital interest in making men sick, and in turning the notions 'good' and 'bad', 'true' and 'false', upside down in a manner which is not only dangerous to life, but also slanders it'.[1] The Jews themselves are thus a tough and strong people of life-lovers, but they used the instincts of decadence, the Nay to life, as a means to domination: Jews have set themselves at the head of decadent movements, because they saw in this procedure a means to power. Nietzsche mentioned Christianity, though in reality, of course, St. Paul was not interested in power. He might have found a better example had he lived since the Great War, and had observed the activities of Jewish Bolsheviks. Nietzsche loathed Socialism, and would doubtless have extended his loathing to Socialism of the Russian type. But he would have detected in Jewish Bolsheviks the presence of the Will to Power. To him this is *in itself* a commendable trait, though to us it is not so admirable, whether found in Jew or 'Aryan'.

What of the relation of Judaism to Christianity? Nietzsche regards Christianity as a development of Judaism, or rather as 'a popular insurrection in the midst of a priestly people—a pietistic movement coming from below (sinners, publicans, women, and children). Jesus of Nazareth was the symbol of this sect'. Christianity is thus represented as a movement of the people against sacerdotal aristocracy. Later, of course, through St. Paul and others, sacerdotalism was carried on into Christianity, but in its origin Christianity was non-sacerdotal and pietistic. Yet Christianity is the

---

[1] The Jewish Table of Values is the expression of their Will to Power. 'A Table of excellencies hangeth over every people. Lo! it is the table of their triumphs; lo! it is the voice of their Will to Power'. *Z.*, p. 66.

direct inheritor of Judaism, for it accepted the Jewish reduction of all sin to sin against God and, going further than the Jewish priesthood, it attempted to alter and falsify the whole history of mankind, making Christianity the most important event in history. (Certainly, if Christianity *were* a fraud, then the Christian philosophy of history would be a falsification.) The Jews had gone some way in enmity towards the noble classes, but they had put the priests in the van of the people against the noble classes—thus creating a sacerdotal nobility. Christianity, scenting in the Jewish priesthood the existence of the privileged and noble minority, did away with priests altogether. It is the 'second degree of power' of Judaism. (According to Nietzsche, the French Revolution is the lineal descendant of Christianity, being also characterized by an insinct of hate towards castes and nobles. The truth underlying this assertion of Nietzsche is that the professed ideals of the Revolution certainly derive from Christianity, the Christian foundation of the ideals having been dropped on the way.)

Nietzsche emphasizes 'Jewish hate'. Now since the supreme moral value of Christianity is *Love*, it might well seem that we should conclude to an opposition between Judaism and Christianity. But Nietzsche is equal to the occasion. He admits that in Christianity there grew up a new phenomenon, 'a *new love*, the most profound and sublime of all kinds of love', but then tells us to 'beware of supposing that this love has soared on its upward growth, as in any way a real negation of that thirst for revenge, as an antithesis to the Jewish hate'.[1] Rather is it true that Christian love grew out of Jewish hate: it is merely a new means of asserting Jewish values and Jewish ideals, bringing salvation and victory to the poor, the sick, and the sinful. It is all part of the Jewish policy of *revenge*. Israel crucifies the very instrument of its revenge in order that all the world, i.e. all the enemies of Israel, might nibble without suspicion at the bait of Jewish ideals. It is certain, says Nietzsche, that '*sub hoc signo* Israel, with its revenge and transvaluation of all values, has up to the present always triumphed again over

[1] *Genealogy of Morals*, p. 31.

all other ideals, over all more aristocratic ideals'. In other words, Christianity is but Judaism returning again to the attack—on aristocratic ideals—and attacking this time more completely, more ingeniously and more dangerously than before. (We should prefer to say that in Christianity all the best of Judiasm is taken up and contained, and that Christianity involves a far more complete vision of the *true* ideals.)

A similar thought occurs in *The Will to Power* when Nietzsche declares that the principle of love comes from the small community of Jewish people, and that 'the song in praise of love which Paul wrote is not Christian; it is the Jewish flare of that eternal flame which is Semitic'.[1] Christianity, developing this flame, has increased the temperature of the soul among peoples cooler than the Jews: 'It discovered that the most wretched life could be made rich and invaluable by means of an elevation of the temperature of the soul'.

Nietzsche, as we have seen, recognizes in the Jews the Will to Power, but insists that they have used 'decadence' and lying as a means to power, and that Christianity is the final outcome of Judaism. ('With Christianity, the art of telling holy lies, which constitutes the whole of Judaism, reaches its final mastership, thanks to many centuries of Jewish and most thoroughly serious training and practice. The Christian, this *ultima ratio* of falsehood, is the Jew over again—he is even three times a Jew'.)[2] Nietzsche is, of course, anti-sacerdotal and is violently opposed to the Jewish—and to the Christian—valuations, which he regards as the contradiction of the noble or aristocratic valuation. But at the same time he recognizes in the Jewish people a persistent vigour and ability, believes that they have contributed to European culture, and will do so in the future. He therefore decries anti-Semitism. With Nietzsche's opposition to anti-Semitism we can only have sympathy— if anti-Semitism be taken to mean opposition to Jews on principle. That Jews should not be permitted to corrupt

---

[1] *Will to Power*, i, aph. 175.   [2] *Antichrist*, p. 188.

others, so far as they can be prevented, is only reasonable—
but the same applies to corrupt 'Aryans'. A Jew is a human
being and has a right to be treated as a human being; and
it is revolting to hear Christians speaking of 'dirty Jewish
blood' as though a different blood flowed in Jewish veins to
that which flows in our own. And was it not Jewish Blood
that redeemed the world? Is not the Mother of God, the
Mother of all the redeemed, a Jewish Virgin? Christianity
sprang from the soil of Judaism, and is the fulfilment of
Judaism—'I came not to destroy, but to fulfil'. The reason
why non-Christian Jews are strangers, anomalies in the
world, is not because Semitic blood runs in their veins, but
because they will not recognize the very purpose of Judaism,
to be a preparation for Christianity, because they will not
accept the divine vocation of their people but cling to a past
that is gone for ever.

CHAPTER X

IN CRITICISM OF NIETZSCHE

THIS book has been entitled *Friedrich Nietzsche, Philosopher
of Culture*, and in the foregoing pages we have attempted
to show how the ideal of an ascending culture runs as a
leitmotif through the whole of Nietzsche's thought. Thus
although his ideas on art, morality, religion, society, history
are set forth for the most part in aphoristic form, which tends
to give them a disconnected and disjointed appearance, they
are to be viewed in function of Nietzsche's guiding desire,
the desire for a higher culture than has ever been attained
before. For example, in so far as the State aids culture
(as Nietzsche understands it) it is commended; in so far
as it obstructs the growth of a higher culture and of more
highly cultured personalities, it is condemned. It should,
therefore, be sufficiently obvious, that the philosophy of
Nietzsche is not to be identified with the Nazi *Weltanschauung*. The Nazis proclaim a race-theory—Nietzsche
called racialism a mendacious swindle: the Nazis exalt

Germany—Nietzsche derided *Deutschland über Alles* and denounced the German Empire: the Nazis worship the State—Nietzsche called the State a 'cold monster': the Nazis make science subservient to propaganda—Nietzsche was sceptical and critical of all dogmatic assertions (with the strange exception of the doctrine of the Eternal Recurrence). The philosophy of Nietzsche has indeed its place in the anti-voluntaristic reaction that followed on the *Blütezeit* of German Idealism, and many of his doctrines (e.g. the doctrines of Superman and of a 'master-class'), especially when misinterpreted and misunderstood, lend themselves for use in the Nazi *Weltanschauung*, so that one can scarcely deny a *de facto* influence on Nazism, but one cannot justly make a philosopher responsible for all the uses to which his doctrines have been put by unscrupulous people. I have argued elsewhere that the philosophy of Nietzsche is not at all the same thing as the 'philosophy' of Nazism, and I do not want to labour the point again here: that Nietzsche would have had little sympathy with the Nazis should be clear to all who have read the foregoing chapters of this book.[1]

Yet though the difference between Nietzsche's philosophy and the Nazi *Weltanschuung* is, in my opinion, so clear that only the ignorant or the malicious can deny it, the assertion of this difference is very far from being an assertion of the truth of the Nietzschean philosophy. For the matter of that the philosophy of Schopenhauer is far removed from the Nazi creed, yet the philosophy of Schopenhauer is none the less fundamentally false and pernicious. In this chapter I hope to show that Nietzsche, while possessed of an ideal of culture, falsified the true nature of culture and that his philosophy, however far removed from Nazism, is fundamentally erroneous and that its influence would be, in certain essential aspects, pernicious.

Nietzsche is a philosopher of culture. Now what is culture? Culture obviously implies cultivation and development.

---

[1] See my 'Nietzsche and National Socialism' in the *Dublin Review* for April, 1941, and 'Nietzsche *versus* Hitler' in *The Month* for Sept.–Oct., 1941.

Of what? Of human nature, of men's faculties, for it is clearly human culture with which we are dealing and not that of bees or ants. Culture therefore implies the development and true use of *all* the faculties of man, and the more the higher faculties of man are developed the higher will be the stage of culture attained. Now the highest faculties of man are those which raise him above the plant and animal world below him and bring him near to the Divine, i.e. his reason and rational will. This truth was clearly seen by Plato and Aristotle some centuries before the birth of Christ. For Plato the soul is the most precious possession of man and man's end is the closest possible approximation to the Divine, a truth that reappears in Middle Platonism and Neo-Platonism. For Aristotle, too, man's reason is what differentiates him from the brute creation and gives him his peculiar status in the material universe, and his reason is best employed when devoted to the contemplation of eternal and unchanging objects.

But culture is not simply an affair of the individual: man is social by nature and the development of his faculties is attained in union with other men. Culture is therefore essentially social in character: man begins his life in the society of the family and it is in society and in intimate co-operation with his fellow men that his cultural development is attained. This was also clearly realized by Plato and Aristotle—they could hardly do otherwise in the Greek world, where the good life was unthinkable apart from the City-State. Even Aristotle, who stresses the fact that the philosopher, more than other men, is independent and can pursue his vocation in comparative solitude, never doubted the essentially social character of human culture. Human culture, therefore, implies the highest possible development of man's faculties, both as individual and as member of society, while, conversely, the cultural development of society implies the highest possible development and perfecting of all its members. If the individual is insufficient to himself without society, society is certainly unthinkable apart from its members: the cultural level of individuals reacts on the general social level and the common cultural level of society reacts on the level of the members who compose that society. Culture must be viewed as a social phenomenon, in function of society and of human nature, not in function of great individuals merely, even if they are geniuses and 'free spirits'. Culture is built up by society or by individuals within the social framework, and though, owing to differences of ability between individuals and differences of social functions, the same level will not be attained by all, culture, directed to human nature as such, must be seen in its relation to society as a whole. To attempt to confine culture to certain strata is to overlook the relation between culture and human nature, and such an attempt involves a falsification of culture and a misunderstanding of its social character. It is true that Plato, for instance, emphasized the hierarchic aspect of the social structure, but it must not be forgotten that he also emphasizes the social duties of the higher classes and that they exist, not simply to serve their 'egoism', but also to serve the whole community. In other words, culture is to serve man, the rational and social animal, whereas Nietzsche tends to place man at the service of culture.

Now man is rooted in the sensible, material, phenomenal world, and the need to preserve life by material means is logically the primitive need. It is obvious that we cannot think—so far as this world is concerned—or practise art or religion, unless we eat: it is then only to be expected that there should be tribal communities in which the satisfaction of material needs is the primary consideration. But as the satisfaction of corporeal needs becomes more highly developed, it is possible for a state of society to emerge in which man's higher faculties are devoted to securing 'comfort', convenience, and so on. We have then a state of what is sometimes called 'civilization' in contrast to 'culture'. In this sense civilization is taken to imply railways, electric-cookers, a good drainage system, factories and all the paraphernalia of modern society in its material aspect. If this aspect is over-stressed materialization results, bourgeois civilization—to use a somewhat unhappy term. With due qualification we might say that a state of materialistic happiness constitutes the Utopia of the Communist. Material civilization is not to be depreciated in itself, but it is insufficient: it is not culture in the full sense, for it inclines to neglect the cultivation of man's higher faculties, save in so far as they tend to the service of material needs. In such a society applied science is unduly elevated above pure science, art is regarded merely as a bodily recreation and sensual pleasure, and religion receives but scant attention. Man's higher faculties are certainly used and are employed to serve 'Life', but they are employed to serve life in an inferior and incomplete sense.

Yet just as material civilization may be over-stressed and over-valued, so may particular functions of man's higher faculties be over-stressed. It might be possible to have a type of culture in which art (art for art's sake) was the guiding *motif*, but though æsthetic expression and appreciation are functions of man's spirit and stand on a higher level than purely corporeal activity, a predominantly æsthetic or literary culture would still not be culture in the full sense—no more than a predominantly 'historical' culture in which knowledge of past cultures was regarded as the highest activity. The truth is that (as Plato and Aristotle saw) the objects of man's faculties differ in grade, and his faculties are most nobly employed when directed to the most noble and the highest objects. Any state of culture that neglects the employment of man's highest faculties in regard to the highest of all objects, God, will accordingly be inadequate, for God is the supreme Object of man's intellect and will. Moreover, since culture has a social character, this will involve social recognition of morality and social recognition of religious values. It is one of the great glories of Plato that he asserted a universal and absolute morality, a moral law binding on both State and individual, a realm of values that is not merely relative. Again, Plato's recognition of the social character of religion is obvious from the famous passage in the *Laws* where he provides for the punishment of atheism by the State. Culture in the full sense, therefore, cannot neglect the employment of man's higher faculties in regard to their noblest objects: to do so is to have a low idea of culture in practice even if one pretends to be striving after a higher and more advanced culture. Nietzsche was impelled by his atheistic doctrine to neglect the highest reaches of culture (even though he had little sympathy for 'bourgeois' civilization), and so proves himself to be in practice—even if not in theory—an enemy of culture. This is one of the reasons that makes it so easy for the Nazis to use Nietzsche for their own purposes, i.e. to use a philosophy of culture in the service of an anti-cultural movement, since the Nietzschean philosophy of culture harbours in its heart a denial of true and full culture. It would be fatal then for anyone to allow himself to be seduced by Nietzsche's enthusiasm for a higher culture and the valuable observations he often makes on culture in general into accepting his beyond-morality and beyond-religion doctrines.

It cannot be denied that there may be culture in a sense, or in a certain degree, without religion. Soviet Russia is officially atheistic (though of course the people are by no means universally so), but as far as railways, telegraphs, etc., go, it is civilized. Moreover, there are, as we know, many valuable cultural activities encouraged by the Soviet Government in the spheres of art, literature, and science. But that the social recognition of religion is essential to *all* culture, we have never maintained—it is obviously possible to cultivate the body and to use the soul's higher faculties in many functions without direct reference to religion. But it seems clear from cultural history, that when culture grows on its this-worldly side a need for a spiritual religion sooner or later makes itself felt. Thus in the Roman Empire, when State organization and a this-worldly civilization had reached a marvellous pitch of development and had become overemphasized, there manifested itself on the other side a need for a more spiritual religion than the official cult could supply. Hence the introduction of oriental mystery-cults, the popularization of philosophy—as, for instance, in the Stoic School—and the tendency of philosophy itself to pass over into religion, as we witness it in the Plotinian doctrine of ecstasy. The swamping of the individual in the great cosmopolitan Empire was of course partly responsible for the desire of a more personal religion, a religion of personal 'salvation', but it was also due to the over-stressing of the *Diesseitigkeit* aspect of culture, which made more obvious and more articulate the need of a complementary satisfaction of man's spiritual and religious capacities (cf. the rise of Methodism in the eighteenth century). Thus the prevalence of Eastern cults in the Empire—and the rise, growth, and victory of Christianity—show clearly enough that culture in the full sense, ideal culture, requires the development of *all* man's faculties in relation to *all* their proper objects. The problem of balance and harmony may not be easy to settle in practice (we get extremes of this-worldliness and 'extremes' of other-worldliness), but the ideal of culture demands such a balance. Now Nietzsche aimed at a pure *Diesseitigkeit* and so excluded important elements of culture. It is true that his thought tends towards 'transcendence', for he was never content with the given and never could be content with the given—he was too much of an 'idealist' for that—but as far as his declared principles go, his was a purely *this*-worldly philosophy, proposing a *this-worldly* culture. The effect of such a philosophy must be a stunting of man's cultural growth. Nietzsche urges us to be true to this earth, and inveighs—often blasphemously—against the transcendentalism of religion, but his philosophy is itself untrue to this earth, untrue to man, since it neglects the necessary relation of this earth to its Creator, of man to his First Cause and Final End.

As for morality, how can a true culture subsist without respect for the Natural Law? The Natural Law is not an arbitrary command of God, but expresses God's plan for man and is founded on human nature: the man who develops his faculties in accordance with right reason is acting in accordance with the Natural Law. There is accordingly a close relation between culture and the Natural Law, for both have reference to human nature. Now human nature is a constant and so the Natural Law is constant, universal, and absolute (founded ultimately of course on the Immutable Divine Essence) and, though moral insight into moral values and the dictates of the Moral Law may differ in succeeding stages of culture, where there is no respect at all for the Moral Law there can be no real and full culture. Plato and Aristotle were aware of this fact and Plato especially stressed the universal and absolute character of moral values, judging that the man who does not try to realize these values in practice is untrue to himself and that neglect of the Moral Law spells ruin for the individual and the State. If we want an illustration of this fact we have only to look at the Roman Empire, where refusal to respect moral values led to appalling results of human degradation, those who disregarded conscience being permitted by God to fall into fearful depths of sensuality and brutality. This degradation of human nature—the very antithesis of true culture—is observable also in the Nazi movement among those who deny the absolute and universal character of morality. A man who has comparatively little insight into moral values and yet endeavours to live up to the light that he has, is very different from the men who deliberately neglect conscience and the Natural Law: these latter bring upon themselves a just retribution, as Plato observed centuries ago. A culture such as that of the Chinese is therefore no objection to our thesis, for even though the Confucian or the Buddhist has less insight into moral values than the Christian, if he lives up to the light that he has got, he is showing respect for the moral values as he knows them and is thus a true bearer of human culture.

In the Ancient World, then, there was morality and there was religion, and where these were respected—according to the lights men had—there was a flowering of culture. But when men sinned against the light, degradation was the result. Those who strove to go beyond good and evil went —not *up*—but *down*. The same thing is observable to-day in relation to Christianity. Culture existed before Christianity, but when once the Revealed Religion has entered the world, nations that reject the light they once had inevitably *descend*. Some are inclined to think that it is possible to reject Christianity and yet hold to moral values, and they point to the cultures of Greece and Rome. But they show merely that culture could exist before the coming of Christ and that those who have not known Christ can possess a true culture: they do not show that those who deliberately reject Christ once they have known Him, can succeed in preserving a true culture. We must not be deceived into thinking that we can get along very well without Christ by the fact that nations who are in great part non-Christian (even if still officially Christian) still preserve culture and civilization. For these nations have, as a matter of fact, retained a large part of their Christian heritage, even if it is not always consciously possessed as such; and we cannot argue from this that if *all* Christian elements were excluded these nations would succeed in preserving for long a true culture. Greek and Roman culture was a preparation for Christianity, Medieval Europe was inspired by the Faith, our European culture rests on a Christian foundation, and if men will accept Christianity and allow Christian values and standards to penetrate our social and industrial structure, we may reach a state of culture hitherto unattained. But if men discard the Revealed Religion or try to go beyond it, they will inevitably fall. The Romans who neglected the light of conscience were given up to shameful vices: the Nazis who reject the moral law and the Kingdom of Christ are a fearful example of human degradation and anti-culture. We cannot go *back* to Greece, we cannot go *above* Christianity: if we abandon Christianity we go, not higher, not even simply 'apart', but *down*.[1]

Nietzsche, therefore, while professing to pursue culture, undermined it. As his personal life ended in madness, so his philosophy ends in a contradiction, for, though a philosophy of culture, it contains within itself the seeds of anti-culture. From his philosophy we can expect no salvation. It is, indeed, a stimulus to thought, to self-examination, to higher endeavour; but if adopted as a philosophy it leads to ruin. We are not called upon to be super-moral nor to be above

---

[1] This refers to deliberate rejection of the Christian religion and morality in the sense of sinning against the light. There are many men to-day who observe the moral law and yet are not Christians, but whom we cannot suppose to have deliberately sinned against their conscience.

Christianity, but to be true Christians and truly moral men and women. Nietzsche desired the highest development of man's faculties, but at the same time he tried to deprive them of their best objects. If it be pointed out that Nietzsche left religion intact for the masses and desired only 'free spirits' to transcend morality and religion, I can only answer that this is tantamount to saying that Nietzsche would spoil and stunt and bring to ruin the finest flowers of the human race. He did not *intend* to do this of course, but such would be the effect of his doctrine. He intended to be a friend of culture: in reality he is an enemy of culture and his philosophy is a danger to the race, all the more dangerous in that it is embellished with his gifts of imagination, literary ability, flashes of insight, and intense earnestness. What a tragedy that a man of Nietzsche's talents should devote himself to such a cause, that the man who foresaw the European catastrophe and longed for European cultural unity should himself help towards the catastrophe through his atheism and his denial of absolute moral values! Just as Socialistic-atheistic civilization tends to reduce man to a machine, to a cog in the wheel of economic progress, so the individualist-atheistic culture proposed by Nietzsche would end in the degradation of the finest men and women. If highly cultured personalities allow themselves to be seduced by the dream of *Eritis sicut dii*, creating their own values and passing 'beyond Good and Evil', they are guilty of a refusal to accept Reality, they deny the bounds and limitations of human nature and so are *untrue* to this world and to every other world—except a world of their own imagination. And that is the road to madness, for ὕβρις spells ruin in the end.

It is indeed a terrible thing that in spite of all material progress man has been unable to create a true, full, and lasting culture. But to throw the blame for this on morality and on supernatural religion is but a poor way out of the difficulty. The root of the trouble is rather that man has in general failed to recognize the supremacy of moral and spiritual values and has failed to live up to the light that he had. Some are inclined to say that Christianity has done little for human culture. In the first place this is not true—what nobility of character, what a flowering of the arts, how many works of charity, we owe to Christian inspiration!—and, as Nietzsche himself saw, even those who in our modern world have upheld the ideal of justice and co-operation in our social and industrial life have drawn, even if often unconsciously, on Christian sources. In the second place, if Christianity has failed to do all that it might have done, this is not the fault of Christianity itself but of us men and women. In a *fully* Christian culture, in which the ideals of Christianity had really permeated all departments of life, what room would remain for social injustice, war, national envy, jealousy, suspicion, and hatred? The future of culture after this war depends on us men and women, it is true, but this means that it depends on the degree in which we realize and put into practice the ideals and demands of the best gift that has been given to man and the highest inspiration that has been set before him, the Christian Faith and the Christian Morality. Those who strive to turn men from this path and to delude man with the dream of something still higher, which shall be exclusively man's creation, are seducers of mankind and, even if unconsciously, instruments of Satan. When a man brings to this work of seduction out-standing talent and earnestness, a naturally noble character and a hatred of sham and pretence, the tragedy is all the greater. Such is the tragedy of Friederich Nietzsche, in whom the world gained perhaps a great writer and a goad to its conscience, but in whom the world lost—what it might otherwise have gained (had Nietzsche so willed)—a true guide and friend.

CHAPTER XI

CONCLUSION: THE PHILOSOPHY OF LIFE:
NIETZSCHE AND BERGSON

By way of conclusion I wish to draw a comparison between Friedrich Nietzsche and Henri Bergson. Nietzsche, who died in 1900, and Bergson, who died in 1941, are both great figures on the European stage, though the outward circumstances of their lives were so different. Nietzsche, the 'Aryan', came to pass an ever severer and more bitter judgment on his own land and people, and after a short period of professorship at Bâle, lived abroad, lonely and neglected by his own countrymen: Bergson, the Jew, was a patriotic Frenchman, a celebrated and honoured professor in the foremost University of France, a man whose word was listened to with respect and attention. Nietzsche, the son of pious Lutheran parents, became an implacable foe of Christianity: Bergson approached nearer and nearer to the Christian religion and is said to have been baptized into the Catholic Church before his death.[1] Yet with both these great men we associate the notion of 'Life': the concept of 'Life' was essential to the philosophy of Nietzsche as to that of Bergson. Precisely what influence, direct or indirect, the thought of Nietzsche exercised on the mind of Bergson the present writer is not at present competent to say; but this much is clear, that the philosophy of life took very different forms in the hands of the two men. In the hands of Nietzsche the philosophy of life, in spite of all claim and superficial appearance to the contrary, becomes, I maintain, fundamentally pessimistic and falls into that very 'no' to life which it professes to decry and repudiate: in the hands of Bergson, on the contrary, the philosophy of life becomes fundamentally optimistic and utters a triumphant 'yes' to Life in its highest manifestations.

There are, of course, similarities to be discerned in the thought of Nietzsche and Bergson: this is the very reason that makes a comparison between them reasonable and profitable. That life is central to the philosophy of Nietzsche, should be clear from the pages of this book. Nietzsche regards life as the highest product of Nature, he calls for more life and higher forms of life; the attitude of soul, which he would inculcate, is a joyful and triumphant 'Yea' to life. To Bergson, too, Life is the highest phenomenon of Nature: we have but to read *Matière et Mémoire, Évolution Créatrice,*

[1] v. footnote, Preface, p. x.

and *Les deux Sources*, to realize the central and irreducible vitalism of the Bergsonian philosophy. Bergson, like Nietzsche, is in a sense anti-rationalist, anti-dialectical : there is an emphasis or intuition that has some kinship at least with the method of Nietzsche. The Philosophy of Bergson is, of course, much more firmly anchored on empirical fact than is that of Nietzsche : moreover the approach is different— Bergson approaches his metaphysical philosophy slowly and carefully, from a scientific and biological standpoint (routing the positivists and materialists with their own weapons), whereas Nietzsche tends to make his particular observations and assertions in function of a preconceived ideal, which he generally disdains to support by any attempt at scientific proof. Yet in both these men we can discern a strain of poetry and enthusiasm, an atmosphere of freshness and reality, which reacts against the conceptual rationalism of Hegel on the one hand and the arid wastes of positivistic and modernistic science on the other hand. In both philosophies, again, an important position is attributed to the great man, the 'hero' : we have only to read Nietzsche's *Zarathustra* and *Will to Power* and Bergson's *Deux Sources* to realize this. Human life in its ascent culminates in the hero.

But though there are marked similarities between the philosophies of Nietzsche and Bergson—we may truly say that Bergson stands in the current of that *Lebensphilosophie* which includes Nietzsche—there are yet strongly marked and vividly contrasting differences ; and it is on these differences that I wish briefly to dwell. It is precisely these differences which reveal the root defects of Nietzsche's thought and the superiority of the philosophy of Bergson. The present writer has no intention of subscribing to the entire philosophy of Henri Bergson ; but he certainly believes that Bergson has a message for modern man, and that his philosophy, when seen in the light of its author's later development, appears as fundamentally sane and true.

What is life as it appears on this planet in the eyes of Nietzsche ? It is 'Will to Power', yes, but what is its ultimate standpoint? We can only say that it is a throw-off of Nature, a continually recurrent phenomenon in the cyclical process. As remarked before, we cannot speak of Nature's 'purposes' in connection with Nietzsche's philosophy. Nature, atheistic and blind, can have no 'purpose'. Life simply appears, it is an undeniable phenomenon, which we have to accept, but it can have no integral place in a teleological scheme: in other words, it can have no ultimate meaning. For Bergson, on the contrary, life as it appears on this planet derives from an impulse of Life itself, it is a manifestation of Creative Life, that 'Pure Act'—to borrow a term of the Aristotelian Schoolmen—which brings into existence all phenomena. Life, for Bergson, is not a phenomenon hung in the void of an atheistic Nature, but it has to be seen against the ultimate background of Creative Life, God, Who works in Nature, creating, in the upward movement of Nature, fresh and higher forms. Although Bergson speaks very cautiously of teleology in *Évolution Créatrice*, he makes it quite clear in *Les Deux Sources* that life has a meaning and that human life reaches its deepest fulfilment · in the moment of union with God. Though Bergson, as a philosopher, may not take it upon himself to 'explain' the teleology of the universe, he certainly leaves room for the teleology indicated by Christian revelation and theology. If Bergson speaks, as he does, of Nature's purpose, the phrase is with him—as it is not with Nietzsche— legitimate, since the purpose must ultimately be referred to the Creative God, Who manifests Himself in this world. While it could occasion no surprise if the author of *Les deux Sources* embraced the Catholic Faith, it would have indicated a decided *volte-face* on Nietzsche's part had he returned to the religion of his childhood.

In *Zarathustra*, as we have seen, the doctrine of the Eternal Recurrence is given a central position along with the doctrine of Superman and the Transvaluation of Values. Now the Eternal Recurrence involves the conclusion that there is no given meaning or 'sense' in the Universe. It cannot explain itself and it cannot *ex hypothesi* be explained by anything outside itself: it is a fact which we must accept, renouncing all hope of explanation—'explanation' is simply a 'will-o'-the-wisp', a fiction of theologians and idealist philosophers. Plato, Kant, Hegel, and their fellows, are the great mytho-logists, who would not *accept*, but who invented an ideal world or an Absolute Reason or what not, seeking to 'explain' what cannot be 'explained', but has simply to be accepted. They slandered Reality in favour of an ideal—and fictitious—world. But man cannot renounce explana-tion, he cannot renounce the search for the 'beyond'—unless he be content to relapse into an irremediable pessimism. Nietzsche certainly attempts to have it both ways, to com-bine a metaphysical pessimism with a psychological optimism, but in so doing he attempts to force human nature to the breaking point. Serious-minded thinkers, those who are con-cerned with the establishment and conservation of values, cannot rest content with the absence of metaphysical Ground, and this fact is surely an indication that there *is* such a Ground, which will reveal itself to the humble and patient seeker. Nietzsche was a serious-minded thinker, and he attempted to establish values without a metaphysical Ground, but the way of Nietzsche is the way of madness. Not all 'pessimists' follow the way of Nietzsche to its disastrous conclusion, but not all who adopt the Nietzschean position are possessed of Nietzsche's intense inner seriousness. Philosophy was no game for Nietzsche but an earnest and passionate struggle, motived by the firm resolve to shut his eyes to the truth.

For Bergson, on the other hand, the Universe has an ultimate and metaphysical Ground. Behind and within the evolutionary process of Nature is the Creative Life, and the world proceeds from the creative hand of God. Meaning is therefore realized in the Universe: the reality of experience is not a blind fact but a creative effort, a progressive mani-festation of God. Bergson stands, in this respect, in the line of great philosophers, of Plato, Plotinus, St. Thomas Aquinas and St. Bonaventure, of Leibniz, Fichte and Hegel, of Whitehead in our days (I do not mean to place all these thinkers on a par, still less to express agreement with all they have said—an impossible procedure, in view of their differences!), in the line of those who attempt to supply a metaphysical Ground for the Universe and to reveal the meaning of life. The Gound asserted by this or that thinker may be fictitious, but once a Ground is asserted then there is justification for speaking of 'meaning'. In Nietzsche's case there is no justification; and if there is no 'meaning', what sense can there be in appealing for the advent of Superman? We might just as well seek after what happiness we can get and let 'nobility' look after itself. In the name of Values? But values are relative according to Nietzsche, and in any case what are values in the void, devoid of ultimate basis and justification?

The ascent of life, in the philosophy of Nietzsche, is towards the Superman, who is the fine flower of culture, the surpassing of man. The Superman stands in the light of the future in his solitary splendour, strong, independent, intellectual, noble, but a law to himself, the egoistic 'master', clad in the armour of hardness, free from the 'softness' and degeneracy of Christianity. But why should we work for the coming of such a man, why should the millions be sacrificed to egoism on a colossal scale, however 'noble' and devoid of pettiness? Superman is but the natural man elevated to the nth degree: in him the highest potentialities of man, the highest vocation of man, are unrealized: he cannot be held up as an ideal without at the same time lowering, dwarfing, and stunting man. How different is the 'hero' of Henri Bergson, who is pre-eminently the Christian Saint and Mystic. These 'Supermen' of Bergson are a great army in which are found the 'Founders and reformers of religion, mystics and saints, obscure heroes of moral life whom we have met on our way and who are, in our eyes, the equals of the greatest'.[1] They are conquerors, but they are conquerors because 'they have broken down natural resistance and raised humanity to a new destiny'. They are men of action and not mere passive 'degenerates', because they are filled with the life that comes from God. 'Sure of themselves, because they feel within them something better than themselves, they prove to be great men of action, to the

[1] *Two Sources*, p. 38.

surprise of those for whom mysticism is nothing but visions, and raptures, and ecstasies. That which they have allowed to flow into them is a stream flowing down and seeking through them to reach their fellow men; the necessity to spread around what they have received affects them like an onslaught of love'.[1] They are the recipients of a vast current of Life, 'from their increased vitality there radiated an extraordinary energy, daring, power of conception and realization. Just think of what was accomplished in the field of action by a St. Paul, a St. Teresa, a St. Catherine of Sienna, a St. Francis, a Joan of Arc, and how many others besides'.[2]

And these 'Supermen', these 'heroes' of Bergson, are armed, not with the mail of hardness and aloofness, but with the panoply of a warm and radiating love—'A love which each of them stamps with his own personality. A love which is in each of them an entirely new emotion, capable of transposing human life into another tone. A love which thus causes each of them to be loved for himself, so that through him, and for him, other men will open their souls to the love of humanity. A love which can just as well be passed on through the medium of a person who has attached himself to them or to their ever-green memory, and formed his life on that pattern. Let us go further. If a word of a great mystic, or some of his imitators, finds an echo in one or another of us, may it not be that there is a mystic dormant within us, merely waiting for an occasion to awake?'[3]

And this love is a love of humanity, of all men, a love that is a participation of the very love of God for men. 'For the love which consumes him' (i.e. the Saint and Mystic) 'is no longer simply the love of man for God, it is the love of God for all men. Through God, in the strength of God, he loves all mankind with a divine love. This is not the fraternity enjoined on us by the philosophers in the name of reason, on the principle that all men share by birth in one rational essence: so noble an ideal cannot but command our respect; we may strive to the best of our ability to put it into

---

[1] *Two Sources*, p. 81. [2] Ibid., p. 194.
[3] Ibid., p. 81.

practice, if it be not too irksome for the individual and the community; we shall never attach ourselves to it passionately. Or, if we do, it will be because we have breathed in some nook or corner of our civilization the intoxicating fragrance left there by mysticism. . . . The mystic love of humanity is a very different thing. It is not the extension of an instinct, it does not originate in an idea. It belongs neither to the sensitive nor to the rational. It is implicitly both and effectively much more. For such a love lies at the very root of feeling and reason, as of all other things. Coinciding with God's love for His handiwork, a love which has been the source of everything, it would yield up, to anyone who knew how to question it, the secret of creation. It is still more metaphysical than moral in its essence. What it wants to do, with God's help, is to complete the creation of the human species and make of humanity what it would straightway become, had it been able to assume its final shape without the assistance of man himself'.[1] Truly *die schenkende Tugend* is much more represented in the philosophy of Bergson than in that of Nietzsche. Humanity in general is not a mere means, a footstool for the 'Superman' of Bergson, but the object of his love, which he would fain help to rise above itself and realize those potentialities imparted to it by God. There can be no question which is the nobler aristocracy, that of Bergson or that of Nietzsche. The Superman of Nietzsche pales into a terrible spectre, a monstrosity, beside the noble-hearted, loving and living hero of Bergson, who is not a mere figure of the future, but has actually lived and walked among men.

Nietzsche was possessed of an ideal for man, he was not content with man as he is, in his pettiness and misery—all honour to him for it!—he was in temperament idealist and even religious, though not by open profession; yet he falsified the position of man and the goal of man, and his philosophy—in spite of all claims to the contrary—is radically pessimistic. His desired culture is but a bubble on the river of the Eternal Recurrence, a passing phenomenon without lasting worth: true culture finds its

[1] *Two Sources*, pp. 199–200.

justification and character in its relation to God and the divine vocation of man (do not the Fathers and theologians say that 'God became man in order that man might become God'?) and its value is eternal, for man himself proceeds from the Creative Life and is designed to return to that Creative Life in company with his fellow men in the union of a living love. Only by recognition of this divine vocation will mankind be set once more on the true path of ascent and so, while indeed accepting the suffering inseparable from life here and now, pass into the splendour of the Divine Glory and Life.

REMARKS ABOUT NIETZSCHE

I

IN 1944 I attended a small dinner-party in the house where Dr. Oscar Levy, the eaitor of the English translation of Nietzsche's works, was then living. The dinner was in commemoration of the centenary of Nietzsche's birth. I found myself next to a young Greek who told me that he was subject to invasion by the dark forces of Dionysus. Appropriate enough for a Greek, I dare say, even if the Dionysian cult came from outside Greece—but less appropriate perhaps for the cerebral atmosphere of Oxford. I have always regretted that English inhibitions prevented me from asking precisely what he was referring to. However, he might not have told me, even if I had tried to probe.

Dr. Levy was an ardent Nietzschean, though he conjured up in my mind the thought of Voltaire rather than of Zarathustra. Besides editing the translation of Nietzsche's works, Dr. Levy wrote some books of his own, to spread the Nietzschean gospel. One of them was entitled *The Idiocy of Idealism*. It is a very long time since I read the book (if I ever read it properly). But I think that it is safe to say that by 'idealism' Dr. Levy did not mean the doctrine that we know only our own ideas. For unless this doctrine is interpreted in a sense which makes it both obviously true and innocuous, it is simply a curious philosophical extravaganza. Under the term 'idealism' Dr. Levy included, if I remember right, both theistic religion and the metaphysical idealism of thinkers such as Hegel. Belief in God and belief that the world was a rational process, the unfolding of an absolute idea, were, for Dr. Levy, idiotic—though he was too polite to express this point of view in conversation with a believer. In any case his main desire was that interest should be taken in Nietzsche, even if this interest was shown by benighted Christians.

Nietzsche himself would doubtless have endorsed the title of Dr. Levy's book, *The Idiocy of Idealism*. His world was, *in itself*, a world without purpose or goal—a world which certainly did not represent either the fulfilment of a divine plan or the self-unfolding of absolute Thought or Spirit. It was, in a sense, an absurd world—this absurdity being symbolized in the theory of the Eternal Recurrence, the theory that the world-process consists of infinitely repeated cycles, in which the same events recur again and again. In each cycle Friedrich Nietzsche is reborn, suffers the same loneliness and the indifference of his contemporaries, and succumbs, presumably, to general paralysis of the insane. An unpleasant thought. Camus remarked that the world cannot properly be described as absurd in itself. The absurdity arises in the confrontation of the human mind with the world in itself. But I do not suppose that Nietzsche would quarrel with this explanation of what it means to say that the world is absurd.

As we are all aware, though Nietzsche believed that the world has no meaning or purpose in itself, he also believed that man could *give* it a meaning. And he himself called upon his readers to make Superman (the more-than-man) the meaning of the earth. Like Sartre after him, he thought that meaning is not discovered but man-made. Values too were, for Nietzsche, created by man, not discovered by him. Here again he anticipates Sartre.

It is in the light of these convictions that we have to see Nietzsche's increasingly shrill and violent anti-theism, or, more precisely, his polemics against what he believes to be the Christian idea of God. He does not really object to belief in God on the ground that it is *false*. A man who defined truth as a biologically useful form of error would hardly be in a good position for objecting to any belief simply on the ground that it was false. His real objection is that Christian belief in God, when taken with all that it entails or is thought to entail, is an obstacle to human development, to human creativeness and to man's taking his rightful place as lord of history. Most people no longer believe in elves—not because their existence has been positively disproved, but because there is no good evidence for thinking that there are any such beings. But if it pleases some people to believe that there are elves in the woods, what does it matter? It is a harmless eccentricity, which has little, if any, effect on conduct. In Nietzsche's opinion, however, belief in the Christian God entails looking on man as sinful, miserable and powerless. It means canonizing a set of values—such as humility, love of the neighbour, human equality and so on—the effect of which is to encourage the preservation of the human race in its present state, and which militates against the development of the intellectually free and independent and of the strong characters who break through the bonds of conventional morality and create their own values. It means looking on history as having a predetermined goal and on human beings as instruments of God in the fulfilment of a divine plan—instead of looking on history as plastic and seeing that man's future lies in his own hands.

For Nietzsche, much the same can be said in regard to metaphysical idealism, which he regards as a kind of concealed theology. Hypostatized Thought or Reason is substituted for the personal God. But to look on man as an instrument of cosmic Reason or as a means whereby some eternal Idea works itself out is not much better than to look on the course of history as predetermined by God. Both Christian theism and metaphysical idealism refuse to see the world as it is—a world which, in itself, has no meaning or purpose. Both say No to the world as it is—a world in which each centre of energy exemplifies the will to power. In fact, the idea of God is the supreme example of a no-saying attitude to the world and life. All perfection is ascribed to an alleged transcendent Being: *this* world is depreciated in contrast with an imagined *other* world, in which the meek will inherit the earth and the human embodiments of the will to power will be cast into the outer darkness or consigned to unquenchable flames. And the values useful to 'the herd' are raised to the rank of universal and absolute values, so that the potentially free and independent and strong are stunted and crippled or tyrannized over by the majority in the name of a non-existent God.

The death of God therefore—the news that the old God is dead—is for Nietzsche an event of the greatest importance. For it is only through the disappearance of belief in God that man can at last face the boundless sea—*his* sea—which lies open before him as a field for his creative energy.

II

Now one of the favourite games played by philosophers is the detection of inconsistencies in their colleagues' theories. And Nietzsche's world-vision provides plenty of opportunities for playing this game. For example, it has doubtless seemed to many readers (whether justifiably or not) that having described all metaphysical systems as fictitious, Nietzsche then goes on, with his doctrines of the will to power and the Eternal Recurrence, to tell us what the world is *really* like. Again, it is a stock objection against Nietzsche that he denies absolute values and then proceeds to speak in such a way as to imply that a certain set of values—the values of 'ascending life'—are objectively superior to the values of the herd. It can also be argued, for instance, that Nietzsche caricatures Christianity.

Objections of this sort can be multiplied and developed. At the same time the Nietzschean can endeavour to meet them. On the subject of values, for instance, he can argue that when Nietzsche proclaims the superiority of his own set of values, he is not necessarily making an implicit admission of the objectivity of values. He has chosen a certain value-system and is speaking from within it. When Bertrand Russell, who also denied absolute values and interpreted the value-judgment as an expression of desire, was taxed with the fact that he vehemently asserted certain values, he replied on these lines: 'According to me, value-judgments express desires. I have strong desires. Why should I not express them strongly?' Nietzsche might make an analogous reply. In regard to Nietzsche's attack on

Christianity, the Nietzschean might reply that the philosopher was well aware that he often indulged in caricature, but that he thought that this was the only way of breaking through the indifference with which his writings were met at the time and of bringing out his point.

Needless to say, the Nietzschean's replies to objections can be met by counter-objections, and the counter-objections by further answers, and so on until the discussion is abandoned, each side thinking that it has won a victory. From one point of view, however, such discussion seems irrelevant or academic. Hegel spoke of the death of God. Feuerbach developed the idea in his own way. But it was Nietzsche who tried, in a dramatic and impressive manner, to bring home to the man for whom God was no longer a reality his situation in a godless world and the possibilities open to him in such a world. Nietzsche divined the breakdown of the old Christian culture of Europe and the consequences of this breakdown. He was the prophet of the twentieth century. He offered myths, such as the myth of Superman and the myth of the Eternal Recurrence, to take the place of myths which he regarded as outmoded or as positively harmful to man. Whether we accept these myths or not is a matter of secondary importance. Nor does it matter very much whether or not they fit in well with one another. The challenge of Nietzsche has an importance which is independent of such considerations. And the only way of countering it successfully, if it can be countered, is to produce a different but equally compelling world-vision. If we think that history has a goal independently of human choice, we have to exhibit this goal in a persuasive manner. The finding of ambiguities and inconsistencies in Nietzsche's writings is a pastime for historians of philosophy; but it has little relevance to the general theme of the death of God. We might just as well think that we can dispose of the psychologies of Freud and Adler by remarking that if everything is blue, nothing is blue. If everything is libido, nothing is libido. If everything is will to power, nothing is will to power. We lack the contrasts required to give meaning to the statement that something is x rather than y. Perhaps so. But this consideration does not alter the fact that the pioneers of depth psychology have had a profound effect upon our ways of thinking. Similarly, logical objections to Nietzsche do not alter the fact that he gives explicit and powerful expression to the situation of modern man.

III

Is Nietzsche however simply a visionary and a prophet—a man who proclaimed the death of God, the breakdown of traditional beliefs and moral codes, and man's freedom to create his own myths and values? Has he nothing to say to the more sober-minded philosophers who steer clear of world-visions, prophesying the future, preaching new values, and who tend to leave everything as it is—giving their attention to meta-ethics rather than to moralizing, to examining religious language rather than to saying whether there is a God or not? Nietzsche anticipated, it is true, the psychology of Alfred Adler. But nobody would deny that he possessed a measure of psychological insight. The question remains whether he has anything to say which is relevant to philosophy as we know it in this country.

Some British philosphers have given the impression of thinking that whenever philosophical theory clashes or seems to clash with common sense, as expressed in so-called ordinary language, the philosophical theory must either be false or a very odd and eccentric way of drawing attention to something which is obviously true. To be sure, the late Professor J. L. Austin disclaimed any such dogmatism and explicitly recognized that ordinary language itself embodies theories and interpretations. It can hardly be denied however that there has been in recent philosophy a cult of ordinary and everyday language, accompanied at times by a tendency at any rate to contrast it with theory and interpretation. Even if they have not regarded ordinary language as incorrigible, some philosophers have given the impression of thinking that in comparison with philosophical theory it constitutes pretty well a criterion of truth. Disclaimers appeared to Professor Gellner, in his well-known book *Words and Things*, as an example of hedging one's bets.

According to Bertrand Russell, ordinary language embodies the metaphysics of the Stone Age. However this may be, Nietzsche looks on ordinary language as shot through with interpretations and assumptions. And he sets himself to question these assumptions in a radical manner. For instance, in ordinary language we assume a distinction between appearance and reality: we assume that there are, so to speak, hard facts: and we assume a clear-cut distinction between truth and falsity. Obviously, we are well aware that on many occasions we do not know what the truth is, or that we do not know it clearly or with certainty. But in our very admissions of this fact we presuppose that truth and falsity or error are mutually exclusive. Nietzsche calls in questions such assumptions. For him, what we regard as hard facts are interpretations. What we would describe as 'reality' or as 'really the case' is also interpretation, fiction. And propositions which we regard as evidently and necessarily true are simply man-made 'fictions' which have proved their utility for life over a long tract of time and so have come to be accepted without question. In other words, he proposes an instrumentalist theory of truth, a theory in which the distinction between truth and error loses fixity and clear-cut lines.

Again, when left to ourselves, we assume that some actions are right, others wrong. We are probably aware that moral convictions have differed in different societies. And we are certainly aware that people hold different moral ideas to-day. But we assume, for instance, that an action such as torturing a child to death is simply wrong. And if someone were to maintain seriously that it was not wrong, we would look on him as devoid of moral sense or as, from the moral point of view, a 'monster', unable to appreciate moral distinctions. Nietzsche, however, calls such assumptions in question. Needless to say, he has no intention of defending the kind of action to which I have just referred. His thesis is that there is no such thing as moral truth and falsity apart from a given code, which depends on human choice and convention. There are no absolute values; but all values are man's creation—expressions of a certain 'perspective'.

In brief, we tend to think that our language mirrors reality, with greater or lesser success. Nietzsche goes so far as to question whether there is any reality to mirror. At any rate if there is, we cannot know it. What we call the world is our creation, a painting painted by man. The world of the artist, the world of the scientist, the world of the religious man, the world of everyday common sense—they are all perspectives, interpretations, human creations.

In other words, Nietzsche is a great questioner, an experimenter with the art of calling in question cherished assumptions and presuppositions. To regard ordinary or everyday language as in any way a criterion of truth would be for him the expression of blind prejudice or of philosophical superficiality. Many philosophers of course would agree that part at any rate of the philosopher's business—perhaps the main part—is to examine presuppositions critically. It has been a common enough occupation. Kant and Russell, for example, tried to make explicit the presuppositions of science. But Nietzsche tries to carry the process of questioning as far as he can, even to the limits of the unsayable—or unthinkable.

This process seems to me to have its utility. For unless a philosopher is prepared to question presuppositions and assumptions, he can hardly hope to come up against the unquestionable, if there is an unquestionable. It is certainly arguable that there is. After all, the instrument for questioning the assumptions of language is language itself. And it is arguable that language sets limits to what can be said or thought. Can we claim intelligibly, for example, that we have only interpretations and that there is nothing to interpret, no reality in itself, which is interpreted? Can I really seriously maintain that the 'g' is a 'logical construction', as Nietzsche held in effect that it is, though he did not actually use Russell's term? For am I not then committed to saying that I construct myself?—which seems overparadoxical.

My point is that reflecting on Nietzsche's radical questioning is not a bad way of immersing oneself in philosophical problems and of examining the limits of the sayable and thinkable. The activity may not attract everyone. But it seems to be a reasonably respectable form of critical reflection.

IV

In his book on Nietzsche, Professor Crane Brinton remarks that the great yea-sayer spent of his life saying No. The remark is apt. For example, Nietzsche said No to man as he is and proposed the myth of Superman. But we can be pretty sure, I think, that if anyone were presented to Nietzsche as embodying the qualities of Superman, the philosopher would very soon dismiss him as human-all-too-human. Incidentally, this is one good reason why the notion that Nietzsche would have regarded Adolf Hitler and his associates as 'higher men' or even as supermen is, to my way of thinking, incredible. Elizabeth Förster-Nietzsche, his sister, may have thought it credible. But her brother was never satisfied with the actual, in spite of his exhortations to say Yes to the world and life.

Metaphysicians have been accused of being profoundly dissatisfied with this world, for some deep-seated psychological reasons, and of inventing other worlds (reality as contrasted with appearance) to satisfy their longings. Nietzsche invented a world—the world of the Eternal Recurrence—which horrified him. He may have tried to affirm it—he *did* try—but it did not give him satisfaction.

For Karl Jaspers, who wrote one of the profoundest studies of Nietzsche, Nietzsche's ceaseless questioning and his refusal to be satisfied with anything are an expression of a hidden drive towards truth, which (interpretatively) is the drive towards the Absolute, to God—or to what Paul Tillich has described as the God beyond 'God'. At the same time this drive towards the Absolute, ultimate reality, is accompanied by a resolute will to 'this-sidedness', this-worldliness, to the exclusion of God. The doctrine of the Eternal Recurrence, which identifies Being with the cyclic Becoming of the world, expresses this resolute will. In

Jaspers' judgment, therefore, Nietzsche is the man who, *with the idea of God*, rejects him. Nietzsche thus embodies in himself one possibility of human *Existence* (which for Jaspers is always *mögliche Existenz*, the possibility of self-determination). The opposite and complementary pole of human existence is represented by Kierkegaard.

For my own part, I have a very strong sympathy with Jaspers' interpretation of Nietzsche. His existential analysis seems to me a profounder account of the philosopher than those psychological interpretations which depict him as a sick, rather ineffective and somewhat comical intellectual who compensated for his own shortcomings and limitations by admiring 'blond beasts' and indulging in megalomaniac utterances. However, it must be admitted of course that Jaspers' interpretation presupposes a certain philosophical point of view: an existentialist point of view, that is to say.

It may be objected that though studies of Nietzsche the man certainly have their interest and value, as a philosopher he must be judged by his writings, by the ideas which he committed to paper and which take on, as it were, a life of their own, outliving their author. There is obviously truth in this contention, even if, in the case of Nietzsche, it is rather difficult to separate understanding of the ideas from understanding of the man. If we consider the ideas, it is clear that Nietzsche explored and tried to overcome what he called 'nihilism', defined as loss of belief in all values and realization of the fact that history has no goal and that there is no answer to the question 'Why?' In my opinion his attempt to overcome nihilism was a failure. My friend Dr. Oscar Levy seemed to take. Nietzsche's myths, such as Superman, with literal seriousness. In other words, he was a disciple, a Nietzschean. The myths, however, seem to me weak and unconvincing, even if they express Nietzsche's struggle to overcome nihilism and to rise out of the depths of unlimited doubt. For me at any rate the significance of Nietzsche consists to a great extent in his embodying in himself the predicament of the man for whom traditional beliefs and values have lost their meaning and relevance and who is searching desperately for something to take their place.

NIETZSCHE AS A PHILOSOPHER

I

IN A well-known essay Rudolf Carnap maintains that meta-physicians are people who have chosen the wrong medium of expression. If they had the requisite gifts, they should express their emotive attitudes to life or to the universe in poetry or symphonies, not in prose treatises which claim to give (but do not give) the objective truth about reality. Carnap then remarks, doubtless by way of confirmation of his thesis, that when Nietzsche wished to play the role of a metaphysician, he very properly turned to poetry and wrote *Thus Spake Zarathustra.*

Carnap's general account of metaphysics is, in my opinion, precisely the sort of slapdash judgment which one would expect from a member of the Vienna Circle. However, I agree with him, though with some misgiving, that Nietzsche can be described as a metaphysician, even if he was other things as well.

To describe Nietzsche as a metaphysician may seem to be a perverse act. So it would be, if one were suggesting that he defended what Professor W. H. Walsh has described as transcendent metaphysics. That is to say, he did not seek the explanation or ground of phenomena or of finite things in any reality transcending this world, God or a transcendent Absolute. As everyone knows, he rejected all forms of theism, panentheism and pantheism. At the same time he can reasonably be described as a metaphysician, if one includes under this term all philosophers who provide world-views which go beyond the sphere of empirical science. We can then say, in Professor Walsh's terminology, that Nietzsche offered an immanent metaphysics.

It might be as well however to go on to borrow a term from Professor P. F. Strawson and describe Nietzsche's metaphysics as 'revisionary'. That is to say, he wanted to alter our way of seeing the world, to see it in a new way, Nietzsche's way. It seems that his first idea of the appropriate title for his contemplated but never finished *magnum opus* was *The Will to Power, a New Interpretation of Nature* or *The Will to Power, an Essay towards a New Interpretation of the Universe*. Later on he changed the title of the projected work, laying emphasis on the transvaluation of values. But the first tentative titles clearly express a concern with a revisionary world-view.

I now wish to explain briefly why I think that Nietzsche can reasonably be described as a metaphysician, in the sense indicated, and why at the same time I have a certain misgiving in so describing him.

II

Nietzsche often refers to a yea-saying attitude to life and the world. In his view Christianity, with its doctrines of a supernatural reality and of man's vocation to a goal or end which transcends this world and this life, inevitably adopts a negative attitude to this world. The world as we know it is transitory and this life is a vale of tears and a preparation for the next life. The body is despised; strength, beauty and so on are devalued in favour of asceticism, humility, meekness and self-abasement. The Christian religion teaches man to seek true reality beyond this world. It is the spiritual heir of Platonism, only worse.

Christianity is not of course the only sinner in this respect. Arthur Schopenhauer, with his thoroughly pessimistic view of human life and of the world, called upon man to turn away from his world through self-denial and mortification, with a view to attaining the Nirvana of non-existence. True, Schopenhauer was not himself given to self-denial and mortification. But this is irrelevant. The point is that his philosophy, like Christianity, represents a no-saying attitude to life and the world, the worst of all possible worlds in Schopenhauer's opinion.

Against this negative attitude Nietzsche sets a yea-saying attitude. It may indeed be the case that, as Professor Crane Brinton remarks in a book on Nietzsche, the great yea-sayer spent most of his life saying No. But he exhorted his readers at any rate to say Yes, to affirm life and the world as they are, without inventing another world or another life, and without disguising the nature of the world and of life by religious or metaphysical fictions.

Well, what is the world like, according to Nietzsche? In the posthumously-published notes, labelled *The Will to Power*, he asserts that '*this world is the Will to Power—and nothing else*! And you yourselves too are this Will to Power—and nothing else!' These words are an adaptation of Schopenhauer's statement at the end of his chief work (*The World as Idea and Will*) and express a transformation of the Will to Existence or the Will to Live into the Will to Power. It would indeed be a mistake to interpret Nietzsche as meaning that the phenomenal world is an appearance of an underlying or transcendent reality, the Will to Power. He is not a metaphysician in this sense. The Will to Power is what he calls the 'intelligible character' of the world. That is to say, everything, from atoms to human beings, can be seen as manifestations of a Will to Power which exists only in its manifestations. The world is a unified process of Becoming in which all members are centres of dynamic energy, manifesting what can be described as the Will to Power. Though, however, Nietzsche certainly tries to avoid hypostatizing the Will to Power as a reality which transcends its manifestations, he is obviously presenting a world-view or world-vision, an overall interpretation of reality. And in this sense he is a metaphysician.

Nietzsche also resurrects the old Greek idea of the repetition of cycles, the doctrine of the 'Eternal Recurrence'. The process of Becoming does not resemble a straight line stretching out indefinitely. It consists of a series of cycles, in which events are repeated. In each cycle Nietzsche recurs, writes *Beyond Good and Evil*, *Zarathustra* and so on, suffers from increasing loneliness, and succumbs to general paralysis of the insane (if this is what it was). Becoming and

Being are identical. And the world is without purpose or 'meaning'.

On the face of it at any rate this is clearly a metaphysical view of the universe. In one sense it may recall Hegel, in the sense, that is to say, that Being is identified with Becoming. In another sense however it is diametrically opposed to the philosophy of Hegel. For Hegel reality was a teleological process, moving towards the attainment of an ideal goal, the self-realization of the Absolute. But this is a view which Nietzsche consciously excludes. The world has not been created by God for a purpose. Nor has it any immanent teleological dynamism. It is a series of endless cycles, a universe which has no meaning in itself and no purpose given from outside.

III

Nietzsche seems therefore to be telling us what, in his opinion, reality or the universe as a whole is really like. And unless we insist on understanding the term 'metaphysics' exclusively in the sense of what Professor Walsh calls 'transcendent metaphysics', there appears to be ample ground to describe Nietzsche as a metaphysician. Why then do I feel some misgiving in regard to this description?

One ground, though not a very serious one—and certainly not the basic ground—is this. The doctrine of the Eternal Recurrence may appear to be simply a piece of metaphysical speculation. At the same time Nietzsche looks for scientific support and tries to turn it into an empirical hypothesis. He suggests, for instance, that 'the principle of the conservation of energy *demands* the Eternal Recurrence'. If we assume, he argues, that the world is a determinate quantum of energy and that there is a determinate number of centres of energy or force, the number of possible successive combinations of these centres will be finite. And in infinite time the totality of possible combinations will be repeated an infinite number of times.

It seems clear to me however that Nietzsche is simply

looking for scientific confirmation of a theory which is not in itself a scientific hypothesis at all. The idea of the Eternal Recurrence came to him one day at Sils-Maria in the Enga-dine as a kind of revelation. For him it was a horrifying idea. But he embraced it as a trial of strength. The weak man will reject the idea of the Eternal Recurrence, as he has not the strength to affirm a meaningless world and insists on representing the world as a purposeful or teleological process. The strong man however will show his strength by affirming the meaningless world and by imposing *his* purpose on a world which in itself is without purpose.

All this has little to do with empirical science. And one can hardly do anything else but describe the theory as a metaphysical theory, for which indeed Nietzsche proceeded to seek some scientific support.

In regard to the metaphysics of the Will to Power, the situation is really the other way round. That is to say, when Nietzsche was an undergraduate at Leipzig, he read Schopen-hauer with pleasure; but he was not inspired by his reading to transform Schopenhauer's Will to Live into the Will to Power. On the contrary, he seems to have arrived at the generalized theory of the Will to Power by a process of extension and extrapolation. Having discussed the operation of the Will to Power in human beings—thus anticipating the psychology of Alfred Adler—he proceeded to unify the activities of all living things in terms of this concept. And he then extended the concept to cover all phenomena, the world as a whole. The generalized theory of the Will to Power can thus be presented as a sweeping empirical hypothesis.

The general hypothesis is, however, the result of a striving after conceptual mastery over reality as a whole. I do not wish to deny that this tendency is present also in science. But science takes the form of the particular sciences, whereas Nietzsche goes beyond the distinguishable fields of particular sciences to the statement of a general view, an overall vision of the universe. So it seems to me quite natural to speak of 'inductive' metaphysics, as contrasted with an *a priori* metaphysics, of which Spinozism is, I suppose, the paradigm case.

Further, if we look for criteria to enable us to distinguish between a scientific hypothesis and a metaphysical theory, and if we adopt, for example, Sir Karl Popper's criterion of falsifiability in principle as a necessary and sufficient criterion for describing something as a scientific hypothesis, it seems to me doubtful whether Nietzsche's generalized theory of the Will to Power can count as a scientific hypothesis. After all, Popper has suggested that Adler's psychology of the Will to Power cannot count as a scientific hypothesis, inasmuch as any counter-instances which one may mention will be interpreted in the light of the theory and therefore as supporting the theory. In other words, the theory is so conceived as to be empirically irrefutable. And though it would sound odd to describe the Adlerian psychology as a metaphysical theory, it seems to me that one can perfectly well describe Nietzsche's generalized theory in this way. It may indeed be difficult to find any clear dividing-line between very general scientific hypotheses (i.e. hypotheses advanced by scientists) and the theories of inductive metaphysics. Perhaps philosophers are at fault here for trying to tidy things up to an extent which would seriously inhibit the scientific genius. It may very well be the case that at a certain level there is a clear similarity between some scientists and some metaphysicians. However, while recognizing that other points of view are possible, I am inclined to describe Nietzsche's generalized theory of the Will to Power as an essay in revisionary metaphysics. If one disagrees with it, it is not so much a question of falsifying it, in a scientific sense, as of producing a different theory and trying to exhibit it as more adequate, less one-sided, more consistent and so on.

In any case to describe Nietzsche as a scientist would be extremely odd, whereas to describe him as a metaphysician is not odd, unless, as I have said, one persists in identifying metaphysics with what Professor Walsh calls transcendent metaphysics. It may be the case, as Karl Jasper maintains, that we can discern in Nietzsche the will to transcendence or a desire to transcend all phenomena. In fact I am inclined to agree with Jaspers. But this does not alter the fact that on the level of explicit theory Nietzsche rules out any reality transcending the world and sets the seal on the identification of Being with Becoming by means of the doctrine of the Eternal Recurrence.

IV

I come now to another, and more basic, line of reflection. We generally think of a metaphysician as one who claims to tell us what the world is really like or to exhibit the nature of reality. He need not of course produce startling and paradoxical theories or world-visions to be described as a metaphysician. He may be concerned primarily with analysis of the basic concepts or categories in terms of which we can unify things on the most common level of being, concepts which are often implicit in the concrete expressions of ordinary language. Some metaphysicians have of course produced striking and revisionary world-views. But to equate metaphysics with paradoxical utterances seems to be an idiosyncrasy of Professor John Wisdom, who likes to dwell on this aspect of the matter. However, we generally think of metaphysicians, it seems to me, as people who profess to give the objective truth about the world, even if in some cases we believe that their claims are unjustified or improbable.

In this case it may appear that Nietzsche is about the last person to qualify for classification as a metaphysician. He rejects the idea of absolute truth and defines truth as '*that sort of error* without which a particular type of living being could not live. The value for *life* is ultimately decisive'. This notion must be seen in context. For many people, I suppose, Nietzsche was a wild man who talked about the Will to Power, the miserable 'herd', 'blond beasts' and Superman, while for others he was a prophet of the future who foresaw the breakdown of the old culture of Europe, the great wars of the twentieth century, the rise of Socialism, the menace of totalitarianism, and even the emergence of Russia as a great power. At the same time Nietzsche had an acute and critical mind. And he tried to subject to doubt all that could be doubted. Scientific theories were for him 'fictions', useful fictions it is true, but still fictions, the constructions of the scientist, imposed on phenomena. Values were not eternal realities, subsisting in some Platonic realm, but simply the expressions of value-judgments, which in turn express the human will. Man creates his own values by the act of evaluation. Even the truths of mathematics and the laws of logic are fictions. And the same can be said of the assumption that there are permanent physical objects and of the law of causality. In other words, Nietzsche anticipates, to some extent at least, the interpretation of scientific theories advanced by writers such as Pierre Duhem and Emile Meyerson and then turns his critical attention to the stronghold of the defenders of absolute truth, namely logic and pure mathematics, and also to the natural beliefs embodied in ordinary language. Some 'truths' are useful to individuals or groups but are not essential to life in general. We cannot but evaluate, for instance; but one set of values is relative to the weak, to 'descending' life, while another set is relative to the strong, to 'ascending' life. But there are fictions which have proved their worth or utility to such an extent that they have taken on the status of unquestioned truths. Such is the law of non-contradiction. We cannot get on without it. Similarly, we cannot actually live in a world of purely discrete successive phenomena. In order to live we have to make certain 'logical constructions', as Bertrand Russell would put it. Such concepts as that of enduring physical objects and such beliefs as that in the principle of causality are necessary to live, and they become enshrined in ordinary language. 'A philosophical mythology', Nietzsche remarks, 'lies hidden in language'. It is indeed an indication of 'natural beliefs' (to borrow a Humean phrase) which are necessary for life, in the sense that they are requisite pre-suppositions of life and action. But it is a mistake to think that ordinary language gives us the key to reality in itself. It tells us more about ourselves and our needs than about reality in itself.

What I have just been saying exhibits an aspect of Nietzsche's thought which is rather different from talk about 'blond beasts' and Superman. But my purpose in referring to Nietzsche's view of truth, in the present context, is of course to raise the question whether we can seriously suppose that in the doctrines of the Will to Power and the Eternal Recurrence he intended to tell us what the world is *really* like. If he did intend to do this, it would hardly be consistent with his general theory of truth. Indeed, it would be so flagrantly inconsistent that we can hardly ascribe to him such an intention. If however he did not intend to tell us what the world is really like, can we legitimately classify him as a metaphysician? Would it not be preferable to describe him as a story-teller or as a creator of myths?

V

Perhaps no simple answer can be given. On the one hand Nietzsche often gives the impression that he thinks of himself as revealing the real nature of the world. And the fact that he looks for scientific confirmation both of the doctrine of the Eternal Recurrence and of the general theory of the Will to Power tends to strengthen this impression. On the other hand scientific theories are for him 'fictions'; and it is natural to suppose that his general metaphysics is also intended as an 'as-if theory'.

After all, Superman is clearly a myth. Nietzsche does indeed say that 'Superman is the meaning of the earth'. But he does not accept the view that the world has any meaning in the sense of purpose or goal. And it is significant that he immediately adds: 'Let your will say: Superman *is to be* the meaning of the earth'. Speaking at Naples in 1922, Mussolini said: 'We have created our myth. The myth is a faith, it is passion. It is not necessary that it should be a reality. It *is* a reality by the fact that it is a goad, a hope, a faith, that it is courage. Our myth is the nation, our myth is the greatness of the nation'. Mussolini looks to the idea of the nation, of Italy as a great power, as an instrument for *creating* the reality—for welding together a divided people and one which is not exactly militaristic. So

Nietzsche looks to the idea of Superman as an instrument for spurring on the potentially higher men to develop themselves freely and to prepare the way for man's surpassing the condition of human-all-too-human. Again, in spite of talk about the conservation of energy, the doctrine of the Eternal Recurrence can quite well be regarded as being essentially a myth, in the sense that its primary purpose is to serve as a test of strength of will and character. Am I strong enough to embrace a theory which highlights the meaninglessness of the world and yet at the same time to *give* a meaning or purpose to the world and to strive after its realization?

Even if, however, Superman is a myth in the sense mentioned, and even if the doctrine of the Eternal Recurrence is an hypothesis which is embraced for a moral purpose rather than as the conclusion of a theoretical argument, it seems pretty clear that to some extent at any rate Nietzsche is committed to saying what the world is really like or, more precisely, what it is *not* like. If, for example, we define values in terms of the act of evaluation, as products of and depending on human will and decision, it seem so me that we are committed to saying that there are no values 'out there', subsisting independently of human choice. And if we maintain that theological or philosophical statements which assert that the process of Becoming has a determinate meaning or purpose are all examples of man's will conferring a purpose on the world-process, it seems to me to follow that we are thereby committed to asserting that the process is not meaningful or purposeful in itself, apart from human decision. Moreover, this is quite clearly what Nietzsche held. He regarded the so-called 'death of God' not simply as the disappearance of an old fable but also as man's liberation. That is to say, in Nietzsche's opinion the 'death of God' set man free to give to human existence what meaning he chose and to create values freely or to carry through the 'transvaluation of values'. The presupposition of this point of view is obviously that the world in itself, apart from human decision, is without meaning or purpose and without value.

Let me make my point quite clear. I am not blaming Nietzsche for trying to say what the world is really like or, if preferred, what it is really not like. Nor am I primarily concerned with the job of finding inconsistencies, a favourite pastime of critics of other people's philosophies. What I am primarily concerned with arguing is that we cannot give one simple answer to the question whether Nietzsche's world-view is intended to tell us what the world is really like. Some elements in it can be interpreted in terms of his theory of truth as biologically useful fiction. But I do not think that the whole of it can be so interpreted. For his rejection of Christian theology and idealist metaphysics seems to me to commit him at any rate to the statement that the world, considered in itself, is without meaning or value. To this extent at least he professes to tell us something about the world in itself.

Would that the matter were as simple as this! But *can* Nietzsche talk about the world in itself? In one sense of course he can and does. That is to say, he makes or implies statements of which the subject-term is 'the world'. But in another sense he cannot talk·about the world in itself. That is to say, any statement about the world in itself which claimed to be true in an absolute sense would be incompatible with Nietzsche's theory of perspectives. All truths are fictions; all fictions are interpretations; and all interpretations are perspectives. The world which I see is *my* world, the world as it appears to me. And I cannot transcend this perspective. Any statements therefore which I make about the world in itself are really about the world as it appears to me, *my* world. There is nothing at all that I can say about the world as not appearing to me. In fact, can I even say that there is such a world? Does it make any sense to talk in this way?

We might perhaps wish to say that it makes no sense to talk about a non-phenomenal or metaphenomenal world and that to talk about the phenomenal world *is* to talk about the world in itself, so far as this phrase ('the world in itself') has any meaning. Or we might prefer to say that Nietzsche's perspectivism forbids him to talk about the world in itself, and that if he does so, he involves himself in inconsistency. But I do not think that Nietzsche ever really teased the matter out. On the one hand he tells us that it is we who impose order and form on the multiplicity of impressions and sensations to satisfy our needs. This point of view would seem to imply a Humean scepticism in regard to what, if anything, lies beyond the succession of phenomena. And for all we know this might be a teleological reality. On the other hand Nietzsche tells us that reality is Becoming, and that we transform it into stable concepts for the purpose of mastering it, of expressing our will to power. And this statement seems to refer to reality in itself, implying that reality in itself is an unintelligible process which owes its intelligibility simply to man.

VI

Well, let us take it, for the sake of argument at any rate, that Nietzsche would be prepared to admit that his own world-view is a fiction, in the same sense that other world-views are fictions. What criteria does he use for differentiating between them? The answer seems to be pretty obvious, namely that the criteria are moral, judgments of value that is to say. The philosopher Fichte remarked, apropos of the choice between materialism and idealism, that which one chose depended on what sort of a man one was. Similarly, Nietzsche sees in different religions and philosophical systems expressions of different types of human beings. All systems express the Will to Power; but the people who embody the Will to Power and who express it in their beliefs are of different levels of value. Some of them represent ascending life and many of them represent stagnant or descending life. Nietzsche's own world-view is, in his opinion, a challenge to the potentially higher man, the genuine aristocrats, the few. It is not suited for 'the herd' which cannot face up to the vision of a meaningless world and yet resolutely impose their own meaning on existence and history, but has to find comfort in Christianity or Communism or some such set of beliefs.

Although therefore Nietzsche could, when he chose,

pursue critical analysis, the basic motivation of his metaphysics seems to have been the expression of certain judgments of value. He put forward a certain world-view as an
instrument for leading those who were capable of following in a
certain direction, the creation of a higher type of man.
Looked at from this point of view, his metaphysics can of
course be described as a 'fiction', in the sense in which he
himself used the word, namely as a 'biologically' useful
perspective or interpretation, justified pragmatically. At the
same time he is, I think, committed to certain beliefs about
reality which can hardly be fitted into his theory of truth
as fiction. There is also of course the question how far
Nietzsche's talk about ascending and descending life, about
higher and lower men, expresses an implicit acceptance of
values as absolute. We might perhaps allow Nietzsche the
same sort of answer which Bertrand Russell made when
taxed with his firmly asserted judgments of value. 'I hold
that judgments of value are expressions of desire. I have
vehement desires. Why should I not express them vehemently?' In both cases, however, that of Russell and that of
Nietzsche, it is very difficult to avoid the impression that in
spite of their ethical theories and in spite of marked differences between the value-judgments which they respectively
made, both men implicitly believed in absolute values. The
impression is not, it seems to me, without foundation. The
difficulty is, of course, to explain precisely what one means
by absolute values. Instead of talking about absolute values,
as though they were subsistent entities, should one perhaps
speak of committing oneself absolutely to certain evaluations?
I am not at all sure what the proper way of speaking is.

VII

This paper has probably been a great disappointment to
some of you, either because you expected me to concentrate
on the Death-of-God theme and Nietzsche's attack on
Christianity, or because you expected more about the
idea of nihilism and of the overcoming of nihilism, or because

you hoped for an existentialist interpretation of Nietzsche in the style of Karl Jaspers. 'After all', some of you may be thinking, 'even if Nietzsche was a very different type of philosopher from those who flourish in Oxford, for example, he was one of the great prophetic figures of recent history. His thought has given rise to many different interpretations and misinterpretations; but there can be no doubt of his posthumous influence and stimulating power, quite apart from the fact that he was a master of German prose. You however have read us a paper on academic questions which fail to exhibit the man who claimed that his thought was "dynamite".'

Well, I can only plead 'guilty, My Lord'. But I have after all been speaking to a philosophical society; and this must be my excuse, if excuse is needed. I add that if anyone wishes to raise questions on other aspects of Nietzsche's personality and thought, I am quite prepared to join in discussion, though I certainly do not pretend to have all the answers.

APPENDIX 3

TWENTY-TWO YEARS AFTER

I

SOMETIME after the end of the second World War a Frenchman kindly sent me a copy of an article which he had published on Nietzsche's ideas about women. He evidently thought that this topic was a matter of considerable interest and expected me to carry on a correspondence. The exchange of letters, however, soon flagged on my side. In the end I received a rather charming letter in which the Frenchman hazarded the guess that as a Reverend Father I had probably been shocked. He apologized for this, and I do not recollect having heard from him again. In point of fact I had been bored, not shocked, by the topic. Apart from some famous and provocative sayings, Nietzsche's statements about women did not seem to me to attain the standard of Schopenhauer's amusing passages on the subject. In any case I did not regard this particular theme as constituting an important element in Nietzsche's thought. To be sure, the philosopher's relations with other people and the reflections to which they gave rise provided data for the psychologist. The same could be said in regard to Schopenhauer. But I felt that if by Nietzsche's thought one meant the ideas which he expressed on paper and which began to exercise a real influence only when their author was no longer capable of appreciating his growing reputation, his utterances about women were of peripheral interest and importance. To delve into them was all very well for the type of scholar who delights in collecting all that Aquinas said about health or Hegel about phrenology. But in comparison with other aspects of his thought Nietzsche's remarks on women did not seem to me of much importance.

What then did I consider to be the most significant element in Nietzsche's thought? In the preface to my book I stated that Nietzsche's 'work may be said to centre round the problem of human culture: he summoned man to a new cultural ideal, the surpassing of man in Superman, *der Übermensch*' (p. xi). Later in the book I asserted of Nietzsche's thought that 'though a philosophy of culture, it contains within itself the seeds of anti-culture' (p. 203). And I was at pains to argue that the German philosopher was wrong in regarding Christianity as an anti-cultural factor. Such criticism does not alter the fact that the book was intended to show 'how the idea of an ascending culture runs as a *leitmotif* through the whole of Nietzsche's thought' (p. 195). Hence the sub-title of the book, 'Philosopher of Culture'.

One critic of my book remarked that the interpretation of Nietzsche's thought as centring on the problem of culture was by no means a novelty. This contention was true enough but, in my opinion, not much to the point. I do not think that I regarded my thesis as novel. The point was that I regarded it, whether rightly or wrongly, as relevant to the contemporary historical situation, to the significance of the war which was being waged at the time at which the book was written. In the preface I advanced the view that one of the essential aspects of the war was the attempt to preserve 'the cultural heritage of Europe against the attack of the New Barbarian'. Looking back, one may regard this view of the situation as over-simplified. But, this consideration apart, I argued that it was a matter of importance to consider the nature and foundations of genuine culture, and that this was a matter in which Nietzsche was passionately interested. I did not suggest that Nietzsche provided any adequate solution to the problem. My point was rather that he gave it serious consideration, and that in one way or another his philosophy was relevant.

The critic went on to maintain that the problem of culture was a peripheral element in Nietzsche's thought and that the really central problem was religious. If I remember correctly, the reviewer was not suggesting that in my book I had neglected the bearing of Nietzsche's ideas on religion. I think that his point was rather that though I was personally more interested in the religious relevance of Nietzsche's philosophy, as far as explicit emphasis was concerned I had laid it on surface elements, on what Nietzsche had to say about cultural development.

This was a more substantial point than remarks about novelty; and I alluded to it, without mentioning the reviewer's name, in an article which I wrote for the 1944 centenary of Nietzsche's birth. I there suggested that if by cultural interest one meant little more than a devotion to works of art and other cultural products, this interest was certainly not Nietzsche's central theme. If however one was thinking 'of man as such, his nature, his potentialities, his development, his relation to the world, his destiny'[1], the philosopher's mind was indeed preoccupied with this subject. After all, it was in function of man's potentialities and needs that he passed judgment on morals, politics, the State, the Church, religion and philosophy. At the same time I allowed

[1] 'Centenary of Friedrich Nietzsche' in *Studies* (Dublin), December, 1944, p. 472.

that 'even if the cultural problem constitutes the chief
interest of Nietzsche on the conscious level, this does not
mean that the religious interest was not, or did not become,
the central interest on the unconscious or repressed level'.[2]
This remark had nothing to do with Freud. It was clearly
an expression of the influence on my mind of Karl Jaspers'
profound work on Nietzsche[3] and of his analysis of the
relation between Nietzsche's actual philosophy and his
search for God, a search which belonged to the existential
level rather than to that of conscious reflection. Whereas
however Jaspers was thinking of the way in which Nietzsche,
in spite of his proclamation of a yea-saying attitude, was
constantly transcending the given and actual in a movement
towards the unobjectifiable ground of all empirical existence,
it is clear that I was thinking more of specifically Christian
belief.

The same sort of view reappears in a short contribution
which I wrote for the International Congress of Philosophy at Amsterdam in 1948. Having already specified the
'problem of culture' in terms of a philosophy of man, I
related Nietzsche's demands for a higher culture to his idea
of man. I contended that by rejecting man's relation and
openness to the Transcendent, Nietzsche made 'the integration of the human personality (and so true culture) impossible'.[4] Nietzsche connected belief in objective and absolute
values with the Transcendent (with belief in God, to put the
matter more concretely). And if, as I argued, he was right in
making this connexion, and if the recognition of objective
and absolute values was essential for 'true humanism and
true culture',[5] it followed that recognition of the Transcendent was also required for genuine humanism and culture.
Remarks about 'the tension in Nietzsche himself between the
resisted impulse to accept the Transcendent and the conscious will to "this-worldliness" and anthropocentrism'[6]

[2] Ibid.
[3] Nietzsche: Einführung in das Verständnis seines Philosophierens
(Berlin, 1939). Translated by C. F. Wallraff and F. J. Schmitz as Nietzsche:
An Introduction to the Understanding of His Philosophical Activity (Tucson,
Arizona, 1965).
[4] Proceedings of the Congress, Vol. 1, p. 258.
[5] Ibid.   [6] Ibid, p. 257.

show the evident influence of Jaspers. For the term 'this-worldliness' had nothing to do with the 'worldliness' to which Christian moralists have often referred. It was a translation of Jaspers' *Diesseitigkeit* and referred, for example, to the way in which, through his doctrine of the Eternal Recurrence, Nietzsche endeavoured to close the circle of Becoming (or to identify Being with Becoming) and to the way in which he demanded that man should make himself, in the form of the ideal projection of Superman, the meaning or goal of history. My contention was that in terms of this line of thought there was no issue from the nihilism which Nietzsche wished to overcome. In brief, I accepted to a considerable extent Nietzsche's diagnosis of nihilism, while rejecting his solution or at any rate representing it as inadequate.

Since the forties I have devoted little serious attention to Nietzsche, apart from reading and reviewing two or three books on him and, of course, writing the two relevant chapters in the seventh volume of my *History of Philosophy*. It seems to be true however that I have come to see him principally in relation to the nihilism of which he wrote, his experience of nihilism and his attempt to transcend it. By saying this I do not mean that I have come to agree with those writers who appear to think that Nietzsche's ideas can be adequately discussed simply in terms of their relation to his psychological make-up. A psychological or a psychoanalytic treatment of Nietzsche is of course legitimate; and it can doubtless throw light on his philosophizing. After all, Nietzsche himself refers to 'masks', adopted for the sake of mental health and development. It does not follow however that a purely psychological treatment is adequate. The belief, for example, that the world and human history have no determinate purpose or meaning, independently, that is to say, of man's will to confer a meaning, can be discussed without reference to Nietzsche's personal psychology. So of course can the belief that while there are human evaluations, there are no absolute values, independent of man's act of evaluation. At the same time Nietzsche experienced in himself a spiritual crisis which has affected others too, as he foretold. And while he strove to transcend nihilism in himself, he offered to man in general a way of transcending it. For my own part, I do not find his positive message either attractive or convincing. I could not be a 'Nietzschean'. But I regard Nietzsche's 'existence', in the sense of Jaspers' *Existenz*, as possessing historical significance, a cultural significance one can say, provided that the word 'cultural' is not understood in terms of the external products of human culture. In other words, I am still inclined to agree with what I wrote in 1963, namely that is arguable that 'what is really significant in what one may call the non-academic Nietzsche is not his proposed antidotes to nihilism but rather his existence and thought considered precisely as a dramatic expression of a lived spiritual crisis from which there is no issue in terms of his own philosophy'.[7] This point of view reappears in the talk entitled 'Remarks about Nietzsche' which was written in 1971 and is printed in the present volume (p. 215).

II

If we say of a given philosopher that what is 'really' significant in his thought is this or that element or aspect, we are obviously giving expression to a value-judgment or to a set of such judgments. These judgments imply criteria which may or may not be made explicit. In regard to Nietzsche, if we claim with Jaspers that what is really important in Nietzsche is his existential significance (when 'existence' is understood in terms of Jaspers' concept of *Existenz*), the natural conclusion is that Nietzsche's positive theories and ideas are deemed of secondary importance, or at any rate that importance is attributed to them in so far as they are factors in an existentialist interpretation of Nietzsche's life and philosophizing, and that they are relegated to a subordinate position when they are considered in themselves or abstractly. Similarly, if we regard Nietzsche's thought as important primarily in so far as it is an expression of nihilism as a cultural phenomenon, as an expression of

[7] *A History of Philosophy*, Vol. 7, p. 420.

what the philosopher described as 'the death of God', this point of view may well imply, even if it does not do so necessarily, that Nietzsche's antidotes to nihilism are not to be taken very seriously.

As far as Jaspers is concerned, Professor Walter Kaufmann has found fault with him for discounting Nietzsche's 'philosophy' as distinct from his 'philosophizing'. In Kaufmann's opinion Jaspers is so intent on exhibiting the existential significance, as he sees it, of Nietzsche's life and intellectual activity that he refuses to take seriously such concepts as those of Superman ('overman' is the term used by Kaufmann), the eternal recurrence, the will to power and sublimation, and indeed 'any other definite concept'.[8] Jaspers is not prepared to look on Nietzsche as a theoretical philosopher in the sense in which Kant was a theoretical philosopher, but rather as a striking manifestation of nihilism; and he uses Nietzsche's restless striving as an introduction to his own line of thought.

There is clearly a good deal of truth in what Kaufmann has to say about Jaspers' treatment of Nietzsche. As Jaspers was an original philosopher, it is not altogether surprising that he should interpret Nietzsche in the light of his own thought.[9] It may of course be objected that even if Jaspers was an original thinker, this fact did not exempt him from the obligation of giving an objective treatment of any other philosopher about whom he proposed to write. Jaspers however saw in Nietzsche an 'exception', a man who represented one extreme possibility of human *Existenz*, while Kierkegaard represented another. And Nietzsche's definite ideas and theories were for Jaspers simply temporary resting-places, as it were, in a movement of thought which constantly tended to pass beyond all determinate positions. Given this approach, Jaspers could hardly treat Nietzsche's philosophy, in the sense of his definite theories, with the

---

[8] *From Shakespeare to Existentialism* (Anchor Books, New York, 1960), p. 311. The original version of the essay in question was written by Kaufmann for the Jaspers volume in the Library of Living Philosophers. But in this new version he comments on Jaspers' reply to the original version.

[9] Much the same, *mutatis mutandis*, can be said of Martin Heidegger's two-volume *Nietzsche* (Pfullingen, 1961).

sort of seriousness which Kaufmann doubtless has in mind. Though however we can understand Jaspers' line of thought and the presuppositions which influence his treatment of Nietzsche, it can indeed be objected that the treatment involves an unverifiable hypothesis, namely that if Nietzsche had retained his sanity and mental vigour, he would have discarded and passed beyond such concepts as those of the eternal recurrence and of *Übermensch*. For if, as Jaspers suggests, Nietzsche's 'godlessness is the increasing agitation of a search for God that perhaps no longer understands itself',[10] the concept of superman would sooner or later be revealed as a substitute which had to be transcended. And we have obviously no means of knowing whether in point of fact Nietzsche would have passed beyond the determinate theories which are associated with his name and which can be regarded as forming his 'philosophy'.

The influence of Jaspers is clear enough in an article published a long time ago in which I suggested explicitly that Nietzsche's thought was 'a philosophizing' rather than 'a philosophy' and referred to it as a restless quest which 'passes beyond all horizons'.[11] Such remarks evidently exposed me to the same sort of objections which Kaufmann has made against Jaspers' treatment of Nietzsche. These objections may seem also to apply to an assertion which I made in a fairly recent review-article. The article in question is entitled 'Foreground and Background in Nietzsche', and in it I say that Nietzsche's thought is 'much more than a set of theses or doctrines [and] has a lasting historical importance, as anticipating, with remarkable insight, the upheavals and convulsions of the twentieth century, and as representing in himself the spiritual crisis of modern modern man'.[12] This assertion does not lack foundation in what Nietzsche says about himself. In *Ecce Homo* he refers to himself as being not a man but dynamite. He emphasizes the destructive effect of his thought on all established 'lies' and values; and he foretells the coming of politics on a

---

[10] *Nietzsche* (English translation, see note 3), p. 435.
[11] *Philosophy*, Vol. 17 (1942), p. 244.
[12] *The Review of Metaphysics*, Vol. 21 (1968), p. 523.

grand scale. At the same time he does indeed deny that he is a purely destructive thinker and claims to have overcome nihilism both in himself and for future man, if the latter will heed and accept his message. In other words, though there is much in Nietzsche which justifies the interpretation of his thought as a diagnosis and intensification of nihilism, one can also appeal to what he says in support of the demand that his positive theories and ideas should be taken seriously.

Nietzsche may however have been mistaken in thinking that his constructive ideas, his antidotes to nihilism, possessed real value. And if this is what someone thinks, he has every right to say so. It can however be demanded that before saying so he should consider the ideas seriously. This is doubtless true. But it is perhaps not immediately clear what taking seriously means in the context or contexts. In different contexts it may involve rather different procedures.

Consider the idea of Superman. Whatever some writers may have said, Nietzsche did not maintain that Superman would emerge as the natural product of further evolution. He was not proposing a falsifiable empirical hypothesis. Nor did he claim to have deduced from self-evidently true or unquestionable premises the conclusion that man would surpass himself in Superman. He was proposing an ideal goal designed to act as a spur to the human will. 'Let your will say: let Superman be the meaning of the earth'.[13] This exhortation was obviously the expression of a set of value-judgments and of desire, Nietzsche's personal desire for the coming of *Übermensch* and his desire that others should share this desire. If therefore we are considering Nietzsche's own attitude, taking the concept of Superman seriously can hardly mean, or should not be interpreted as meaning, weighing the empirical evidence or the proofs that Superman will arise. It involves reflection on Nietzsche's judgments of value. This does not of course exclude argument. When writing about Nietzsche in his *History of Western Philosophy*, Bertrand Russell says that the ultimate 'argument' against Nietzsche must take the form of an appeal to the emotions.

[13] Preface (*Vorrede*) to *Zarathustra* (*Werke, Kritische Gesamtausgabe*, VI/I, Berlin, 1968, p. 8).

But even if we accept Russell's analysis of the nature of the value-judgment, the operative word is 'ultimate'. We can, for example, draw attention to what we believe to be the probable consequences of Nietzsche's idea of differentiation in rank and of the notion that the 'herd' should find the meaning of their existence in the emergence of a higher type of man. If we believe that such ideas are objectionable and dangerous and that they would have consequences which we reject, we can hope, by drawing attention to these consequences, to persuade the follower of Nietzsche to change his conviction. If however he agrees that Nietzsche's ideas would probably have the consequences in question but welcomes them, an intended persuasive argument will obviously be ineffective. We can of course consider the presuppositions of the different sets of value-judgments and argue about them. But if we come to the conclusion that the Nietzschean and we have basically different desires, there will come a point at which further argument becomes profitless.

It is not a question of arguing that Nietzsche would have seen in Adolf Hitler an embodiment of the ideal of *Übermensch*. Apart from the fact that he would doubtless have judged any actual man to be 'human, all-too-human', he is much more likely to have seen in Hitler a manifestation of active nihilism and of the new barbarism. Rather it is a question of objecting to the whole idea of finding the goal of human history in the production of a number of outstanding individuals. There is a sense, as it now seems to me, in which I took the idea of Superman too seriously in my book on Nietzsche. I there suggested that the saints were the genuine Supermen, and that the surpassing of man as he is could be achieved only through an influx of that divine life and love to which Henri Bergson refers in the *Two Sources of Morality and Religion*. As far as this suggestion goes, it is equivalent to accepting the idea of *Übermensch*, while altering the content to fit in with Christian beliefs. But does it fit in? In my book I tried to combine the idea of Superman with belief in the value of man as such, of all human beings. Nietzsche's idea of *Übermensch* however involves thinking of human beings in general, the 'herd' that is to say, as attaining the goal of their existence in the emergence of an aristocracy of talent. Nietzsche himself did not look on this idea as Christian. And I think that he was justified. In this case it can well be doubted whether the idea of Superman is much improved by the substitution of saints and mystics for the admittedly somewhat vaguely defined content given it by Nietzsche. Though however I should not now wish to take the concept of Superman seriously in the way in which I did so in my book, there are other ways in which it can be taken seriously. For instance, one would not wish to commend any policy of levelling down, of inhibiting the free development of outstanding individuals, whether artists, poets, philosophers, scientists or saints. And in so far as Nietzsche condemns attempts to mould all members of society to one pattern and to impose uniformity in the name of an ideology or as the expression of what he describes as 'resentment', his protest is justified. To emphasize the desirability of a free or open society, as against any form of totalitarianism, is not however the same thing as to make *Übermensch* the meaning of the earth.

When Nietzsche says, 'Let your will say: let Superman be the meaning of the earth', it would be inappropriate to ask whether what he says is true or false. For Nietzsche is exhorting or commending a certain policy rather than making a statement of fact or what is claimed to be such. If we disagree with his judgment of value, we can of course try to support our counter-judgments in appropriate ways. But we are not treating of questions which can be settled simply on the plane of logic. We can however ask, what analysis of the value-judgment as such is implied by what Nietzsche has to say about values? And the answer seems to be that it is similar to Bertrand Russell's. For when Nietzsche denies that there are objective or absolute values, waiting, as it were, to be recognized by man, he is obviously not denying that there are evaluations. If, for example, he asserts that the world in itself is without meaning or value, he is not denying that human beings are capable of attaching meaning or value to the world. He is saying that there are only evaluations or acts of evaluation. And it is reasonable to argue that such evaluations are for Nietzsche, as for Russell, expressions of desire, though in the case of Nietzsche desires are seen as relative to different types of human beings considered as manifesting the will to power in different ways. In other words, reflection on what Nietzsche says about values gives rise to the question of the correct analysis of the nature of the value-judgment. And even if we were prepared to follow Bertrand Russell in excluding substantive judgments of value from moral philosophy in a strict sense, this meta-ethical question would still remain open for serious discussion on a strictly philosophical level.

There are of course other such questions to which Nietzsche's writings give rise. Some of the topics which he discusses might indeed be more properly described as psychological than as philosophical. The will to power is a case in point. But the distinction is admittedly rather difficult to apply. While Nietzsche's anticipation of Alfred Adler in regard to the operation of the will to power in human beings would naturally be considered as pertaining to the area of psychological theory, he extends the concept of the will to power in such a way that it can reasonably be described as a metaphysical theory. Again, while Nietzsche has a lot to say about the psychology of morals, his ideas on this subject can also be regarded as constituent elements in a philosophical anthropology. If however we consider his theory of truth, his view of the status of logical principles, his idea of the nature of scientific hypotheses, his account of the nature of the self, his assertions about the systematically misleading features of ordinary language, it is evident that they are all amenable to philosophical discussion. It is true not only that Nietzsche is given to introducing psychological considerations in a way which may not be acceptable to all philosophers. It is also true that these ideas are often simply stated or supported in a hurried and impressionistic manner. Though however he had little use for academic philosophy and philosophers, he certainly raises a number of philosophical questions which merit serious treatment. In other words, it is hardly adequate to assert that Nietzsche was not a philosopher at all but rather a visionary or prophet or what not. If we wish to do so, we can extract an academic Nietzsche, as it were, and treat him as such.

If we do this, it seems to me that it is the critic and questioner who emerges. If we except Nietzsche's preferred antidotes to nihilism, associated with the ideas of *Übermensch* and the transvaluation of values, his philosophical reflection is largely destructive, in the sense that it consciously aims at undermining hitherto established or traditional and firmly entrenched beliefs and 'prejudices'. It is not simply a matter of religious beliefs and moral convictions. Nietzsche carries his questioning into all spheres and spares nothing, including of course ordinary language and its implications. And it is natural to see in his critical and destructive thought an expression of what he describes as nihilism. After all, he himself regarded it in this light. He is undoubtedly one of the great iconoclasts; and his historical significance is missed, if his thought is reduced to a set of theses. To look on Nietzsche as a striking manifestation of European nihilism does not however entail a refusal to admit that he raises philosophical questions which can be discussed seriously on an abstract or academic level. It is largely a question of where one chooses to place the emphasis. In view of the not uncommon tendency to depict Nietzsche as an eccentric visionary it is doubtless useful to draw attention to those elements in his thought which fit most easily into conventional ideas of philosophical reflection. The suggestion however that the analytic movement in philosophy might 'reclaim him as a predecessor'[14] sounds rather odd. It is not a matter of there being no grounds at all in Nietzsche's philosophical activity for making such a claim. If we look for some grounds, we can find them. At the same time it would be an odd procedure if we tried to tame, as it were, a man who looked on himself as 'dynamite' by over-emphasizing those elements in his thought which, taken by themselves, might qualify him for membership of a department of philosophy in a British or American university.

[14] *Nietzsche as Philosopher*, A. C. Danto (New York & London, 1965), p. 14.

III

What has been said in the last section may have given
the impression that in my opinion only those elements in
Nietzsche's thought which can be brought under the heading
of critical analysis count as philosophy, and that other
elements, unless they pertain to the area of psychology,
constitute the dreams of a visionary. It is not however my
intention to deny that the word 'philosophy' can legitimately
be used in a variety of ways. Nietzsche may not have been
much of a philosopher in terms of a rather narrow and
antiseptic view of the nature and function of philosophy.
His aphoristic works are hardly distinguished either by
sustained argument or by systematic and logically developed
arrangement, except in a general manner. And those who
regard argument as a philosopher's chief concern are naturally
inclined to question the propriety of describing Nietzsche as a
philosopher. But how else is he to be described? As a
psychologist? He certainly pursued psychological reflections; but so have a good many other philosophers. And the
professional psychologists might jib at any suggestion that
Nietzsche was primarily a psychologist. 'Poet' is a description which has sometimes been used. Though however
Nietzsche certainly wrote some poetry, this was a side-line.
And to classify him as a poet simply because his best known
work, *Thus Spake Zarathustra*, is written in what might be
described as a poetic style seems to me misguided. Philosophy can be expressed in poetry. Witness the *De rerum
natura* of Lucretius. There is of course the term 'visionary'.
But philosophers can presumably be persons of vision.
Indeed, it has sometimes been said that this is precisely
what the great metaphysicians were. And if we are thinking
of fanciful and highly imaginative speculations, it can
hardly be claimed that Nietzsche's vision of a world bereft of
meaning or purpose was simply the product of a disordered
mind or a feverish imagination. We can, if we like, define
philosophy in such a way that persons such as Kierkegaard,
Nietzsche or Unamuno cannot count as philosophers. But

we are not involved in transgressing all reasonable linguistic limits if we recommend a wider concept of philosophy in terms of which Nietzsche can certainly be described as a philosopher, and as being primarily a philosopher.

The retort might be made to the foregoing remarks that though they are true, they also miss the point. They are true in the sense that the words 'philosophy' and 'philosopher' have been used and are often still used in such a way that it is quite proper to describe Nietzsche as a philosopher. They miss the point in the sense that refusal to call Nietzsche a philosopher is not equivalent to a denial that a meaning can be given to the word 'philosophy' which would make this description permissible. It expresses a recommendation that the word should not be used in such a loose manner but that it should be confined to 'scientific' philosophy, with a view to drawing attention to the very real differences which are concealed if the word is used to cover a variety of very different activities. Nietzsche regards the genuine philosopher as a creator of values and as a lawgiver, as one who determines a goal for the human race. And it is desirable to make a clear distinction between this sort of activity and, say, analysis of the value-judgment as such or consideration of what is meant by speaking of the human race as having a goal or of history as having an end or purpose. The distinction can be best made by reserving the epithet 'philosophical' to inquiries of the second sort and finding some other term to describe the activities which Nietzsche assigns to the philosopher. In the field of meta-ethical questions, for example, there is some hope of arriving at definite results. But once we start talking of the creation of values as an exercise of the will to power, we pass beyond the limits of what can properly be described as scientific philosophy. To put the matter in another way, we pass beyond the area in which we can speak of truth and falsity and enter the area of personal choice or, as Nietzsche sometimes says, of 'taste'. It is desirable to distinguish between these areas, whereas use of the same word to cover both is confusing.

This point of view is perfectly understandable, and arguments can of course be adduced to support it. To put the matter very briefly, it expresses a certain view of the development of philosophy, a development in which the philosophical field is seen as having been progressively narrowed through the hiving off of areas which either have become separate disciplines or have come to be seen as comprising unanswerable questions or questions which at any rate cannot be answered by employing recognized philosophical methods. The point of view also expresses an evaluation of this development, namely that it has contributed to the benefit and not to the detriment of serious philosophical reflection. Philosophers cannot answer, for example, astronomical problems. And it is to the benefit of both philosophy and astronomy that they have become separate disciplines. Nor can the philosopher be properly expected to tell people what value-judgments they ought to make or what goal, if any, they should assign to human history. If the philosopher does act in this sort of way, he is simply expressing personal options or decisions which lie outside the reach of anything which can properly be described as proof. And if he sets himself up as a social or moral reformer or as a legislator of the future, it should be understood that he is going beyond the limits of philosophy as an academic discipline.

In comparison with this point of view Nietzsche's idea of genuine philosophy appears as highly idiosyncratic. But his idea is none the less the fruit of reflection. Nietzsche was of course perfectly well aware of contemporary notions of what philosophy should be. And he rejected them. He saw all established beliefs and values as crumbling; and in his view academic philosophers were either engaged in the vain attempt to support what was doomed or occupying themselves with niggling questions which had little relevance to man's predicament. To be sure, Nietzsche did not have the benefit of acquaintance with twentieth-century philosophical movements. But it is pretty obvious that he would have had scant sympathy with those philosophers who consider it their main business to remind people of what they already know or think that they know. He would doubtless have had even less regard for them than he had for Neo-Kantians and other philosophers of his time. In his estimation academic philosophy was sterile and irrelevant. It could serve as a preparation for those who were prepared to go beyond it, but this was about all it was good for. The true philosopher, in his opinion, must be an adventurous spirit, prepared to question all cherished assumptions and beliefs and to accept the consequent alienation from his contemporaries. In other words, he must embody in himself the spirit of nihilism. At the same time he should overcome nihilism in himself and be prepared to provide others with the vision required to emerge from it. It is no use looking for help either to Christian theologians and priests or to those concealed theologians, the idealist metaphysicians. For it is precisely their pictures of the world and of human life and history which have been dissolved or are in process of dissolution. As for the 'mishmash-philosophers'[15] who call themselves positivists and the followers of 'the great Chinaman of Königsberg'[16] who have reduced philosophy to the theory of knowledge, the only relevance of their activities to the task of the genuine philosopher of the future is to serve as instruments in his formation: 'The real philosophers are commanders and lawgivers',[17] who determine the order of rank of values and set a goal for man.

Nietzsche's reference to the philosophers of the future as lawgivers and as embodying the will to power tend to suggest that he envisages philosophers as rulers. This is not however what he has in mind. The true philosopher is for Nietzsche a solitary figure, like Heraclitus. He expresses the will to power not by acting as a tyrant in a political sense but by giving meaning to what is in itself without meaning. And he is a lawgiver not by drafting laws for a parliament to endorse but by creating a scale of values in a world which has been stripped of value. The critical intellect sees that the world in itself is without meaning or purpose, and that there are no such entities as absolute values. But human beings cannot live in a

---

[15] *Beyond Good and Evil*, section 204 (*Werke, Kritische Gesamtausgabe*, VI/2, p. 135.
[16] *Ibid.*, section 210 (p. 148).
[17] *Ibid.*, section 211 (p. 149).

world bereft of meaning and value. Someone has to supply a goal or goals for life, create values and determine their order of rank. And Nietzsche envisages the philosopher as understanding the preconditions of the development of a higher culture and as 'legislating' accordingly. He sees the vision which is called for and which will be accepted in the future, if not by the philosopher's contemporaries. During his lifetime he may be a voice crying in the wilderness; but he helps to mould the future through his power of vision.

We have therefore two ideas of philosophy and its function. There is the idea of those whom Nietzsche describes, rather disparagingly, as 'philosophical workers', who consider philosophy as 'science' (*Wissenschaft*), as a particular discipline, that is to say, which is concerned with a particular subject-matter of area of inquiry, such as theory of knowledge, in which assured truths are attainable. And there is Nietzsche's idea of the philosopher as a man for whom knowing (*Erkennen*) is creating (*Schaffen*). We may be inclined to interpret Nietzsche simply as making a plea for a greater breadth of interest and vision. He recognizes, at any rate at one stage of his development, that there is a place in philosophy for 'little unpretentious truths'.[18] And it may appear that he is concerned simply with saying that these little truths should serve as a preparation for something wider and more impressive. In this case of course many people would agree with his attitude. Though however Nietzsche obviously does desire a breadth of vision, we have to bear in mind his theory of truth. He does not suggest that in a restricted area patient and meticulous work can establish a number of objective truths, corresponding with reality itself, and then argue that there is a place for comprehensive theories, even if they do not attain the same degree of certainty as can be attained in the case of 'little' truths. For in his view all truth is 'fiction'. Consider, for example, the principle of non-contradiction. It may be the case that we are unable to think of X as being simultaneously X and non-X. But this does not prove that the principle of non-contradiction reveals the nature of reality 'in itself'. For the

[18] *Human, All-too-Human*, I, section 3 (*Werke*, IV/2, p. 21).

principle presupposes a concept of 'thing' which is open to question. To maintain the principle of non-contradiction is required for life; and this biological necessity makes it 'true'. But the biological necessity of accepting it does not show that the presuppositions of the principle correspond with reality in itself. It shows how human beings have to think if they are to live. And when a philosopher enunciates the principle of non-contradiction, he is issuing an imperative. He is telling us how we ought to think if we want to live. When therefore Nietzsche speaks of the genuine philosopher of the future as a lawgiver, there is continuity between this view of the philosopher's function and what he says about more humdrum 'truths' than *Übermensch* and the order of rank. Nietzsche does not assert that while at certain levels absolute truth can be attained by the philosopher, there is place for speculative theories which lie beyond the reach either of demonstrative proof or of empirical verification. He rejects the concept of absolute truth and gives an interpretation of truth which applies not only to striking theories about Superman and the eternal recurrence but also to logical principles, scientific hypotheses and truths of common sense. Similarly, if Nietzsche demands of the philosopher of the future that he should create values, it must be remembered that for him values were always created by man, even if man chose to ascribe their creation to God.

It is doubtless true that in an attempt to arouse the attention of uninterested and unreceptive contemporaries Nietzsche became more and more inclined to speak in ways which suggest conclusions which do not necessarily follow from his premises. For example, his talk about smashing the old Tables and substituting new ones tend to suggest that in his view all previous values should be rejected and all previously held moral convictions thrown overboard. It is necessary however to make a distinction. Nietzsche does indeed see the system of value-judgments and moral imperatives traditionally accepted in Europe as linked with Christian belief. Moreover, the link is for him not simply a contingent historical fact but a relationship of such a kind that the ethical system cannot survive when it has been separated from its theological basis. To take a simple example, Nietzsche has no sympathy with the assumption that if the existence of a heavenly Father has been denied or discarded, this abandonment of religious belief makes no difference to the moral imperative that human beings should love one another as brothers. Again, Christian sexual morality is part of the general framework of Christianity; and if Christian belief is once subjected to radical questioning, Christian sexual ethics must sooner or later suffer the same fate. In brief, Nietzsche sees the 'death of God' as entailing the death of the Christian morality which, even if it has often not been practised, has formed, as it were, the moral horizon of Europeans for centuries. It is thus quite true that for Nietzsche the death of God means that all traditional moral precepts and value-judgments are subject to radical questioning and put in suspense. At the same time it does not necessarily follow from Nietzsche's premises that no judgment of value which was made before the death of God, before, that is to say, the decay of traditional theological and metaphysical beliefs, is to be re-asserted in a godless world. Nietzsche does indeed talk about smashing the old Tables and substituting new ones. And his attacks on Christian morality are often vehement and expressed in shrill and strident tones. For he sees Christianity as the enemy of 'life', as calumniating natural impulses and qualities and as inhibiting or preventing the development of the higher type of man. Though however his own judgments of value differ in specifiable ways from those of Christianity as he sees it, it does not necessarily follow from what he says that the new values, which the philosopher of the future is expected to proclaim, will bear no resemblance whatsoever to the old values. If, for instance, there is no heavenly Father, we obviously cannot claim that all men ought to love one another as fellow children of God. But it does not necessarily follow that we have to proclaim hatred as the supreme value and exhort all men to hate one another. If we take it that human beings desire to live in a tolerable society, we could hardly demand what would make social life intolerable. Besides, proclamation of universal hatred as a value might well be rejected on aesthetic grounds, as something ugly and repugnant.

Nietzsche obviously thinks of the genuine philosopher as carrying out his task of determining the rank of values without having recourse to any alleged divine revelation or to supposedly metaphysical truths. But it does not necessarily follow that he envisages the embodiment of Zarathustra as acting in a purely arbitrary or capricious manner. After all, Nietzsche defines truth as the sort of error without which a particular type of being could not live. And in proposing 'new Tables' the philosopher would presumably take into account different types of human beings. It is doubtless quite true that talk about ascending and descending life, or about lower and higher types of man, presupposes the judgments of value implied by such distinctions. But the thesis that basic judgments of value are insusceptible to proof is by no means peculiar to Nietzsche. And the point is that, given certain basic value-judgments, criteria of coherence and consistency can then be brought into play. The concept of creating values or determining the hierarchic structure of values does not entail acting in a purely arbitrary and capricious manner.

At the same time Nietzsche's idea of the philosopher's task is obviously very different not only from that of the metaphysicians who believed that they could exhibit the nature of reality as it is but also from that of the philosophers who have recommended a more restricted and modest view of the philosopher's task on the ground that objective truth, proved to be such, can be attained only by leaving on one side speculation about reality as a whole and concentrating attention on sharply defined questions relating to particular issues in a restricted field. For in Nietzsche's opinion there is no absolute truth to be attained. Again, there is an obvious difference between Nietzsche's idea of the philosopher as lawgiver and that of Plato. Plato's philosopher did not create values: he recognized them. And it was in accordance with his insight into the sphere of unchanging values that he directed society. Nietzsche's philosopher however had no such unchanging model before him: he would have to create his model. He would have to open up to people's

minds the possibilities of evaluation and commend a hierarchy of values within the framework of basic value-judgments which he would endeavour to persuade others to
endorse and make their own. However, as this conception
of the philosopher's task is based on a philosophical theory
about values, including truth, and on a philosophical theory
of perspectivism, there seems to be no good reason for
refusing Nietzsche the title of philosopher. We can of course
state certain criteria fulfilment of which is demanded by us
before we are prepared to describe someone as a 'real'
philosopher. But it is open to anyone else to state other
criteria. And by Nietzsche's own criteria those who decline
to recognize him as a 'real' philosopher would probably be
themselves disqualified from membership of this class. All in
all, it is simpler to call him a philosopher and have done with
it. It may be said that he envisages the philosopher as
usurping other people's functions. But as Nietzsche believed
that theologians and metaphysicians, preachers and moralists,
were practically all bankrupt, he had to choose between
passive acceptance of nihilism and allotting to the philosophers of the future the task of overcoming it.

IV

In my 1942 book on Nietzsche I criticized the philospher from
a Christian point of view. This was obviously a case of
external criticism, in the sense that it was based on presuppositions or beliefs which Nietzsche did not share. Similarly, when Bertrand Russell rejected Nietzsche's judgments
of value or what he took to be Nietzsche's judgements, he did
so in the light of his own ethical convictions. In ordinary
life we are obviously given to judging people's actions in
terms of the concepts of right and wrong as we understand
them; and we criticize other people's opinions and beliefs in
the light of what we ourselves think to be true or probable.
As Nietzsche is a writer who is apt to arouse strong feelings or
reactions of one sort or another, there is nothing surprising in
his being treated in a similar manner.

Provided that one does not lay claim to complete neutrality, external criticism is a normal and legitimate procedure. It can of course be superficial. But this is not necessarily the case. For example, Christian criticism of Nietzsche can vary between a mere registering of pretty obvious facts on the one hand and, on the other, discussion which involves a genuine effort to grasp Nietzsche's meaning and intentions and to explore the extent to which his judgments may be justified. At the same time criticism which presupposes a particular point of view, whether Christian, humanist, Marxist or what not, can amount to a refutation of Nietzsche only in the eyes of those who share all or some of the relevant presuppositions on which the criticism is based.

Is a presuppositionless criticism possible? To put the question in another way, is a purely neutral criticism a possibility? Not on Nietzsche's premises at any rate. In his view there are only perspectives; and criticism of one perspective necessarily presupposes another. Criticism can be intelligent or unintelligent, profound or superficial; but it cannot be neutral. Not even if we try to presuppose simply the principles of logic. For these too, according to Nietzsche, express a perspective. If anyone claimed to be speaking from an absolute point of view, Nietzsche would tell him that he was suffering from self-delusion. There are only interpretations of the world; and one interpretation can be challenged only in terms of another. Further, as every interpretation expresses judgments of value, we arrive in the end at clashes between different value-judgments and imperatives. On Nietzsche's premises therefore there can be no purely neutral criticism of his philosophy, free of all presuppositions.

This view of the matter is of course part of Nietzsche's philosophy. And any radical criticism of his philosophy would presumably include an attempt to show that in point of fact we can arrive, by a process of reductive analysis, at the unquestionable. Without however getting involved in this task, we can at any rate ask whether Nietzsche's perspectivism and his theory of values are coherent and self-consistent theories which can be held without self-contradiction. To be sure, this procedure presupposes that there is something wrong with any philosophical theory which involves one in self-contradiction. But the presuppositions are obviously minimal in comparison with assuming, for example, the truth of a particular religious faith or of a given system of metaphysics. Moreover, though Nietzsche refuses to admit that we have any right to claim that the principle of non-contradiction reveals the nature of reality in itself, he allows that it is a necessity of thought, in the sense that it is required for life. The world in itself may not be a logical world; but man has learned by experience that he cannot attain his aims without developing a logical view of the world. If therefore Nietzsche is serious in maintaining that we require a logical view of the world for life, we can properly apply logical tests to his theories. To this extent at any rate criticism can be internal in a sense in which criticism based on presupposition of the truth of Christianity or Hegelianism or Marxism would not be internal.

A common enough objection against, for example, Nietzsche's attack on Christian morality as expressing the will to power of the herd and as inhibiting the development of a higher type of man is that it presupposes an objective distinction between higher and lower, between ascending life and descending life. The vehemence with which he attacks the slave-morality, as he calls it, shows clearly enough that he considers it objectively inferior to the master-morality. He thus contradicts his own denial that there are objective or absolute values.

One has to be careful here. When Nietzsche attacks one set of value-judgments and extols another, he does of course take the second set as a criterion and so presupposes it. It does not necessarily follow however that he presupposes its absolute character. For it is always open to him to say that human beings cannot live without evaluating, that he has made certain value-judgments, and that it is open to anyone else to make different judgments of value. As for the vehemence with which he often writes, he can always reply that he has strong feelings and that there is no reason why he should not express them strongly. If anyone else also has strong feelings, but different ones, he too is entitled to express them strongly. If we allow Bertrand Russell this sort of reply, we have to allow it to Nietzsche too. If value-judgments express desires (or, as Nietzsche would claim, the will to power), and if such desires are strong, one is entitled to express them strongly. It does not follow however that one claims, even implicitly, to be able to prove that one's basic judgments of value are the only valid ones.

It is of course true that acceptance of a general theory about the nature of the judgment of value does not entail acceptance of a given set of substantive judgments of value. In other words, rejection of some of the particular value-judgments made by Nietzsche does not mean that we have necessarily to reject his general theory about the nature of such judgments. We can attack Nietzsche's judgments on the basis of our own basic value-judgments. At the same time it is difficult to avoid the impression that, whatever his general theory of values may have been, Nietzsche did in fact believe that one type of human being was objectively superior to another, just as it is difficult to avoid the impression that Bertrand Russell believed love to be objectively better than hatred. It is not simply a matter of both men having been given to vehement or strong assertion. Suppose that we attach great value to X and desire that others should do likewise. We are likely to feel that there is something wrong with people who deny value to X and attribute it to the opposite of X. If, for instance, we value very highly mutual love among human beings, we would be likely to think that those who professed to value hatred instead were afflicted with some deficiency or flaw. And this, it might be argued, would express a conviction that love is intrinsically valuable, something which human beings ought to value because it is what it is.

If however we claim, as against Nietzsche, that there are objective values, how is this claim to be understood? It might be understood as involving the assertion that there are values as subsistent entities. But this is an ontological theory which it is difficult to defend. And if we do not mean this, what do we mean? Perhaps that certain things or qualities or activities are objectively of such a kind that they are worthy of being valued and that human beings ought to value them. This way of speaking has its own difficulties. If we say that X ought to be valued because it possesses characteristics a, b and c, we have to face the problem of the relation between judgments of fact and judgments of value.[19] If we mean that X has an objective quality of being valuable, over and above or in addition to a, b and c, we have to meet the objections which have been brought against G. E. Moore's theory of the 'non-natural' quality of goodness. Could we however allow that 'value' is a relational word and still find a meaning for the assertion that values are objective? Consider colour. Talk about things possessing this or that colour 'in themselves', apart from any relation to a perceiving subject, is open to objection. At the same time we talk about things being coloured. We attribute colour to the leaf, not to the eye. It is the leaf which is green or yellow or brown, even if it is such only in relation to a perceiving subject. And we would normally say that we see or recognize its colour, not that we attach colour to it or confer colour on it. Analogously, to speak of recognizing love as a value is preferable to talk about attaching a value to love or creating the value. Though however love *is* a value, it is so in relation to man.

This suggestion is not of course a new one. As far as the analogy with colour is concerned, this can be found in the case of those philosophers who have referred to values as 'tertiary' qualities, on an analogy with 'secondary' qualities such as colour. As for the relational aspect of the term 'value', it has often enough been noted that use of the term invites a question such as 'value for whom?' The suggested account doubtless gives rise to difficulties. But it has at least the merit of trying to effect a synthesis of objective and subjective elements. It thus makes it easier to explain the

[19] Perhaps this particular problem would not arise in the context of Nietzsche's thought. For if all judgments of fact are interpretations, and if all interpretations express judgments of value, there seems to be little question of breaking out of the circle of value-judgments and having to cope with the relation between the judgment of fact and the value-judgment.

development of divergent theories. For it is clearly possible to emphasize one element at the expense of the other.

If the question is asked 'value for whom?' I should wish to answer 'for man as such, for all human beings'. Nietzsche asserts the existence of two moralities, that of the slave and that of the master. If however the moral judgment is held to be essentially universal in character, this theory of two moralities will not do. Human beings act in different ways of course; and we can doubtless find sets of empirical facts about human behavior which enable one to speak of 'slavish' and 'masterful' behaviour. But it does not necessarily follow that talk about two distinct moralities is appropriate. Indeed, Nietzsche himself tends to transcend this distinction by proposing an ideal for mankind, *Übermensch*. In so far as he does this, he appears to acknowledge implicitly that value-judgments and moral judgments are universal not only in the sense that they express a desire that all would endorse them but also in the sense that the development and integration of human nature, or of a human person, demands a striving after certain goals or ideals recognized as values for man as such. In other words, it can be argued that Nietzsche tends to transcend his own theory of the two moralities. Indeed, this is only to be expected if, despite what his professed theory may have been, he believed that one type of man was objectively superior to another. His attacks on Christian morality as being an enemy of life and anti-natural suggest that he did believe that the development of man in one way was better than man's development in another way, in a sense of 'better' which was stronger than a mere expression of taste.

It is not a question of trying to make out that Nietzsche 'really' accepted Christian ideals. He certainly rejected these ideals as he saw or interpreted them. Rather it is a question of arguing that though in theory he denied the objectivity of values, in practice he tended to reassert it, not in the sense that his philosophy implies belief in a world of subsistent entities called values, but in the sense that we can speak meaningfully of the development or perfecting of human nature and that this implies an objective relationship between man and certain goals recognized as worthy to be striven after by man and so as values. Nietzsche's philosopher of the future may have had the task of substituting new values for old. But unless we envisage him as acting in a purely capricious and arbitrary manner, it is natural to think of him as 'legislating' in accordance with an ideal of man which implies that certain qualities, for example, are in some sense objectively valuable for man, or which are objectively of such a kind that they should be valued and desired if man is to become what he is capable of becoming. To state a theory of the objectivity of values which does not give rise to any further problem is extremely difficult. And, as has already been noted, the present writer does not claim to be able to do so. But it is also very difficult to propose any goal for man without implying that there are in some sense objective values. And it seems to me that Nietzsche's philosophy illustrates this difficulty. Nietzsche's attitude can be described as anti-moral, if morality is understood in the specific sense which he gives it when he speaks of morality as hostile to life, or at any rate to ascending life. And he likes to claim that what the Christian calls 'bad' he calls 'good'. But this is not of course simply a matter of whim. Nietzsche has an idea of human nature, which serves as a basis for his evaluations. And it is in relation to this idea of man that he asserts certain values.

V

If we are looking for an opportunity of accusing Nietzsche of inconsistency, we can find an obvious one in his theory of perspectives. In his view all so-called facts are really interpretations; and every interpretation expresses a perspective. There are of course different perspectives. Some are required for the welfare, or even for the continued existence of the human race, while others are not necessary in the same way, though they may of course correspond to the needs of a given type of human being. All perspectives express in some way the will to power, the will to impose intelligible form and meaning with a view to obtaining mastery over what is in itself without form and meaning. Within the area of perspectives we can distinguish between 'truth' and 'falsity'. An interpretation which is required for human life, belief in the existence of definite things for example, we call 'true', whereas one which got in the way of increasing conceptual mastery over phenomena we would call 'false'. Though however we can perfectly well speak of truth in an instrumental sense, all interpretations are fictions, constructions of the human mind which create 'reality' rather than reflect or mirror it. It is doubtless necessary for life that we should create, for instance, a world of substantial and relatively permanent physical objects and selves. But this practical need does not alter the fact that this world of things and selves is a human construction, an interpretation. We have no right to assume that it reflects reality as it is apart from human interpretation. Indeed, we could not know reality 'in itself'. For to know is to interpret, to create. There are no such things as knowledge and truth in an absolute sense. There are only interpretations and perspectives. And what we call 'truth' is simply a special kind of 'error'.

An obvious comment is that Nietzsche claims implicitly to be able to occupy an absolute standpoint from which he can judge the fictional character of all truth and the relativity of all perspectives, and that this claim is incompatible with his own theory. It may be said that Nietzsche would not in fact claim to occupy an absolute standpoint. He would be quite ready to admit that his own view of truth is an interpretation and perspectival. In this case however he would leave open the possibility that there could be absolute truth. And if Nietzsche replied that this was impossible, in as much as he had shown that all truth is relative, we would be back again with the claim to be able to occupy a point of vantage from which the whole field could be surveyed and universal judgments passed which were absolutely true. Nietzsche might perhaps reply that to talk about perspectives is not the same thing as to express a given perspective, just as to talk about the nature of the moral judgment is not the same thing as to enunciate a moral judgment. What he says about truth however is expressed in universal terms. And if his theory about truth is supposed to be itself true, it is affected by what he says about the nature of truth.

Though however Nietzsche makes categorical assertions about the nature of truth, we can perhaps regard him as questioning and experimenting rather than as dogmatizing. We can see him, that is to say, as questioning entrenched assumptions and trying out a different view. And there is of course no good reason why he should not question and experiment in this way. It remains however questionable whether his proposed experimental theory can be consistently maintained. Nietzsche may indeed help us to see that some or perhaps many propositions and beliefs which we think true do not in fact enjoy the certainty which we are inclined to attribute to them. But if all truth is fiction, there seems to be no possibility of judging that it is fiction. It is not enough to refer to the distinction between fictions which are required for life and those which are not. For if we are to be able to distinguish between the two classes, we seem to require some firmer foothold than fiction itself.

Questions of consistency can also be raised in regard to what Nietzsche says about the nature of reality. According to him, to know is to schematize, to impose form and regularity on what is constantly changing. In metaphysical language, it is man who transforms Becoming into Being, or who at any rate constructs stable beings out of the flux of becoming. But how does Nietzsche know that reality is becoming? If the objects of knowledge are constructions, 'fictions', how can Nietzsche possibly know what the 'real' world is like? In the case of values one might argue that 'value' is a relational term, that it therefore makes no sense to speak of things having value out of all relation to a subject, and that we are thus entitled to talk about the world as having no value 'in itself'. But to assert that reality in itself is simply a flux of becoming is to make a positive assertion which we are not entitled to make, if every view of the world is a mental construction. For even if things as they appear to us were fictions, it might be the case that there were things in themselves which were irreducible to a flux of becoming. If all views of the world are perspectival, we cannot get beyond our perspectives. And that is that. Nietzsche does indeed sometimes say that the phenomenal or apparent world is the only real one. And if he held this constantly and consistently, he could, and indeed should, avoid any statement about the real world as distinct from the apparent world. In this case however he would find it difficult to justify his talk about things as they appear to us being fictions, mental constructions. Sometimes he seems to be saying that the phenomenal world is our construction, a 'fictional' world, and that it is the only world which there is. But if our world is a perspectival interpretation, it is very difficult to believe that it is an interpretation of nothing. In other words, Nietzsche is sometimes inclined to rule out the problem of the relation between appearance and reality by identifying them. Then there is no place for a metaphysics of the beyond, of 'reality in itself'. But at other times he makes a distinction between appearance and reality which his view of the nature of our knowledge give him no warrant for making.

There is indeed a sense in which criticism of this kind is unfair to Nietzsche. For much of what he has to say about truth and knowledge is found in the notes which constitute the *Nachlass* and which were published posthumously. And some writers on Nietzsche are insistent that one should look for his philosophy in what he himself published rather than in unpublished material. While however there is a good deal to be said in support of this contention, it seems clear enough that Nietzsche did not really think through his theories in a thorough manner. He was a great questioner and experimenter; and he can stimulate others to question and to open up avenues of thought. But he was not so good at providing answers to the questions which he raised. It is not a matter of finding fault with him for not having produced a system. For if by a system one understands a systematic reconstruction of reality, it is evident that Nietzsche did not believe that reality was of such a kind as to make such a reconstruction possible. Rather is it a question of suggesting that he did not really think out the implications of the assertions which he made.

The obvious comment is that he had other things to do. He had, or believed that he had, a message to convey, a vision to impart. He was concerned, we may say, with opening men's eyes to the consequences of the 'death of God' and with the overcoming of nihilism. He was concerned with a radical attack on all that he saw as hostile to life and as threatening the freedom of man to surpass himself. He wanted man to face up to existence in a godless world, bereft of meaning and value, and at the same time to give a meaning to his existence and history, to defy, as it were, the meaningless world and to assert his own freedom, strength and creativity. In attacking what was to his mind dead or decaying or hostile to man and in proposing his own vision of the future he certainly put forward philosophical theories. But he was too intent on his prophetic role to devote the time and energy which would be required to work out these theories in what academic philosophers would consider to be an appropriately thorough manner. Nor of course did the state of his health allow him to do so. What energies he had he concentrated on his 'mission', on trying to make himself heard. Hence the increasing vehemence and exaggeration. Nietzsche was not suited for an Oxford Common Room. But he did of course make his mark, not simply as a writer of German but as a thinker with a power to stimulate others to a variety of lines of thought. He said on occasion, and pretty emphatically, that he did not want disciples. In view of his increasing isolation and loneliness and of his failure to make any real impact before the onset of madness, there is a natural tendency to look on such protestations as a matter of sour grapes. But this interpretation is hardly adequate, even if it has some foundation in fact. For Nietzsche did not construct any take-it-or-leave-it system or set of doctrines. He clearly did not seek Nietzscheans in the sense of followers who would concentrate their attention in a heavy-handed way on the letter of what he wrote. He wanted to be heard by the type of man who was capable of understanding him and then of pursuing his own line of thought. He was of course pleased when he heard that someone of note, such as Georg Brandes, was paying attention to his writings. But the people whose attention he really wished to arouse were those whom he was prepared to regard as his equals and as potentially creative thinkers. After all, he was concerned with the future of Europe, not with founding a school. There is obviously room for specialists in Nietzsche studies. Nietzsche himself regarded the scholar as worthy of respect. But such people are not necessarily Nietzscheans. And the sort of Nietzscheans whom the philosopher desired were creative thinkers who shared his vision of the 'death of God' and its consequences and who were prepared to make their own contribution to the overcoming of nihilism.

It is Nietzsche's fate that his ideas have been appealed to by persons for whom he would have had scant regard and in favour of a German nationalism for which he had no use at all. But he has also exercised a stimulative influence on philosophers such as Karl Jaspers and on literary figures such as Thomas Mann and poets such as Stefan George. His power to stimulate remains. But it can hardly be claimed that his vision of *Übermensch* has turned out to be an influential and successful myth in the twentieth century. We can all think of a myth which was certainly not to Nietzsche's taste but which has exercised a far greater influence in the modern world than the idea of Superman. And it is perhaps significant that Sartre, who shares in important ways Nietzsche's theory of the 'death of God', has looked to Marxism as the living philosophy of the twentieth century. Nietzsche's protests however against levelling-down, against fear and suspicion of independent minds and against the totalitarian spirit in general are still applicable, not least in the country which, according to Nietzsche, would one day astonish Europe.

INDEX